From Servants to Workers

From Servants to Workers

South African Domestic Workers and the Democratic State

SHIREEN ALLY

ILR Press
an imprint of
Cornell University Press
Ithaca and London

Copyright © 2009 by Cornell University

First published 2009 by Cornell University Press
First printing, Cornell Paperbacks, 2009

Printed in the United States of America

Librarians: A CIP catalog record for this book is available from the
Library of Congress.

ISBN 978-0-8014-4832-4 (cloth: alk. paper)
ISBN 978-0-8014-7587-0 (pbk.: alk. paper)

Cornell University Press strives to use environmentally responsible sup-
pliers and materials to the fullest extent possible in the publishing of its
books. Such materials include vegetable-based, low-VOC inks and acid-
free papers that are recycled, totally chlorine-free, or partly composed
of nonwood fibers. For further information, visit our website at www
.cornellpress.cornell.edu.

Cloth printing   10 9 8 7 6 5 4 3 2 1
Paperback printing   10 9 8 7 6 5 4 3 2 1

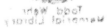

For AK,

(22 April 1946–23 August 2008)

And anon,
Like Snow upon the Desert's dusty Face
Lighting a little hour or two—
is gone.
—*Rubaiyat of Omar Khayyam*

Contents

Acknowledgments

This book would not have been possible without the intellectual, material, social, and emotional contributions of a number of people who deserve acknowledgment.

I am deeply indebted to the domestic workers who gave of their limited time to share with me their most personal experiences. I am especially grateful to Mrs. Selinah Vilakazi and Ms. Monica Dube at the Johannesburg offices of the South African Domestic Service and Allied Workers Union (SADSAWU). And, to the remarkable Mrs. Eunice Dhladhla, within whose spirit resides a silent energy and strength that shaped this project and my commitments to it in ongoing ways.

Thanks, too, to various officials—especially Annemarie van Zyl at the Department of Labour—who assisted me in securing information and materials relevant to the project. Neva Makgetla deserves particular thanks for sharing not only useful ideas but also invaluable data. For research assistance, thanks to Elizabeth Zuze. And, for their financial assistance, I am grateful to the Fulbright Foundation, Compton Foundation, Skye Trust, and the Equity Development Unit at the University of the Witwatersrand.

Many colleagues and friends provided various forms of intellectual companionship that, either directly or indirectly, brought this project to completion, and to whom I am grateful: Peter Alexander, Nurina Ally, Eileen Boris, Charles Camic, Jacklyn Cock, Jane Collins, Marcelle Dawson, Matt Desmond, Jo Ellen Fair, Laura Griffin, Shireen Hassim, Jon Hyslop, Abby Kinchy, Heinz Klug, Amy Lang, Cameron MacDonald, Kate McCoy, Darlene Miller, Bekisizwe Ndimande, Leigh Payne, Seemin Qayum, Raka Ray,

Cesar Rodriguez, Melanie Sampson, Lucien van der Walt, Edward Webster, and Michelle Williams.

Irma du Plessis and Kezia Lewins offered not only sincere and generous collegiality but also critical conversations on the politics of race, gender, and generation in a transforming South African academy. And, to my friend and colleague, Bridget Kenny, I owe a huge debt—for intellectual companionship that shaped this analysis in crucial ways, for the many telephone conversations, and the regular Friday afternoons at *The Boekehuis* without which this book would have never materialized—but, most important, for embodying a vision of warm, genuine, supportive, critical, and generous collegiality for which I have found no equal.

To my former adviser, and continuing friend, Gay Seidman, I am immensely grateful. Gay's incredible scholarly acuity has graced this project from its first inception, and it was thanks to her efforts that this work finally made its way to Cornell University Press. Her nurturing friendship, collegiality, and energy have fueled this endeavor from the beginning.

Finally, this book is profoundly influenced by my parents—Sakina and Abdool Kader Ally. My mother's continuous "care work" made this book literally possible and inspired its substantive content. More than subtle inspiration was provided by my father. Not only was he acutely perceptive of social inequality but also daringly, imaginatively—and humorously—disruptive of it. This effort was made possible by, and is in honor of, their lives of struggle.

From Servants to Workers

Introduction

Maid with Rights?

> Political emancipation certainly represents a great
> progress . . . not the final form of human emancipation . . . but
> the final form . . . within the framework of the prevailing
> social order.
>
> Karl Marx, "On the Jewish Question"

One crisp and bright winter morning in South Africa's economic hub, Johannesburg, I met Hazel Sondlo[1]—a woman whose life story typifies the problem that is at the core of this book. That morning, on an ordinary street in the working-class suburb of Bez Valley, I walked past the driveway of the modest home that stood at the address I was given. That was when I first saw her. A buxom but forlorn figure, she was sweeping a section of paved driveway behind the curvy designs of a heavy black iron gate. This was Hazel, but it was not her home. She merely worked there. Wrapped in light blue overalls, behind the bars of the gate, she looked more like a prisoner than a worker. I approached her with a greeting, and she quickly turned to face me, startled by the intrusion into her morning activity. The revealing rays of the sun illuminated her rubbery, wrinkled face, and the smiling eyes hidden within it. Together, they betrayed her unique life as a domestic worker in South Africa.

Born and raised in an impoverished village deep in the country's vast hinterland, fifty-two-year-old Hazel Sondlo's life bore the strong imprint of apartheid's racial regime. Relegated to one of the ten ethnically divided "Bantustans,"[2] dispossessed of the land required to sustain a rural livelihood, she found herself desperate for an income that would feed, clothe, and school her two children. But given the strong racialized urban control policies of apartheid, securing a "pass" and getting to the urban center of Johannesburg to find work was difficult.[3] When she did eventually arrive in Johannesburg with a pass, and therefore urban status attached to the miner husband who had left her a long time ago, she found that without a decent education, there were few prospects for jobs or accommodation—except one. Like most of the black African[4] women of her generation, she found white households willing to pay her, albeit a meager amount, to clean, cook, care for their children, and in general, "serve" them. The backyard room[5] became hers, and she became the family's "maid." And so Hazel Sondlo joined the ranks of the nearly one million women who, today, constitute the largest single sector of women's employment in South Africa.[6] Hidden away in the homes and kitchens of suburbia, they are an open secret—such a normalized part of South African life that they are hardly noticed.

Working sometimes excessively long hours for often terribly low wages many as live-in "servants," black domestic workers serving white families came to represent an iconic image of apartheid's racial logics. "I was like a slave to that family. I was their black slave," Hazel summarized poignantly in one of a series of narrations of her life history to me. "From early in the morning, to late in the night, I would do everything. Even if she was sitting in the lounge and the tea on the coffee table was too far away, she would scream, and then I was supposed to come from the other side of the house just to move her cup of tea closer. She never lifted a finger, because she had me, her servant," Hazel continued, her eyes despondent at the thought.

As Jacklyn Cock's pioneering and classic study *Maids and Madams* (1980) exposed, apartheid was easily one of the most despotic organizations of paid domestic work anywhere in the world.[7] In one of its great ironies, apartheid's maniacal racism enforced a strict separation of races, but at the same time crafted urban and labor control policies that channeled black women like Hazel into the most intimate spaces of white households. Despite this intimacy, or perhaps partly because of it, most found themselves highly exploitable. With almost no legal protections other than common law, paid domestic work under apartheid has been defined by exploitative pay, oppressive working conditions, and dehumanizing racism and sexism.

While Hazel's feeling of being a slave to her employing family reflected some of the feudal, colonial vestiges of the institution, Cock (1980) had theorized paid domestic work as a form of servitude within South Africa's modernizing racial capitalism. Paid domestic work, she argued, reproduced not only labor power for capitalism but also reproduced the racialized logics of apartheid that constructed blacks as a servant class and socialized white South Africans into "the attitudes of racial domination" (8) necessary for its distinctive racial modernity.

But, by 1994, South Africa had changed. Nelson Mandela had been released from prison, and with the eyes of the world watching, a series of remarkable negotiations placed the country on the eve of its first ever democratic elections. This took domestic workers out of the invisible shadows and placed them in the full glare of the politics of transition. In April 1994, in the same month as the historic elections, domestic workers boldly took over the streets of Cape Town, defiantly staking their claim on the "miracle" transition, with banners shouting: "The new South Africa must be for domestic workers also."

Just a decade later, by 2004, the democratic South African state had not only heeded the call of the marching women and their banners, it had crafted what is today, undoubtedly, one of the most extensive and expansive efforts anywhere in the world to recognize paid domestic work as a form of employment. Existing labor legislation was redrafted to include domestic workers, giving them the same rights as all other workers.[8] These were extended[9] with a landmark national minimum wage, mandatory formal contracts of employment, state-legislated annual increases, extensive leave, severance pay, formal registration, a government-sponsored pension fund,[10] access to unemployment insurance benefits (a world first), and a national certificate and qualification in domestic work through government-sponsored training (another world first).

As Pierette Hondagneu-Sotelo (2001) succinctly put it, "paid domestic work is distinctive not in being the worst job of all but in being regarded as something other than employment" (9). It is rarely recognized as employment because of its extension of women's seemingly "natural" roles. Its location in the private household as an apparent continuation of kinship rather than contractual obligations, and in a site of leisure, not work, makes it seem all the more like something other than employment. The efforts by the South African state were thus remarkable in beginning from the premise that domestic work was a form of work like any other, and should be formalized, modernized, and professionalized as a form of employment.

Within a single lifetime, domestic workers like Hazel Sondlo found themselves straddling a divide between two completely different regimes. Having labored as "servants" with limited political rights in the dystopic world that was paid domestic work under apartheid, they now found themselves in a utopia of sorts—beneficiaries of full citizenship rights in, quite possibly, the world's most progressive state effort to regulate paid domestic work. "Can you understand what a feeling it is?" asked Hazel one day as we sat on a street corner soaking in a warm summer's midday. Hazel stared past the cars flitting by and offered the thought that is at the core of this book.

"This thing of democracy," she started, with a slowness to the pace of her voice that signaled the gravity of her reflection. She stopped, and stared at a government brochure educating domestic workers about their rights that I had placed on the grass beside us. With a slightly quickened pace, she seemed to have struck on an idea. "Now, I have rights. Rights like all other workers," she said, soaking in the profundity of the idea as much as the midday sun.

But, what difference has it made that "maids" in South Africa now have rights? Has it overturned relations of servitude so prevalent under apartheid? Has it transformed the lives of these working women and the function of paid domestic work? In the end, what difference has it made to women like Hazel Sondlo, and how do they understand what it means, that the South African state has tried to transform them from "servants" with limited political rights under apartheid into workers with citizenship rights under democracy?

For eighteen months between February 2004 and August 2005, in the homes, workplaces, churches, parks, and on the pulsing inner city, suburban, and township streets of Johannesburg, I collected the life histories of domestic workers like Hazel Sondlo who, within single lifetimes, straddled the divide between the opposing worlds of apartheid servitude and democratic citizenship.[11] In their workplaces, at their homes, in public parks, and on street corners, they narrated the stories of their lives and shared with me their most intimate thoughts. I followed them as they went to union meetings, state-run information workshops, government "celebrations," state-sponsored training, *manyano* (church group) meetings, and as they played *fah-fee* (betting game). I conducted in-depth interviews with state officials, union officials, and training providers. I even shadowed state inspectors as they went into private homes, sat in living rooms, and uncovered the intimate details of the relationships between employers and the workers in their households.[12] What I found was perplexing, and speaks to a debate that has been raging for more than forty years.

"Servants" versus Workers, and the Dilemma of Paid Domestic Work

In the 1970s, Marxist feminists ignited a second wave of one of the century's most powerful social movements from a simple recognition: They argued that seemingly mundane activities—usually the preserve of women—

like cleaning toilets, giving children their baths, and putting dinner on the table, were actually crucial for capitalist accumulation (Dalla Costa and James 1972; Secombe 1974; Hartmann 1976). While a fierce debate ensued about the exact relationship between domestic work and capitalist production (the notorious "domestic labor debate")—there was agreement that women's unpaid labor in the home reproduced the labor power required for capitalism. By this accounting, women shared a "common difference" (cf. Mohanty 2003) within patriarchy and capitalism—unpaid domestic labor—and this became an important new ground of solidarity. Barbara Ehrenreich remembers that, in that moment, "housework was supposed to be the great equalizer of all women. Whatever else women did—jobs, school, child care—we also did housework" (2003, 86).

By the 1980s, however, a vibrant scholarship on paid domestic work shattered this presumption. As it turned out, not all women did housework. Some women employed other women to do it for them. Exploring in detail the extent and nature of paid domestic work, feminists pointed out that here was an institution in which primarily middle-class white women used their race and class privilege to, literally, buy their way out of their gendered responsibility for domestic labor (Rollins 1985). Given that paid domestic work is almost always reserved for poor women, women of color, and immigrant women, feminists showed that in paid domestic work, gender inequality was splintered by race/ethnicity and class (Cock 1980; Rollins 1985; Glenn 1986; Hansen 1989; Chaney and Castro 1989; Colen 1990; Romero 1992; Gill 1994; Dill 1994).[13]

But, paid domestic work not only reflected these structures of inequality, it also constituted and reproduced them. Domestic workers, crucially, make possible the paid work of the men and women they work for, subsidizing the full-time incomes of their employers, displacing them from the drudgery of household work and the demands of child care. As domestic workers do the "dirty work" of cleaning their employers' toilets, or entertaining their employers' children, they free them to engage in accumulating other forms of capital, including cultural, while limiting domestic workers' abilities to engage in these "value-added" activities themselves. In this way, as Roger Sanjek and Shellee Colen put it, "through household work the multiple axes of inequality dividing household workers and employers intensify and harden" (1990, 10).

Given this centrality of paid domestic work in producing and reinforcing structures of gendered, raced, and classed inequality, it was no surprise that it became a seriously intractable "dilemma" for feminists.[14] Employing a domestic worker was not just a choice about how to manage one's household work, it was colluding with an institution that was crucial to the production and reinforcement of raced and classed inequalities. But, given feminists' struggles for women's entry into paid employment as a measure to disrupt gendered inequalities, how else would some women manage their full-time jobs as well as cooking, cleaning, and child care, without employing a domestic worker? This catch-22 made paid domestic work a difficult personal choice for many socially conscious working men and women, and an obstinate political predicament for feminists.[15]

But, for some, this dilemma was partly resolved by considering not so much the *fact* of hiring a domestic worker, but the *terms* on which she was hired. If one could offer a modern, formal, depersonalized form of employment, with decent wages, decent working conditions, and one treated a household worker as exactly that, a *worker*, surely paid domestic work need not be so problematic after all. Dispense with feudal attitudes of domestic servitude, replace them with modern attitudes of a formal, contractual, legally, and politically regulated form of employment, just like any other, and you've resolved part of the dilemma of domestic work.[16]

The urgency of this modernizing solution to the exploitation and oppression faced by domestic workers has been resuscitated in the past decade as we've seen a spectacular return to a form of servitude, on a global scale. Today, hundreds of thousands of women from poor countries in Central and South America, in South and Southeast Asia, and even from Africa, make the difficult choice to leave their families behind and risk the hazardous journeys that bring them, either legally or illegally, to the shores of North America, Europe, and the wealthier countries of the Middle East and Asia. There, despite their qualifications as doctors and teachers, many find work as domestic workers, doing household work and providing in-home child care (Sanjek and Colen 1990; Constable 1997; Bakan and Stasiulis 1997; Chin 1998; Andall 2000; Anderson 2000; Chang 2000; Gamburd 2000; Hondagneu-Sotelo 2001; Parreñas 2001a; Ehrenreich and Hochschild 2003; Silvey 2004; Lan 2006). Far from modern workers with the protections of minimum wages and basic conditions of employment, however, these "servants of globalization"[17] toil for extremely low wages, sometimes under unbearably abusive working conditions, and, more often than not, without any legal recognition that they are engaged in a form of employment.

The recent explosion of studies on this globalization of paid domestic work has analyzed, in particular, the tenuous citizenship status of these migrant workers, and the consequent failure of protective state regulation, as a crucial variable in explaining their exploitability (Colen 1990; Bakan and Stasiulis 1997; Constable 1997; Hondagneu-Sotelo 2001; Parreñas 2001a;

Lindio-McGovern 2003; Lan 2006). Guest worker status, restrictions to live-in programs, measures against family reunification and the like, are reflective of limited political incorporation in many countries, in ways that reinforce workers' vulnerability to the peculiar exploitations of paid domestic work (cf. Bakan and Stasiulis 1995).

In her brilliant study of Filipina migrant domestic workers in the United States and Italy, Rhacel Parreñas (2001a) has shown how the limited political statuses and rights of these women in the countries they migrate to is one major reason why they are so exploited and abused. She calls this "partial citizenship" and argues it is this which ensures that transnational migrant domestic workers "are not protected by labor laws, and [they] are left vulnerable to the exploitation of employers, including sexual harassment and abuse, excessive work hours with no overtime pay, and substandard living conditions" (Parreñas 2001b, 1134). But, if "partial citizenship" is a source of the compromised position of migrant domestic workers, to what extent can more inclusive citizenship rights, and extended legal protections, challenge the exploitation and oppression experienced by domestic workers? Can global servitude be overturned through more protective state regulation and the extension of rights to domestic workers?

In South Africa, domestic workers bear the unique distinction of having experienced both of these political potentials within single lifetimes. Under apartheid, they experienced the most despotic organization of paid domestic work as a relationship of "servitude," with compromised citizenship and only limited legal protection (Whisson and Weil 1971; Preston-Whyte 1976, 1982; Gaitskell et al. 1984; Gordon 1985; Marks 1987).[18] Post-apartheid, with a democratic state committed to their plight, they have become beneficiaries of one of the world's most extensive efforts to recognize them as workers. But, have these extensive citizenship-rights, and the attempted formalization and modernization of the occupation through state-based regulation solved the dilemma of domestic work in South Africa?

Contradictory Consequences, Recalcitrant Realities

Despite the broad-ranging efforts to turn South African domestic "servants" into workers, the iconic apartheid live-in African woman "servant" attending to the lifestyles of white, middle-class suburbia, remains a recalcitrant reality in contemporary South Africa. The continued shift to live-out and part-time "char"[19] work has become more commonplace, and nouveau-riche blacks increasingly employ domestic workers as well.[20] Although the work structure of domestics has continued to shift, the political system under which they labor has altered, and the racial composition of employers has been negligibly blackened,[21] the black woman domestic worker remains one of the enduring continuities of apartheid in contemporary South Africa. Every morning, scores of black women make a journey from their township homes, shacks, or backyard "servants quarters" to the suburban and not-so-suburban homes where they work, literally moving "across the boundaries of race and class" (Dill 1994). Working long hours for meager wages, they do the "dirty work" that keeps South African households functioning and secure.[22]

During their working days, some continue to endure at times slavelike conditions performing manual and emotional labor, often suffering the violation of their psyches through demeaning racism and the violation of their bodies through pervasive levels of sexual abuse and exploitation.[23] At the end of their strenuous working days, in their journeys home, they traverse the landscapes of race and class privilege carved out by apartheid-era inequalities, returning from the islands of racialized affluence where they work to maintain others' families to the seas of squalor where they struggle to do the same for their own.

Once a year, or more if they are fortunate, most of these workers make a journey "home" to a rural town or village, where they continue to maintain a homestead of parents, children, and extended family. As migrants straddling the divides between urban and rural South Africa, their lives traverse the erstwhile physical geography of apartheid. When they return to their urban work lives as domestic workers caring for others' children, it is as mothers seeking to ensure a better life for their own children whom they leave behind in the care of others.

In the few hours during these demanding days when they do not slave away in isolation, however, they construct vibrant associational lives in the public spaces they co-opt as a defiant resistance against their "incarceration" (Bujra 2000). On street corners in their uniforms, animatedly in discussion, on city benches raucously telling jokes, and in public parks playing *fah-fee*, they form vibrant networks discussing everything from their latest dream that will decide the numbers they play, to their family and work lives. In associational unions such as *stokvels* (revolving credit associations), trade unions, mainstream church groups, and the burgeoning industry of Pentecostal churches, they congregate en masse—visible, collective, and vocal.

In these inversions—of their public activity as workers in the private sphere, and their private lives enacted in public spaces—domestic workers in South Africa continue to embody the tenacious legacies of apartheid. At the same time, however, they embody all the aspirations of the post-apartheid era. As the beneficiaries of an extensive crafting of protective rights and mobilization of an extensive state apparatus to translate those rights into a formalization, modernization, and professionalization of the occupation, domestic workers in South Africa have experienced the striking effects of a democratic order.

Part I of the book historicizes the transformations of paid domestic work in South Africa to provide a more textured reading of domestic workers' entry into the modernizing project of the democratic state. The apartheid state crafted a distinctively modern form of servitude (chapter 1), while workers themselves engaged in a "modernizing" of the institution (chapter 2), making their entry into a post-apartheid statecraft seeking to modernize the institution all the more striking.

Yet, as Part II shows, despite the dramatic continuities with apartheid servitude in their working lives, the state's efforts *did* improve domestic workers' lot, with wages and working conditions showing definite improvements. Chapter 3 shows, however, that for workers, more important was the fact that they could no longer be instantly dismissed. It was one of only a few issues that consistently brought tears to many workers' eyes. Job security, and the guarantee of a livelihood as well as the dignity it brought, was what most captured the meanings of democracy for them.

Domestic workers also more actively claimed their new political statuses as workers with rights. Lining government offices to collect unemployment insurance, packing town halls for government "celebrations" of domestic workers, enthusiastically signing up for government sponsored professionalization programs, and boldly cramming into the offices of the governmental industrial relations commission to lay complaints against their employers, South African domestic workers claimed their rights with a frenetic energy and political maturity many imagined them incapable of.

So it was utterly surprising that on asking them what difference democracy had made to their lives, many domestic workers repeated, over and over again, that things were actually "worse than before." They denied any knowledge of the new laws even as they claimed them, some refused to sign mandatory contracts of employment, and others refused their employers' efforts to register them with the government for unemployment insurance. For most government officials, this was confirmation of the political ignorance of domestic workers, and one of the reasons for the slow pace of transformation in the sector.

For some scholars, employers' continuing colonial attitudes are among the most important explanations for the apartheid-era continuities within the sector.[24] Jennifer Fish (2006a) argues that the failure to translate public commitments to gendered rights within paid domestic work is a testament to the constrained possibilities for "engendering" democracy in post-apartheid South Africa. She argues that the institution "manifests" the contradictions between South Africa's public expressions of democratic values and the remaining vestiges of colonial logics in the servitude relations still prevalent within paid domestic work.

This echoes the vibrant scholarship examining the character of paid domestic work in relation to a postcolonial social formation.[25] In Zambia (Hansen 1989), India (Qayum and Ray 2003; Ray and Qayum 2009), Tanzania (Bujra 2000), and Zimbabwe (Pape 1993), among others, democratic values have coexisted with continued servitude relations within paid domestic work. This suggests an urgent need for an *explanation* of this disconnect.

John Pape specifically examined the effects of independence in Zimbabwe for paid domestic work and summarizes that "independence elevated domestic workers to full-fledged citizens and statutory members of the working class. . . . Yet . . . these changes in the daily life of many domestic workers did not enable them to escape the chains of personal servitude or to attain a status anywhere near to equal that of their employers" (1993, 389). Pape argues that the political economy in Zimbabwe following independence limited the gains of democratization, with housing and job shortages ensuring that paid domestic work remained coerced into erstwhile colonial relations of servitude.

In these analyses, there is a similar deference to the power of either the market or employers to retain the employment relationship as noncontractual, poorly paid, and low status. The postcolonial state is presented as the benevolent legislator, and either the market or employers as recalcitrant and noncompliant. In trying to explain this disconnect, the South African case suggests that while the market and employers are part of the explanation, we have to engage the politics of paid domestic work *as an intimate form of labor* to understand why the effort to turn "servants" into workers produced such contradictory consequences and recalcitrant realities.

The Powers of Democratic Statecraft

When the "oppression of women by women" in waged domestic work posed a challenge to the feminist project, it "excavated the microsociology of the relationships between women who employ maids and nannies and those who labor in such jobs" (Milkman et al. 1998, 484). In a series of excellent seminal studies, the micropolitics of paid domestic work were meticulously unearthed, and the gendered, raced, and classed construction of labor markets exposed (Rollins 1985; Glenn 1986; Sanjek and Colen 1990; Dill 1994; Romero 1992). The contemporary resuscitation of analyses of paid domestic work in its transnational mutations has extended this. This proliferating scholarship analyzes the global political economy of domestic work and details its implications for the micropolitics of the employer-employee relationship, especially in its constitutive reinstantiations of hierarchies of race, class, and citizenship (Anderson 2000; Parreñas 2001; Hondagneu-Sotelo 2001; Hochschild and Ehrenreich 2003). This book goes beyond this overriding emphasis on the micropolitics of paid domestic work, however, to examine the macropolitics of paid domestic work. It is an analysis of the power dynamics in the relationship, not between employers and employees, but between workers and the state.

Nicole Constable's (1997) now classic *Maid to Order in Hong Kong*, interestingly, inaugurated the contemporary proliferation of studies on transnational migrant domestic work with a study that focused on the state. She artfully showed how government policies disciplined migrant Filipina domestic workers as state regulation was marshaled for the control of workers.[26] Similarly, Abigail Bakan and Daiva Stasiulis (1997) have analyzed the political economy of the Canadian state's relationship to paid domestic work, and how the state's restrictions on citizenship for migrant Filipina domestic workers is a mechanism of labor and political control, suggesting the state's complicity in the continued exploitations of foreign domestic workers (see also Bakan and Stasiulis 1994; Schechter 1998; Pratt 2004).[27] Christine Chin's (1998) analysis of state elites and the middle classes in Malaysia, as they construct a foreign domestic workforce as part of a "modernity project," was also interestingly concerned with state politics.

These studies have all shown the ways in which state regulation for control disciplines workers, extends state power, and is a crucial vector in structuring exploitation in the sector. But, what about state regulation for protection? The failure of state-based regulation for the protection of domestic workers is lamented continuously,[28] and the enactment of such legislative protections has become a staple prescription as a basic condition for the emancipation of domestic workers. From the International Labor Organization (Blackett 1998) to advocacy groups and academic invocations of the necessity of workplace-based legislative protections to define wages and working hours, protective state regulation is understood as a vehicle for the empowerment of domestic workers rather than as a form of power in itself. This book explores state power as power in one of the most extensive forms of state regulation for domestic workers' protection. It is an analysis of the powers of the state in its relationship with workers, and of the consequences for workers in their relationship to their work.

In this, the state is shown to be not a bounded, formal institution. Instead, the state is laid bare as an entity in the making, whose existence is constituted in the sites of its relationship with its subjects—the legislative process, state-run information workshops, state-sponsored training facilities, and state inspections. As Wendy Brown (1992, 12) has theorized it, the state is an "unbounded terrain of powers and techniques, an ensemble of discourses, rules, and practices, cohabiting in limited, tension-ridden, often contradictory relation with one another." While this Foucauldian reading of the state leads Brown to theorize the state as a disciplining apparatus, that the state "subjects" its citizens has an intellectual lineage that precedes Foucault's "governmentality" (Burchell et al. 1991). Max Weber, after all, had argued that the state was "a *claim* to legitimacy, a means by which *politically organized subjection* is simultaneously accomplished and concealed" (1946, 78; emphasis added). In this theorization of the state as not an identifiable "thing" and as involved in "subjection," even Karl Marx was in agreement, having theorized the state to be "in an important sense an illusion . . . : [It] is at most a message of domination—an ideological artifact attributing unit, structure and independence to the disunited, structureless and dependent workings of the practice of government" (Marx 1967, quoted in Corrigan and Sayer 1985, 7).

This study fuses these conceptions to show that the state is simultaneously *both* a disciplining assemblage of discursive tactics *and* an arena of contestation for an emancipatory politics. In what I call the *democratic statecraft* for domestic workers, the occupation was not just being formalized and modernized, but became a crucial legitimating feature of a state in formation and therefore a mode of power. Chapter 3 shows how this democratic statecraft introduced and enacted the extension of rights to domestic workers on the basis of their "vulnerability." In doing so, domestic workers were presented as in need of a benevolent protector, acting on behalf of subjects presumed too vulnerable to act themselves. In the numerous sites, practices, and moments of the state's relationship to domestic workers, their availing for state protection on the basis of their "vulnerability" rendered workers the *subjects* of state policy. Paradoxically, then, state-based regulation intended to protect workers against the unilateral powers of their employers became a mode of subjection to another practice of power—this time of the state.

Barbara Cruikshank's (1999) analysis of the state argues that the extension of state power through efforts that seek to empower citizens can operate as a "will to empower"—a turn on the Nietzschean phrase that is not just clever but highly instructive. In the democratic South African state's efforts to legally regulate paid domestic work, there was the operation of a similar "will to empower," in which the efforts to empower domestic workers became a mode of power in itself. South African domestic workers were disciplined and made subject, quite unexpectedly, by the very citizenship rights meant to support, protect, and empower them. This dynamic of state power is crucial for understanding why South African domestic workers continually claimed things were "worse than before," and why some refused to be registered. By discursively, and at times in their practice, disowning the state's efforts, they were in fact distancing themselves from their subjectification to the logics of state power. And, at the same time, they suggested the contradictory juxtaposition of the depersonalizing technologies of the state as it confronted workers' practices of power—derived from the personalizing intimacy of their work.

Intimacy and Workers' Power

What many South African domestic workers expressed, at times through parables, at times directly, was that the state's practice of power in the sector had threatened their own, issuing from the intimate nature of their work. Chapter 4 shows how domestic workers are not just like any other workers because their work, especially child care, involves—as a requirement of the work—the development of intimate emotional bonds. Workers explained that if they were to do their job, they had to actually care for the families whose households they maintained, and love the children they took care of. And most really did.

While this form of intimacy can be found in other kinds of care work, too—teachers and nurses, for instance—domestic workers uniquely do this work within the most intimate setting of private homes and lives. Even when involved only in cleaning rather than child or elder care, they work within the emotion-laden intimate spaces of other peoples' most private lives—they wash underwear, overhear (and sometimes become part of) family arguments, and are often the first ones to discover intimate family secrets.

In the absence of state protection under apartheid, South African domestic workers had strategically utilized exactly this intimacy, and the personal relationships bound to develop with their employers, as a way to independently control their work. In the absence of labor rights defining leave provision, sitting down every morning with tea and talking to one's employer about her problems became a way to ensure an extended Christmas vacation.

Even after labor rights defined working hours, one worker preferred to go into her backyard room on days she knew she was not required to work and "pull the blankets" over her head until her employer capitulated.

Why the continuation of these informal mechanisms for negotiating working conditions, when an extensive formal industrial relations system was there? Why refuse registration with the government, when it guarantees legal recourse against unfair labor practices and the material benefits of social security? The answer, as many workers expressed, was that while they strategically utilized their new rights to protect themselves in cases of dismissal, for instance, they also recognized the ways in which the state's efforts at formalization reflected a "will to empower" in ways that paternalistically transferred their erstwhile dependencies on their employers to the state. Their independent powers to control their work based in the personal nature of the relationship were unacknowledged by the state's efforts to depersonalize the relationship through formalization. Worse still, their own practices of power were being challenged.

Employers have been shown to also strategically cultivate personal relationships, albeit hierarchically, as a mode of power. The giving of gifts, for example, is not simply a benevolent gesture but has been keenly analyzed as a form of "maternalism" that ingratiates the worker to the employer, extracts more work, and allows employers to validate themselves as benefactor (Rollins 1985). But, South African domestic workers cultivated personalism and intimate relationships with their employers as an equal strategy of extracting benefits. Seemin Qayum and Raka Ray (2003) provide a brilliant analysis of the ways in which the discursive deployments of love and loyalty among servants in India are not deferential capitulations to the logics of "servitude" but rather important demands for mutual obligation and protective securities that are erased by the modernizing waged contract preferred by some of their middle-class employers.

Very interestingly, however, almost all South African workers (especially full-time live-out workers) preferred a depersonalized, formal, and modern employment relationship. This is quite different from many of the Indian servants in Kolkata (Qayum and Ray 2003), and Latina domestic workers in Los Angeles (Hondagneu-Sotelo 2001). In Los Angeles, some employers with hectic career and family responsibilities, and a discomfort with domestic servitude, tried hard *not* to cultivate intimate or personal relationships with their employees and treated them like depersonalized workers instead. The Latina immigrant domestics who worked for them "crave[d] personal contact" in reaction to this "new sterility" (Hondagneu-Sotelo 2001, 11). South African domestic workers preferred depersonalized relations but were acutely aware of the impossibility of this given the intensely intimate nature of their work. They therefore maintained personal relationships with their employers, more as a practice of power in terms of managing their working conditions than for the validation of their dignity as human beings and workers.

An abstract industrial relations system, it turns out, just cannot manage the daily intimate relations between mothers and the workers who care for and love their children. Cameron MacDonald's (1998) unique and perceptive analysis of the intense micropolitics of the relationships between nannies and the mothers they work for, which she captures in the brilliant theorization of in-home child care workers as "shadow mothers," shows how the intimate nature of the work and its intimate setting within private families, makes the relationships between employers and their workers highly personalized. South African domestic workers' ambivalence about a state-based attempt at depersonalization issued from the complications of intimacy that structures paid domestic work.

For South African domestic workers—who wanted formal, modern, and depersonalized employment relationships but were acutely aware that the intimate nature and setting of their work made this implausible—it was their collective control as workers over the process of depersonalization that was the issue. State efforts that presumed them too vulnerable and thereby acted on their behalf were rejected by some as an affront to their historically cultivated work culture that afforded them a measure of control over their own work. The democratic statecraft's "will to empower" had paternalistically rendered them subjects, rather than agents, of a modernizing of the occupation and was therefore met with contradictory impulses that included *both* the embrace of its protective elements *and* the rejection of otherwise seemingly sensible legislation. But, South African domestic workers' ambivalent response to the state's efforts to transform domestic servitude into modern and formal employment, and the resulting recalcitrance of the institution to change, also issued from another source: skepticism about the potential of rights.

"Maid" with Rights?

In the tenacious continuities of the logics of apartheid servitude alongside some modernizing transformations of the sector lay a commentary about the limited capacity of labor rights as a mechanism for overturning domestic workers' structural location as a reproducing class. Black South African domestic workers, from poor, often rural, backgrounds bestowed rights by democracy immediately confronted white employers who had been bestowed power by decades of apartheid. The formal power of the rights granted in law confronted the informal power of the deeply entrenched race and class inequalities between middle-class white "madams" and their still working-class black "maids." But, while this was a case of rights being rendered inert by powerful social inequalities, it was also more than that.

The extension of rights to domestic workers on the basis of their "vulnerability" presumed, and constructed, a specific kind of political subject—one availed by their lack of capacity—and therefore immediately delimiting their political potential. As Wendy Brown argues, to have a right as a designated category—in this case "vulnerable" domestic worker—"may entail some protection from the most immobilizing features of that designation, [but] it reinscribes the designation as it protects us, and thus enables our further regulation through that designation" (2002, 422). Making domestic workers the subject of rights through their construction as "vulnerable" defined their political status as incapacitated, making them politically inert as the bearers of those rights, and subject to state power to effect change instead.

At the same time, the rights granted to individual domestic workers to improve labor relations within their individual workplaces remained potently unable to change the structural logics of paid domestic work in South Africa. Chapter 5 shows how post-apartheid social welfare policy around child care refused more socialized responsibility and provision, leaving most domestic workers with only familial solutions to their care burdens. This at the same time as labor market policy regulated them as a supply of private caregivers to more privileged households.

Analyzing paid domestic work as part of this broader political economy of care, therefore, the attempt to turn "servants" into workers through liberal democratic rights, rather than empowering domestic workers as a social class, facilitated a conservative care regime in the country. For mostly black, poor women their only options were to leave their children in the care of unpaid family members, mostly grandmothers. At the same time, the state had effectively crafted a system that formally regulated them as a supply of quality, affordable, in-home care to more privileged households, reinforcing social stratification.

The profile of paid domestic work in post-apartheid South Africa, however, is not only a product of these structural forces—the legacies of apartheid's gendered and raced capitalism and the post-apartheid order's continuation of the same structures of privatized care provision. The historical and contemporary shape and substance of paid domestic work is as much reflective of domestic workers' own practices.

From Domination/Resistance to Practices of Power

Part III of the book confronts the tenacious theoretical problem at the core of studies of paid domestic work—domination and resistance. Paid domestic work is constitutively implicated in the most obstinate gendered, raced, and classed inequalities, yet domestic workers are seemingly notorious in their passivity against these structures of domination. They are not only accused of rarely raising organized voices of protest against their subordination, but are known for their deference. Various studies have therefore attempted to recover domestic workers' "agency," to demonstrate that they are not simply passive victims of structure, but that they can, and indeed do, *resist*. For instance, Judith Rollins (1985) theorized "ressentiment" as domestic workers' resistance to psychic domination, and Bonnie Thornton Dill (1988) suggested that workers' "chicanery" and "cajolery" were forms of resistance.

Resonating with the tradition of resistance studies exemplified by James Scott's (1985) *Weapons of the Weak*, recognizing the hidden transcripts of resistance that various categories of dispossessed deploy as subtle critiques of their domination is powerful. But, these forms of resistance rarely transform structures of subordination. Indeed, with domestic workers, cynical forms of deference, mocking modes of silence, or various types of "foot dragging"—wasting water while washing dishes or electricity while pressing laundry—simply confirm employers' racist, classist, or nativist attitudes. Workers' "agency" in these cases reinstantiates and reinforces, rather than disrupts, the logics of their domination. Paul Willis's (1977) classic ethnography, *Learning to Labor*, confronted the same problem. Working-class kids actively resisted the middle-class culture of schooling, but in doing so reproduced their position as working class. How do we reconcile a similar paradox of agency with domestic workers?

Rhacel Parreñas (2001a) offers an interesting possibility. Quoting Judith Butler, she argues that "the analysis of subjection is always double, tracing the conditions of subject formation and tracing the turn against these conditions for the subject—and its perspective—to emerge" (1997, 29; cited in Parreñas 2001, 33). Resistance is therefore never an escape from domination, but a reflection of the "bind of agency" in which the subject simultaneously engages in a "recuperation" and "resistance" of power. But, this theoretical posture still remains framed within the vocabulary of agency as resistance.

Posing the problem as one of the "seemingly simple dualism domination/resistance," Sherry Ortner proposes escaping it through an anthropology of resistance focused on "practice," following Pierre Bourdieu's attempt to dissolve the apposite polarities of structure and agency (2006, 282). But, the attempt to resolve the dualism presupposes it to begin with. Lila Abu-Lughod (1990), intervening in a long-standing debate about "agency" in feminist theory, criticizes feminist theorists and her own previous work for being obsessed with, and therefore romanticizing, resistance. Instead, she proposes a different formulation that bypasses the domination/resistance duality altogether and privileges the theoretical place of a different analytic—power. Instead of trying to document resistance and understand how it ameliorates domination, she argues we should look to social practices as a "diagnostic of power" (42).

A similar approach is attempted in this study of South African domestic workers. An analytic that focuses on the practices of power—of the state and workers—attempts to evade the domination/resistance problematic. The state, in its subject-producing practices of power, confronted workers whose refusal of such subjection also represented a practice of power. In their claims that things were "worse than before," and in cultivating a work culture that relied heavily on intimacy, the practices and narratives of workers are used to diagnose the workings of power. Chapter 6 details workers' collective mobilization in unions and church groups, but the purpose is not to paternalistically represent domestics as capable of agency but to diagnose post-apartheid state practices of power instead. Positioning itself as the articulator and representative of workers' collective interests through the trope of "vulnerability," the state displaced the union from that role, leading workers to eschew a historical tradition of unionism in favor of private forms of protest. At the same time, the collective affirmation of motherhood in the church-based *manyano* (mothers' prayer unions) is used not to suggest worker resistance but instead to diagnose state and employer assaults on workers as mothers and persons (chapter 7).

Within this reformulated analytic focused on power, the book documents the ways in which South African domestic workers have negotiated their lives of hardship with defiant struggles—collectively in trade unions and churches, as well as individually in their workplaces and families. They have, in fact, co-constructed the institution they inhabit. Where democratic reforms have struggled to achieve their desired results, it is as much a reflection of workers' practices of power as it is of the state and employers.

————————

THE experiences of South African domestic workers in the state's efforts to transform them from "servants" into workers complicates dominant current advocacy that presents state-based regulation of paid domestic work as a solution to the exploitation and abuse faced by this highly marginalized workforce.[29] Legally recognizing paid domestic work as a form of employment, and domestic workers as *workers*, with the accoutrements of a formal industrial relations system and the extension of labor rights, requires a more sensitive analysis. It requires paying careful attention to *how* domestic workers are politically incorporated, the kinds of state power and political subjects that may be implied by different modes of political inclusion, and the intimate nature and setting of their work.

For studies that have explored the disconnect between domestic workers' recognition as employees and the continued servitude relations that prevail in those contexts, an analysis of the state as much as employers and workers is required. Explanations that present the democratic state as the benevolent protector and employers as the recalcitrant noncompliers, or employees as the deferential nonclaimants of their own rights, do not take seriously enough the ways in which the crafting of rights-based protection may be part of the problem of the institution's obstinate refusal to transform.

For South African domestic workers, continuities with apartheid in the logic and practice of paid domestic work did not reflect a lack of state will to transform the institution, nor even lack of state commitment in enforcing their own laws, but actually the opposite. An active and energetic democratic statecraft reflected a serious commitment to improving the lot of domestic workers by recognizing their status as workers in an employment relationship. But the "will to empower" (Cruikshank 1999) that constructed domestics as too "vulnerable" to effect change themselves, and as thus requiring the benevolent state to act on their behalf, unleashed a mode of power that ignored workers' existing capacities and practices of power, reinforced domestic workers' dependent statuses, and reflected an insensitivity to the specificities of paid domestic work as an intimate form of labor. In this, the democratic statecraft of turning "servants" into workers is as much responsible for the dramatic improvements that have taken place in the sector as it is for some of the institution's more stubborn resistances to a progressive transformation.

Part I
Apartheid Servitude

1

The Apartheid State and Modern Servitude

In 1905, just as the then colonial government of South Africa entered the twentieth century, an official commission on "native affairs" made the following extraordinary recommendation: "One branch of the Native labour question is the employment of women, and the Commission feels that it is highly desirable that every measure should be adopted which would encourage the employment of native women in domestic work."[1]

It's a remarkable fossil of South Africa's complex history of servitude, and the role of the state in it. Suggesting complicity of the state in legislatively intervening in the sector, it overturns popular understandings of the history of state regulation of paid domestic work. In a poem published in a union newsletter in 1986, for example, Roseline Naapo lamented the life of a domestic as that of "the lonely worker." She ended the poem by addressing plaintively the "rules of our country." "How can you forget me in your house," she pleads, "how can you forget the lonely worker."[2]

Presuming the absence of the state and legislative regulation, Jacklyn Cock, author of the seminal study *Maids and Madams* (1980a), also argued that part of the problem of domestic workers under apartheid was that they were "located in a legal vacuum" (1980b, 10). What she and Roseline Naapo meant was that "domestic workers [were] not protected by any legislation" (ibid.). But, popular and scholarly accounts have extended this to presume the absence of the state in the relationships between "maids" and "madams." The exploitations of apartheid servitude are often imagined as issuing from the failure of state regulation and the resultant power of employers to unilaterally dictate conditions for their "servants." It is not surprising, then, that state intervention in the relationship between employers and employees is proposed as a solution to ending the exploitations of the sector post-apartheid.

Even from as early as 1905, however, the (at first) colonial and (later) apartheid states were not absent as a regulatory force in the sector. Whether attempting, at various historical intervals, to get more immigrant white women or more "native" women into the occupation or deciding whether to manage the relationship as a colonial, feudal one between "masters" and "servants" or as a distinctively modern form of servitude between "maids" and "madams," state regulation has been a distinctive feature of colonial and then apartheid servitude. Excavating the state's relationship to domestic service in the existing historiography of the sector both complicates existing understandings of the conditioning of "servitude" by state regulation and provides a more textured understanding of contemporary forms of state regulation.

Colonial Servitude

Domestic service in South Africa began as a project of colonial servitude. In the settler colony of the mid- to late eighteenth century, especially in the Cape, it was slaves who served as domestics. Not only the local black population but also Africans from as far as Madagascar, and even Asians, were enslaved by the early colonists as domestics (Gaitskell et al. 1984, 98; Cock 1980a). While the women slaves worked as skilled seamstresses, wet nurses, and child rearers, the men (mostly Malay) worked as cooks and butlers (Gaitskell et al. 1984). White immigrant labor was also available, but it is argued that the early colonists preferred black slave labor because "it was cheaper and more controllable and some officials considered that it was more fitting for slaves than free whites to do menial work" (Gaitskell et al. 1984, 98).

Toward the end of the eighteenth century, however, with slavery less politically tenable than before, domestic service transformed from a form of slavery to a form of waged labor marked by feudal relations. On the east coast of the Cape Colony, Dutch farmers reportedly employed local African women as servants (Cock 1980a). On the west coast, various local groups, as well as whites and men, were incorporated into wage labor early on (Boddington 1983). By the end of the eighteenth century, the availability of domestic servants was already not only a staple feature of colonists' lives but also one of the earliest and more significant forms of waged labor in colonial South Africa. Indeed, concludes Jeff Peires, it is in this early history of domestic service that "we see the beginnings of a permanent class of wage laborers" (1976, 170).

By the beginning of the nineteenth century, however, white English colonial settlement at the Cape inaugurated an era in which white women immigrants entered and came to predominate in domestic service. The arrival in 1820 of English settlers to the eastern shores of the Cape saw a shift in the demographic composition of domestic service (Cock 1980a). Accustomed to servants in England, they increased the demand for domestic workers upon their arrival. But, by 1834, emancipation had outlawed the supply of slave labor (Boddington 1983), and local waged domestic labor was in short supply (Cock 1980a). So, many of the settlers who arrived in the first few decades of the nineteenth century brought their own European domestic workers with them (Cock 1980a). Later, primarily in the 1840s, large numbers of European women immigrated to South Africa to work as domestic servants (Swaisland 1993). And, for the better part of the next several decades, European women came to constitute a significant proportion of the domestic labor force in the Cape (Boddington 1983).

This important demographic shift in the patterns of paid domestic work during the first half of the nineteenth century was shaped by European employers' preferences for white servants trained in their cultural tastes and by the choices of the white women who became their servants (Swaisland 1993). Seeking a route of escape from the poor working conditions and limited occupational opportunities available to them in a highly class-stratified Britain, the comparatively high wages for domestic servants between 1820 and 1860 attracted European women to the colonies (Swaisland 1993).

But, the colonial state also played an important role in structuring this supply of labor for white colonists. Far from absent, the state was actually petitioned to become more active in regulating a supply of domestic labor for colonists. At public meetings in the eastern Cape, a government-aided "white labor policy" was urged (Cock 1980a, 192). For the first few decades of the nineteenth century, an embargo had been enforced on the funding of immigration (Swaisland 1993), so the state's hands were proverbially tied. But, in 1844, when that embargo ended, the Cape government quickly voted 10,000 pounds to assist immigration and established the Colonial Land and Emigration Commission that began to recruit the domestic labor that was so in demand (Swaisland 1993). These assisted immigration policies were, in part, responsible for the influx of a relatively substantial 14,000 immigrants to the eastern Cape during this period, many of whom worked as domestic servants (Garson 1976; Hattersley 1969). This state assistance contributed to establishing the 1840s as a decisive decade of white female immigration into domestic service.

In the following decades, the state continued to actively craft a supply of white (female) domestic labor for settlers and colonists. Government Notice No. 742 of 1889 printed regulations for the granting of aided passages to domestic servants from England who were prepared to enter into contracts of at least twelve months (Boddington 1983). And in the interior of the country (the Witwatersrand), the local administration created a "Women's Immigration Department" that arranged for the import and reception of white women immigrant workers, many of whom were destined for domestic service (Van Onselen 1982).

Toward the 1880s, however, the supply of white servants was unreliable and unable to meet the demand for domestic labor in the Cape. The difficulties in enforcing contracts entered into in Britain, combined with the tendency for immigrant servants to marry soon after arrival, led many—though not all—white European women to leave domestic service (Swaisland 1993). "Poor accommodation and loneliness" in households where they were the only servant, and the difficulties of "mixing black and white" servants in multiservant households made domestic service an unsatisfactory form of employment for white women immigrants (Swaisland 1993, 81). Since, at the time, "marriage was easy to come by," they usually quickly opted out of paid domestic work (Swaisland 1993).

From White Women, to Black Men, to Black Women

As European women moved out of domestic service, an important demographic shift was initiated. In the Cape, domestic service shifted from an occupation of largely white immigrant women to predominantly black women (both "Coloured" and "African"[3] while in the interior (the Witwatersrand) and the coastal colony of Natal, white female servants were replaced initially by black African men. While these shifts were connected to the patterns of capitalist development, as well as employer and employee preferences, the shift was also conditioned by the state, which played a significant role in managing the raced and gendered character of domestic service throughout this period.

In the Eastern Cape, as European domestic servants moved out of the occupation, they were replaced by black African women, thanks to the direct intervention of the colonial state. An indigenous local group, "Khoikhoi," were replaced as servants by another group of black Africans, "Bechuanas," who were not originally from the area. This was done actively by the colonial government at the time, distributing the "Bechuanas" among the settlers as servants (Cock 1980a).

In the western Cape as well, black Africans came to predominate in domestic service due to direct state efforts. The report of a Select Committee "on the Labour Question" proposed that "native" laborers should be introduced into the Cape in response to complaints from employers about a lack of cheap (domestic) labor (Boddington 1983, 159–61). So successful was the effort that after 1875, domestic service became a main source of employment for all groups of black women wage earners in the Western Cape (Boddington 1983; Gaitskell et al. 1984).

In the late 1800s, black Africans also constituted a large proportion of domestic workers in the newly established and rapidly growing mining camp of Johannesburg. It was a period of great demand for domestic workers, and one in which white women immigrants came to occupy the top rungs of a segmented domestic labor market (Van Onselen 1982). White women predominated in the homes of the bourgeoisie (the merchant and mining capitalists) and the petty bourgeoisie, where they served as specialist servants, assisted by the more ubiquitous white, black, or "coloured" general servants (Van Onselen 1982). But, while the demand for white women's labor remained generally high, peaking in the 1890s (Van Onselen 1982), "the limited supply of white female labor could not hope to match the demand in all these areas, especially the demand for reliable domestic servants" (Cobley 1997, 70). Various state efforts therefore sought to increase the supply.

The registry office played an important role in this effort, connecting employers and employees (Van Onselen 1982). Such registry offices had operated in port cities such as Durban, Cape Town, and Port Elizabeth for some time (ibid.). In the interior town of Johannesburg, two such registry offices, including the South African Employment Bureau, supplied domestic workers either through local hiring or through the recruitment of immigrant European servants (Van Onselen 1982).

In a rare and stunning study of the domestic life of one household on the Witwatersrand, Ian van der Waag (2007) details sensitively the anxieties and transformations of the servant complement of the Wyndham residence during the early part of the twentieth century. The assault on the aristocracy in Britain led nobles like Hugh and Maud Wyndham to transport their aristocratic traditions of servitude to the periphery of empire. Van der Waag wonderfully traces how the Wyndhams adapted the use of various strategies to ensure a decent complement of servants to attend to their leisured lifestyle, everything from poaching the staff of friends to utilizing the recruitment mechanisms of the South African Expansion Committee (later the South African Colonisation Society) and various registry services in Britain. "But, the overall scale of the problem was clearly beyond the capacities of the registries," argues Van Onselen, resulting in a "steadily increasing demand for the labour of the largest group of servants of all on the Witwatersrand—African men" (1982, 5).

With the limited supply of white women, and (at that time) limited African women's urbanization to the mining areas around Johannesburg, the "houseboy" became the characteristic domestic worker on the Witwatersrand by the beginning of the twentieth century (Van Onselen 1982). In particular, through a combination of factors including a rinderpest (cattle plague) outbreak that most affected the cattle-keeping groups of southern Africa, it was African males from Zululand and Natal who became houseboys. Zulu houseboys became ubiquitous on the Witwatersrand after 1897 (Van Onselen 1982). "By the outbreak of the war the words 'houseboy' and 'Zulu' had become almost synonymous on the Rand labour market," argues Van Onselen (1982, 8). White households relied on them for a variety of tasks, from washing laundry to cooking and even nursing infants (Cobley 1997).

By the 1930s, this dominance of the houseboy had given way to a major shift in which African women came to dominate the serving classes of Johannesburg. While it took a few more decades for this to happen on the Witwatersrand than in the Cape, by the 1930s the dominant demographic pattern of domestic service in South Africa had been established (Cock 1980; Boddington 1983; Gaitskell et al. 1984). The processes through which African women came to dominate domestic service throughout the remainder of the twentieth century were complex, but the state proved crucial.

Black African Women as "Servants"

In the early twentieth century, black African women became predominant in paid domestic work. In Cape Town, from 1911 to 1946, the sector transitioned from "Colored" women as the primary demographic to black African women dominating the occupation (Boddington 1983). Similarly, in Johannesburg, it was the 1930s that marked the watershed when African women came to predominate in domestic service. In 1936, the census there found, for the first time, more African women employed in domestic service than African men (Cobley 1997).

This demographic transformation of paid domestic work suggested the pattern of African female urbanization. While black African women's urbanization had been muted for more than a century since the process began for African men, the first half of the twentieth century saw a major shift in the pace and character of African women's entry into the towns. African female urbanization began only in the 1920s, later than for any other demographic group, but it proceeded rapidly once it had begun: Between 1921 and 1936, while African male urbanization was 44.9 percent, for African women it was 245.3 percent (Walker 1990). The vast majority of these urbanized women, initially, joined the ranks of the domestic working class. For example, in Johannesburg, the vast majority of African women listed as "gainfully employed" before World War II were domestic servants (89.66% in 1921, and 91.56% in 1936) (Gaitskell et al. 1984). Effectively 90 percent of African women employed in the city were domestic servants (Gaitskell 1979).

That such large numbers of African women entered the urban wage-earning labor market, and in particular the domestic labor market, reflected the transformations of capitalism. In both the Cape and the Witwatersrand, processes of capitalist penetration and development, of land dispossession and subsequent proletarianization, played a central role in the mobilization of a black African labor force into paid domestic labor. African women had, however, only belatedly entered the circuit of migrant labor compared to African men. Scholars argued this was because of the developing form of racial capitalism in South Africa. It was theorized that African men had to be urbanized and converted into waged laborers to service the labor demands of a capitalism in formation, while African women's urbanization had to be curbed. This in order to maintain a rural economy in the so-called native reserves that would, by funding the costs of the social reproduction of the worker, subsidize capitalist development (Wolpe 1972).

Feminist historians, however, effectively argued that the differential urbanization (and proletarianization) of African men versus African women arose also, in part, as a result of preexisting gender relations in the countryside and women's negotiation of these (Bozzoli 1983; Walker 1990; Berger 1992). The rapid entry of African women into urban waged labor markets from the 1930s onward reflected the choices of African women to escape the patriarchal relations of the countryside and to seek economic independence for themselves and their children (Walker 1990; Bozzoli 1991).

That they found themselves in domestic service, however, reflected not only these choices on their part, and the changing nature of capitalism, but also direction by the state. The early, nearly equivalent, relationship between African women's proletarianization and their entry into paid domestic work suggested a more structured process of migrancy and capitalist incorporation than that presumed by Cherryl Walker (1990), who argues that, contrary to the coercive male migrant labor system, African women's urbanization reflected "voluntarism." While African women's urbanization certainly reflected their wills and imperatives, it was not a process free of state control.

In various efforts to explain African women's urbanization and entry into paid domestic service, the role of the state and of official attempts to stimulate and control the domestic labor supply have been eclipsed by considerations of the role of capitalism, racism, and responses to these. Cock (1980), for example, in the attempt to explain the transition in domestic service from predominantly whites to predominantly Africans, argues: "because of the low wages, and poor working conditions it involved, whites escaped it as blacks were increasingly coerced into it" (73). The extent to which such coercion was mediated by state control and to which capitalist and racialized demands were materialized through state mandate, resulting in extensive legislative regulation of the sector, have not been fully recognized. Instead, the dominant image of domestic service under first colonial control and then apartheid is of a sector defined by the impunity of employers divorced of regulatory oversight by the state, leading Cock to the conclusion that domestic service under apartheid existed in a "legal vacuum" (1980b, 10). Far from this, however, paid domestic work was a crucial site of control for the colonial, and then apartheid, state. A colonial legal apparatus managed the sector as a feudal relationship from early in the nineteenth century and later, by the time of apartheid in the 1940s, co-constructed a distinctly modern form of servitude.

State Regulation of Colonial Servitude

In the nineteenth century, various pieces of colonial legislation, Union and Republic statutes, as well as the common law remained important legislative devices and mechanisms of control over paid domestic labor.

Most important of these in defining the relationship in specifically feudal terms was the Masters and Servants Act (No. 30 of 1889). This regulation by law of the relationship between "masters" and "servants" maintained state regulatory oversight for control over the sector and defined *servants* in feudal terms as subject to the control of both their "masters" and the state. Cases brought to courts in line with the Act demonstrated the degree of coercion necessary to force and maintain a supply of domestic waged labor (Boddington 1983) and the importance of the state, through its role as enactor and enforcer of the Act, in structuring colonial servitude.

Connected to the interests of farming capital, the Act's extensions and applications signaled the state's class and controlling interests (Boddington 1983). While holding on to farm labor was centrally important in the application of the Act, so was the state's interests in control of the population. Employers were somewhat schizophrenic: They wanted harsher punishments for those who broke their contracts and greater state control of the stimulation of a labor supply, but they also wanted less state "interference" in the relationship itself (Boddington 1983). Amendments to the Masters and Servants Act continued to actively control the supply of domestic labor on farms while refusing to give in to employers' demands for harsher punishments and less state "interference" in the relationships between "masters" and "servants."

While these amendments to the Act gave the state increased control over servants, it did not offer much control over those not already employed. Other forms of legislative control were mobilized to serve that purpose. The Vagrancy Act (No. 23 of 1879), in its primary effort to control stock theft, secondarily produced a supply of domestic labor (Boddington 1983). Together with the opening of servant's registry offices, the state managed the domestic labor market in important ways. A number of "servants registry offices" were opened in and around Cape Town, for instance, to exert "stronger control over domestic workers in the city" (Boddington 1983, 172). A labor bureau was opened in 1902, and in 1906 an amendment to the Trespassers Act was passed that, according to Boddington (1983), was part of the apparatuses of state control over the supply and distribution of paid domestic labor.

Similarly, as already discussed, the demographic composition of domestic service, over time, was also a product of state regulation. The state played an active role in managing the supply of white immigrant women early on. When these immigrant white women were in short supply by the turn of the century, the state first turned to the local white population as a potential source of domestic labor. Indeed, the state sought to establish homes for young white women from poor backgrounds that would assist in securing a supply of cheap domestic labor. The 1906 Select Committee on Labour Settlements for Indigent Whites argued that there was evidence "that institutions such as those contemplated by the Act, may be of some assistance in the solution of the 'poor white' question. The girls are rescued from undesirable and, in many cases, immoral surroundings, and are trained in house-work, so as to become useful as mothers' helps" (cited in Boddington 1983, 170).

The most significant demographic shift in paid domestic work—that of the shift toward black African women in the twentieth century—similarly bore the strong imprint of state control and management of a domestic labor supply. After the Anglo-Boer War in the first decade of the twentieth century, mining and other companies sought male labor for production, and this required the recruitment of alternative labor for reproduction. The 1905 South African Native Affairs Commission (SANAC) report with which this chapter opened reflected state management of capitalist interests, by urging the promotion of a class of African female domestics. The report went on to argue: "The employment of Native women for domestic purposes would, particularly in Natal and Transvaal, release large numbers of men and boys for employment in occupations more suited to them. One of the results which the employment of females may reasonably be hoped to have would be the introduction into Native domestic life of higher standards of comfort, cleanliness, and order."[4]

The report argued that African women's entry into domestic work would not only free crucial male labor for the mines but also "civilize" Africans into more acceptable (i.e., white) aesthetic tastes of domesticity (Boddington 1983). The report intimated the state's active involvement in structuring the domestic labor market. Indeed, as early as 1902, the Milner administration on the Witwatersrand undertook to resolve the problem of the intersectoral competition for labor between the mining and domestic markets by devising a scheme that, for several months, provided black female domestic servants to the citizens of Johannesburg from the military refugee camps (Van Onselen 1982). This was, however, short-lived and unsystematic.

In 1913, in the first major effort to regulate this system actively, the state sought to extend to African women the pass laws that already applied to "native" men. In doing this, it "intended to force African women and girls into domestic service in white homes" (Gaitskell et al. 1984, 99). But, the militant protests against this by women refusing to be proletarianized and controlled by the state reflected the incapacity of the state to enact its vision and delayed women's entry into the sector. Well into the first few decades of the twentieth century, employers also resisted the state's expressed requirement for the urbanization of African women. White women employers on the Witwatersrand, for instance, continued to prefer "boys," arguing that "country girls" were too ignorant, too dirty, and too troublesome for domestic work (Van Onselen 1982). Van Onselen (1982) argues that this often reflected white women's fears that African women would enter into sexual relations with their sons and husbands, aided by the fact that, initially at least, African women were not any cheaper than African men.

By the 1930s, more urgent demands for male labor, particularly in the mines, together with African women's greater willingness to enter the urban labor market, restructured the conditions of supply and demand for domestic labor. In 1937, the report of the official state Commission of Enquiry regarding the Cape Coloured population of the Union suggested the state's consciousness of its role in balancing the racial and gendered composition of domestic service: "Native competition in the field of domestic service is also widening in extent. . . . Here again the Natives, both male and female, often show considerable aptitude, and, as in other fields, their requirements with regard to housing, treatment and wages are more easily satisfied. In addition, there is a decided disinclination . . . among many Cape Coloured menfolk today to enter domestic service, and this helps to provide the Native with an opening for work" (cited in Boddington 1983).

More specifically, the state focused its efforts on restructuring paid domestic work as the preserve of black African women. As Boddington notes, "there was never any question that employers should do without domestic workers. Men who had been incorporated into wage labour as domestic workers were required in other sectors—women were suggested as replacements" (1983, 184). The changing demands of capitalism, and growing African women's urbanization, supplemented by the failure of supply of white women servants (Swaisland 1993), meant that the relative cost of employing African women declined as their numbers in towns grew (Van Onselen 1982). This shift was aided by a series of notoriously sensational "black peril" scares involving cases of alleged sexual assault of white mistresses by black "houseboys" (Van Onselen 1982; Cobley 1997). So intense was the paranoia that a mass meeting held in Johannesburg had "unanimously decreed," "in loud, manly tones," "that the houseboy must go!" While many white women were not ready to let go of their trusted houseboys, it was reported that "within the last couple of years many housekeepers have found out the value of native women as servants, and have discovered that it is possible to get hardworking respectable women to whom they can entrust their children" (*Transvaal Leader*, 1915).[5] If the "black peril" scares accelerated the transition of African men out of domestic service, the state shaped African women's entry into domestic service, and the confused and sometimes contradictory efforts by the different tiers of the state—national versus municipal—reflected the ambivalence of this process.

The government's official commission into the "black peril" investigated the apparent epidemic proportions of alleged sexual assaults of white women by their houseboys and "concluded that only African women could be an effective substitute for the 'houseboy'" (Gaitskell 1979, 50). The state directed this process, in ways that suggested the competing and contradictory imperatives of the different constituencies involved in domestic service. Municipal authorities, undergirded by white property owners desiring African women's urbanization for domestic service, but only under heavily regulated conditions that would control them, attempted to impose at times stricter controls over the African working women within their boundaries. This included, in particular, pass measures that would regulate and control African women's entry into urban areas and tie their urban status to employment (Cobley 1997). The Native Affairs Department of the central state, however, was not willing to impose strict controls at first, both as a result of African women's resistance to these and because their presence was needed in the countryside (Cobley 1997). Julia Wells (1991) shows that women were deliberately omitted from the pass provisions of the Natives (Urban Areas) Act of 1923. By 1930 and 1937, special amendments to the Act did eventually extend controls to African women. This lethargic control by the state over the supply of African female labor has led some, like Walker (1990), to assume the failure of the state in managing African women as a labor force.

But the state's role in controlling African women's labor was not lethargic as much as more nuanced than its control of African men. For African women, the state enacted its efforts at control through third parties with whom they shared an interest, if for altogether different ideological purposes. Key among these were churches and missionaries, and crucial among these joint state-church initiatives that channeled African women into domestic service were hostels for "native" girls. So significant were these hostels in channeling African women into domestic service in concert with the state that Gaitskell (1979) has described them as "Christian compounds for girls." These hostels paralleled the function of mining compounds for male migrant workers, suggesting the ways in which the migrant domestic labor force was as equally structured by the state—if in different forms—as the migrant mine labor system.

It was the original official 1905 South African Native Affairs Commission Report that suggested this would be a necessary institution in coordinating and grooming African women's entry into domestic service. Given African women's defiant resistance to being coerced into towns as cheap, servile labor, the hostels played an important intermediate role in shaping the desires of domesticity among younger African women in their initial urbanization (Gaitskell 1979). The report went on to argue: "Where it might appear probable that organised efforts to secure a supply of Native female servants would be effective, provision might be made for the formation of Societies which would undertake the duty of protecting female workers by securing suitable employment for them and providing them with homes or refuges while awaiting employment."[6]

White employers and property owners were increasingly uncomfortable about the presumed "immorality" of African women in towns, and they resisted government efforts to restructure the supply of African male domestic workers to mines and replace them with African women (Cobley 1997). At the same time, African parents and structures of authority in the countryside equally drew on tropes of the supposed degradation of African women's morality in the towns to justify resistance to their proletarianization (Gaitskell 1979). The proposed Societies would alleviate both of these concerns by providing training grounds in which African women could be "civilized" into the Christian morality that would presumably protect them from the moral degeneration they were purportedly susceptible to in the towns (Cobley 1997). Not only would parents and white urban residents' fears be addressed, but in so doing, training for domesticity could introduce African women as an attractive supply of domestic labor. "For the next twenty years every major government commission and every missionary conference which considered the position of African women in towns reiterated the need for such hostels," summarizes Cobley (1997, 85).

Within a decade of the original report, these Societies had materialized as "native girls" hostels, run by the churches, to domesticate African girls—both within their own homes and for pay in the homes of others (Gaitskell 1979). But, they were run in concert with the state's continuing efforts to manage the distribution of African women as migrant domestic workers.[7] In 1917, the Anglican Women's Missionary Committee proposed cooperation between church-run hostels and an employment bureau to be run by the government's Native Affairs Department in order to find work for hostel residents (Cobley 1997). Over the next two decades, three other hostels for African women would open in Johannesburg: the

Helping Hand Club in 1919, the municipality owned and operated "Native Women's Hostel" at Wolhuter in 1930, and the Wesleyan Hostel in 1934 (Cobley 1997).

The hostels were defined by the training for domesticity of African girls and, undergirded by state support, ensured a demographic transition in the supply of a migrant domestic labor force. The Anglican Native girls' hostel for instance, acted directly as "housemaid employment agency" (Gaitskell 1983, 246). The Girl Wayfarers Movement similarly, according to a missionary quoted by Gaitskell, helped "to make good servants, Housewives and Mothers who will understand how to take care of their children" (Gaitskell 1983, 246). The Talitha Home for Native Girls, too, trained girls in domesticity: "The large laundry took in orders, and girls who proved trustworthy were sent out unaccompanied for daily domestic work" (Gaitskell 1983, 247).

Indeed, the period of the most accelerated replacement of African men by African women in domestic service coincided with "the very decades when hostel advocacy reached its peak" (Gaitskell 1979, 46). So close was the relationship between the state and these church-run hostels in managing the supply of African women as domestic servants, and the contradictory imperatives of national and municipal tiers of the state, that when in 1924 the Johannesburg City Council vetoed plans for the site of a women's hostel because of outrage over African girls being housed in the town, the (Acting) Director of Native Labor intervened personally to reassure householders that "domestic servants had always been a recognized exception to residential segregation" (cited in Gaitskell 1979).

In 1925, the role of these hostels as a form of control over the African female migrant labor system for domestic work (subtly authorized by the state) was confirmed again as the Joint Council of Europeans and Natives directly sought to use hostels as a measure of control that would not require the reintroduction of passes for African women. A Joint Council committee met with Prime Minister J. B. M. Hertzog in January 1925, and came up with a "highly complicated scheme" in which Native girls' hostels were central. It directly planned to control the movement of African women "mainly through the Natives themselves and through those who are interested in their welfare." It would also directly ensure a supply of African women domestic workers as hostels would receive names of work-seekers from the Native Record Offices, and employers would only be allowed to hire servants through hostels and these offices. Although the Joint Council's efforts did not materialize, the consideration within official circles of this mechanism to replace the pass law control is suggestive (Gaitskell 1979, 53).

The necessity of channeling the burgeoning African female urban population into domestic service had further official expressions. The 1930 and 1937 amendments to the Urban Areas Act of 1923, if not strictly enforceable, demonstrated the state's willingness to control the influx of African women. Women could enter the towns and remain there so long as they were under the control of a male (husband or father) and had accommodation. This ensured a steady influx of African women available to constitute a supply of domestic labor, but strictly within the limits prescribed by the state (Gaitskell 1979). These measures of pass controls were firmly enmeshed with questions of the supply of African women as domestic labor, as Boddington notes of the *Report of the Native Economic Commission* in 1932 that considered extending passes to women: "Looking only at passes from the view of domestic service, this was partly in order to give control over an increased supply of women to domestic service, so that men could enter other sectors of employment which suffered greater shortages" (1983, 185).

Furthermore, as a direct result of state policy, the availability of legal self-employment was intensely prescribed by law, leading Denis Hirson to conclude that "the only alternative for most women was domestic service" (1990, 56). Boddington reiterates, with emphasis on the interests served by these state forms of control: "Measures by the ruling class to obtain cheap Black labour were major factors which led to Black women being trapped in domestic service" (1983, 100).

Even before African women entered the sector, pass laws were used to regulate the domestic labor market. Van Onselen argues that the state was responsible for "harshly controlling the majority of servants that really made the system function—the black 'houseboys'" and its major mechanism for doing this was "of course, the pass laws," which while "primarily directed at industrial workers, they also applied to domestic servants" (1982, 29). As pass laws and the influx control machinery served to regulate the domestic sector, the state remained directly involved in ensuring that urbanized African women were channeled into domestic service.

Early on, a government commission that sought to replace white women with African domestic workers, argued that the former "object to menial work, and also have a strong feeling of repugnance against working with natives in any household when these are employed" (cited in Berger 1992, 22). Later, the efforts to replace African men with African women were much more direct. In 1938, the Municipal Employment Bureau was established, which found it difficult to satisfy the demand for domestic labor, and actively placed more women in domestic service than men (Gaitskell 1979).

The Apartheid State's Structuring of Modern Servitude

With the mobilization of a laboring class of black female domestics, the apartheid state actively regulated the sector through a set of distinctively modern forms of labor control. Domestic workers became subject to the extensive system of urban control that characterized apartheid. Labor bureaus remained a staple feature of domestic service throughout the apartheid era, operating as part of the expansive influx control apparatus. In an early example of this, in 1908, on the Witwatersrand, the labor bureau supplied "piccanins"[8] for domestic service (Van Onselen 1982). Later, in the apartheid era, these labor bureaus not only regulated the sector but actively contributed to the demographic profile of domestic work and the transition in the 1930s toward African women's predominance in the sector.

Gaitskell (1983) argues that white approaches to African urbanization and employment in domestic service around the time of World War II crystallized around two positions. While missionaries and urban manufacturers argued that regulating "higher wages" in the sector would be an effective market-driven mechanism for ensuring a controllable supply of African women in domestic labor, state and municipal officials converged on "more influx control" as a way to regulate the sector. In 1936, the South African Native Affairs Commission resolved that debate by arguing that the flow of African women to the towns, and their entry into domestic service, had to be managed and controlled through influx control (Gaitskell 1983).

Iris Berger argues that "the bleak economic situation of the African reserves, the commercialization of agriculture, and more varied alternative openings for African men eventually supplied more black women for domestic labor than any direct state policies" (1992, 26). But, the state was never absent from structuring black women's paid domestic labor. That African women were forced into domestic service because of the failure of alternative legal options, prescribed by state racial policy, is the most obvious of these official coercions. Not only did the apartheid architecture of citizenship directly tie urban residence for African women to employment, but the state also systematically prevented African women from alternative forms of independent economic activity, such as beer brewing and prostitution.

But, the state played a much more varied, even ambivalent at times, role in the management of the domestic labor market than that which is obvious or presumed by the lamentations of the exploitative character emerging from the failure of state protection. Of course, state directives were effective only to the extent that African women chose to follow them. Indeed, it was not the entry of African women into paid domestic work during the early twentieth century that was so distinctive, but in fact, the ways in which African women consistently refused to be incorporated into waged labor on any terms other than their own. Berger concludes: "Although some young women were forced into service because of the scarcity of alternatives, their stubborn reluctance to enter household work was perhaps the most distinct characteristic of women's protest during the early industrial period" (1992, 43).

As the apartheid machinery gathered steam toward the 1950s and an extensive influx control system involving administration boards and labor bureaus regulated the supply of cheap African male labor to the mines and secondary industry, an equivalent bureaucratic machinery of influx control regulated the by now hundreds of thousands of African women who had entered paid domestic work. Domestic workers required work permits to remain in a "white" urban area, and the worker (by 1978, whether part- or full-time, live-in or live-out) had to be registered with one of the Bantu Affairs Administration Boards by employers. Labor bureaus functioned as a mechanism of the state to distribute workers among the employers who came to the state-run bureaus to hire a domestic. The chief director of the Port Natal Bantu Administration Board, in 1978, on announcing the new "directive from Pretoria" that all domestic workers would have to be registered with the Board, noted: "It is not a question of denying a person the right to work. It is controlling that activity in order to avoid a chaotic situation arising, as could happen if there were no control. It is purely to control the number of people in the area and to make sure there is no oversupply" (*The Daily News*, June 22, 1978).

By the late 1970s, domestic work was a sector enmeshed in this web of legal requirements inaugurating a modern system of legislated coercion and control that replaced the Masters and Servants Act after 1974. This was a key moment in which the state officially transformed the legal encoding of domestic "servants" and recognized paid domestic work as a form of modern servitude, akin to employment for the purposes of control rather than protection. As a result, a curiously hybridized arrangement of modern labor control over the work of serving others was instituted. And, the legal regulation was quite extensive.

The characteristic understanding of domestic work during this period is of employers and workers having to ensure the legality of their workers in the white urban areas—or be faced with the threat of fines, raids, or both. In the late 1970s, this network of legal control over the sector by the state was so onerous that a local newspaper ran an advice column for employers of domestic workers, subtitled: "Do you regard the engagement of black domestic help as a burden of bewildering bureaucracy?" (*The Citizen*, July 10, 1978), and then went on to detail the registration requirements of a worker:

> It's really quite a simple procedure. Notify your bureau of any vacancies you have. The staff there will then try to find suitable workers whom they will send to you for an interview. She'll bring a letter with her in which you are asked to indicate in the space provided whether she's acceptable. She will also have two cards, known as "E" and "F" cards, one is a notification of engagement and the other a notification of discharge. . . .
>
> But what if somebody off the street arrives at your home and you wish to employ her? Then you must address a note to the bureau, indicating that you want to engage her, and stating the wages you (cif.) are offering, the type of work, your address and telephone number. . . .
>
> Once a worker is registered, you must pay a monthly contribution. As soon as she (or he) has been registered in your employ, you must complete section "B" of her reference book, indicating your name and address and the date of engagement.

Cock's claim, and others' rehearsal, of the idea that domestic work existed in a "legal vacuum" seems misplaced given these extensive legislative controls. Reports at the time lamented "the vast network of laws governing the lives of Black work-seekers, especially women" (*The Natal Mercury*, June 27, 1978), with employees having to negotiate extensive legal bureaucracies to remain employed: They had to seek permission to work in a city from the "tribal" labor bureau, and for a married woman, from her husband; to obtain a permit to live in the white area of the city and a permit to sleep on the employer's premises; and to be confirmed a legal resident of the area in which they worked before their employer could register them with the local Bantu Administration Board.

Of course, the idea of workers being in a "legal vacuum" related to the failure of protective regulation of the sector and sought to locate the unique exploitation of domestic workers in that failure. Paradoxically, it was exactly the complex legal network of state regulation for control that generated a unique calculus of dependency and exploitation for workers. For those workers who found work through the state network of labor bureaus, these state agencies facilitated the exploitation of workers. The West Rand Administration Board, for example handled the following such requests for employers: "Wanted, girls under 18 who have never worked before. Pay: R10 a week. Must not have boyfriends" (*The Star*, May 3, 1978).

But, a significant proportion of employers simply bypassed this extensive set of state regulations by hiring workers "off the street," and in the classic scenario of apartheid domestic work, required workers to hand over their "reference book"[9] to prove their legal status—a widespread practice that literally bonded domestics to employers in ways that the Masters and Servants Act once did, but under a different regime defined by the dictates of a modernizing racial capitalism. African women work-seekers similarly often risked "illegal" status rather than comply with the state's extensive requirements. But because employment was necessary for legal residence and mobility, employers were given a unique power by the state. Exploitative relations of service were thus deepened by state-mandated dependence on employers.

In the late 1970s, various administration boards clamped down on employers who hired unregistered workers, imposing not only heavy fines but also, in some cases, summarily prosecuting employers without providing the option of admission of guilt through payment of a fine. In doing so, the state mobilized employers as proxies of influx control legislation, establishing domestic work's integration into the bureaucracy of apartheid migrant labor control through direct employer, and only indirect, state control.

In this history, then, the colonial and then apartheid states, together with capital and employers, structured the domestic labor market, not only defining its demographic composition, but shaping apartheid servitude through modern technologies of labor control. Treating domestic workers as a laboring class within capitalism and managing their supply as workers reflected some recognition of domestic workers as workers by the apartheid state, suggesting the necessity of a more nuanced understanding of the postapartheid shift in the regulatory regime for domestic workers. In the democratic state's efforts to turn "servants" into workers, the apartheid state's already existing recognition of domestics as workers was obliquely obfuscated. And, the history of workers' already existing efforts to modernize the institution themselves was bypassed in favor of a script that cast the state as the protagonist of a story in which the transition to democracy became crucial to the narrative of the emancipation of domestics. But, even under apartheid's coercive structuring of the domestic labor market, workers themselves played a role in "modernizing" the institution. Chapter 2 rescripts workers themselves into the history of apartheid servitude.

2

Beyond the Backyard

The Shift to Live-Out and Part-Time Work

In 1963, at the height of apartheid, Sophia Ncobo, a nineteen-year-old mother of two, found herself in Johannesburg. She had just accepted work as a live-in domestic for a white working-class family in an inner-city suburb. Sophia had grown up in a small rural village in an area that had just been declared a "Bantustan. Having no longer attended school from the age of twelve, she got married when she was seventeen and had children right away. Just after the birth of her second child, however, her husband—who had been working on the gold mines in Johannesburg since they were married—suddenly stopped sending home a portion of his pay. Sophia later learned he had abandoned her and their two children for one of his girlfriends in the city. The abrupt end to his remittances caused a crisis in the homestead and, after discussing it with family, it was resolved that Sophia should find work. A sister who worked in Johannesburg, soon after beginning to look, had secured Sophia a job as a domestic worker in the city. Sophia left her one-year-old daughter and her infant son in the care of her mother, and set off for Johannesburg nearly 800 kilometers away.

With limited legal accommodation for "natives" in Johannesburg, as well as the requirements of the pass laws regarding employment, Sophia accepted the job as a live-in domestic, retiring each evening to the basic one-room structure in her employer's backyard. With her two children left behind in the care of her mother, Sophia worked for the Wolfson's[1] for the next nine years. She raised their two children and summarized her relationship with her employers and work with "I had no troubles with those people. I was working very nicely there." But, there was one problem. Sophia had met a man in Johannesburg in 1966, and after five years, she had a son with him.

In 1972, when the child was still an infant, Sophia found it difficult to nego-tiate motherhood within the prescriptive limits of a live-in job: "When my child was *een jaar oud* [one year old], I was seeing the father one time every week. He was coming in the backyard when the lights were all dark. . . . But, that was not nice, you see. . . . When the baby was crying, I was getting hurt. I couldn't be there all the time, you see, for the child."

So Sophia began looking for work that would allow her to be there for her son. Having worked as a domestic for nearly a decade, she was resourced with knowledge of the informal hiring networks that govern recruitment in the sector, so finding full-time live-out work was relatively easy. Even though the work and her employer were sometimes difficult, it allowed her to bring her other two children from the eastern Cape and to maintain a family life in Johannesburg with them, while still working. She explained: "I got the job in Pretoria, there was this Afrikaans *vrou* [woman]. She was saying I must come in the morning. 7am I come and cook the breakfast. . . . She was screaming that day, I say no Sophia, this is a very good job. You are not in the back yard, and you are with your *kinders* [children] six o clock."

In this, Sophia Ncobo became one of countless African women domes-tic "servants" in South Africa who made the transition to live-out work in the 1970s, challenging apartheid servitude. Far from the passive victims of the apartheid structuring of domestic work, they attempted to challenge the coercive labor regime of live-in domestic servitude by trying to trans-form the structure of their work in ways that allowed them to maintain the capacity to be mothers. That shift was facilitated and intensified in the following two decades by the loosening and eventual removal of the labor and residential controls of the apartheid state that had coerced African women into live-in servitude. By the start of the twenty-first century, live-out workers represented the majority of domestics in South Africa.[2] This transformation, however, had been going on throughout much of the twen-tieth century and arguably represents a worker-initiated "modernization" of the sector. The bonds of servitude presumed by live-in work were chal-lenged, and replaced by a different structure that allowed workers to maintain more independence, and autonomy, especially over their famil-ial lives.

Being Present Mothers: The Shift to Live-Out Work

In the 1980s, Suzanne Gordon recorded the life history of Elizabeth Tshayinca, and showed how Elizabeth's mother, Lizzie Pambo, worked from 1909 as a live-out washer woman, taking "in washing from the white people living in the suburbs, laundering and ironing it at her home, and returning it two or three days later. Sometimes she worked in houses on a daily basis" (1985, 70–77). Seventy years later, Lizzie's daughter Elizabeth also worked live-out for a family, making the daily commutes from her home in Soweto to her employer's home in one of the white working-class suburbs of Johannesburg.

Elizabeth's story is useful for historicizing the live-out character of domestic service, given that both she and her mother, collectively working since the middle of the twentieth century, had both worked live-out. Indeed, the first documented attempts by domestic workers to "live-out" was as early as 1902, when paid domestic work for working-class households on the Witwatersrand was done mainly by live-in "houseboys." Charles Van Onselen documents how when the "houseboys" returned to the Witwatersrand after the war, with some "steady cash and new expectations," "a significant number of them refused to re-occupy the old hovels in the back yard. Knowing just how great the demand for their services was, the 'houseboys' pushed the employers into allowing them to live off the premises. What they then did was to club together and collectively rent a house within a Johannesburg suburb like Ophirton or Doornfontein, and live there free from the scrutiny of their employers. Yet others hired a room in a slum yard in old Jeppe or Doornfontein, or lodged themselves in the location" (1982, 28).

Demonstrating the extent to which "live-out" work in South Africa has, from its earliest recorded moments, been a movement initiated by workers to regain control over their lives, "this new pattern of independence persisted right up to 1914." But, as Van Onselen notes, the movement did not last long. "Never again," he writes, did this pattern of independence exist "on the scale of that immediate post-war period. Growing proletarianization, but above all the declining cash wages for 'houseboys,' progressively undermined these black servants' independence and ultimately drove them back to the employers' property" (Van Onselen 1982, 28).

By the 1930s, however, when black African women were predominantly domestic workers, the structure of work on the Witwatersrand reflected a more sustained pattern of live-out work not often acknowledged. Crucially, it issued primarily from these domestic workers' desires to maintain their capacity to be mothers and maintain their own familial lives independent of the employing family.

The apartheid structuring of urban residence patterns for black African women from the 1940s clearly played a very important role in confining more and more African women to live-in domestic service, as their ability to remain in urban areas became conditional on employment, establishing the dominant image of paid domestic work under apartheid as that of the live-in domestic worker. It is not surprising, then, that the shift to live-out domestic work is popularly understood as being connected to the demise of apartheid and the end of its restrictions on urban residence for Africans.[3]

This mirrors Katzman's (1978) and Dudden's (1986) macrostructural accounts of the shift to live-out work in the early part of the twentieth century for African American domestics in the United States, for whom such a shift was a reflection and instigator of changing class relations. Katzman (1978), for example, attributes the shift to the tendency of the domestic labor force to become older and more heavily African-American as industrial and white-collar jobs opened up exclusively for young white women in the first decades of the twentieth century. But, such accounts privilege structural shifts in the transformations of paid domestic work over time, rather than recognizing the role of workers themselves in such mutations in the structure of their work.

The limited, though instructive, life histories of domestic workers in South Africa recorded for this study show that the shift to live-out work began at least as early as the 1960s. And just like Sophia Ncobo, it was motivated primarily by workers' concerns about being present as mothers to their children. The difficulties of live-in paid domestic work are notorious. In South Africa, it is the archetypal image of oppressive work relations, of the deindividuation of the worker through their co-option into full-time servitude relations for the employing family. Cock (1980) likened live-in domestic service in South Africa to Erving Goffman's (1961) "total institution," and Bujra (2000) calls it a "mode of incarceration." Parreñas repeats the carceral metaphor, saying that live-in workers "cannot help but see the enclosed space of the employer's home as a prison" (2001, 162). More than anything, live-in domestic work is oppressive in its denial of independence to the worker to maintain her own family: "The living-in servant . . . no matter how favourable pay and working conditions may be, she is denied the independence of living with her own family in her own place" (Gordon 1985, xxv).

For workers, this—together with the relations of servitude implied by live-in work—were the most egregious aspects of this structuring of paid domestic work. "You can't understand," lamented live-in domestic worker Josephine Kekana. "It doesn't matter. Even [when] you must sit on the *stoep* [porch] and drink from the maid's cup, it pains me. But, the pain to not see my children. . . . And my husband. He has another woman now. That pain, it doesn't go away."

While the servitude relations of live-in service were continually raised by workers as a source of "hurt," "anger," and "frustration," and there was deep resentment for some over the arrangement, many argued that the pain of family separation is what made the situation intolerable. Especially during apartheid when the state urban control apparatus made it illegal for any black person to be on white premises without being a registered employee, employers were able to completely cut domestic workers off from their families. In the South African film *Mapantsula,* which detailed conditions under apartheid,[4] the sneaking into and out of girlfriends' and wives' backyard "servants quarters" without the knowledge of their employers is used as a powerful trope for the race and class relations of apartheid and the complicity of live-in domestic service in the apartheid disorganization of African family life. Phuti Masimane, a retired domestic worker, explained this as well. "My child couldn't come stay," she said with visible distress. "The madam said the police will come give her a ticket for fifty rand. . . . He [her husband] was coming to stay only after eleven, twelve, then I used to put the dog in the room at the back. . . . Four o' clock then he must leave. That was [the] hardest time in my life."

The control of visitors by employers of live-in domestic workers became a crucial mechanism of entrenching servitude relations as the worker's access to any life and identity beyond those of "service" to the employing family were denied. Phuti went on to narrate how she eventually left this live-in job two years later, when her aunt had secured a small house in a township, and she was able to find a "good madam" who allowed her to work five days of the week live-out. "I was coming home every night to my babies," she said as she explained why she found this work better, echoing Sophia Ncobo's preference for live-out work. The early shift to live-out work, according to these workers, issued from their struggle to remain mothers to their own children, a simple requirement made impossible by apartheid forms of live-in servitude.

Monica Seepe, a worker who left Newcastle in 1989 to find work as a domestic in Johannesburg, learned from her mother's experiences as a domestic worker in the 1960s, how domestic workers even then were restructuring paid domestic work to allow them the opportunity to care for their own families. Monica's mother was born in 1944 on a farm, where "it was very happy days for her." She went to Durban in 1964, where she worked as a live-in domestic worker and returned home to see her parents and family only "twice every three months, then five months." When her mother had her first child, Monica relates, "she left him home with the one sister, was working, working . . . Then, one year, two years, she said no, this is too much." When her mother's sister found a job herself as a domestic worker, her mother "told the madam, she must not sleep in the back yard." She eventually found a job with another employer whom Monica described as "very nice people," where her mother worked live-out, and Monica explained "this job was good" because "she was coming home in the night time."

So workers negotiated live-out conditions of service to allow them the capacity to be present in raising their own children. Sometimes this was out of necessity, as with Monica's mother, but often the need to be good, and not simply present, mothers shaped workers' decisions. Hazel Sondlo recalls that her choice to take a live-out job was informed by the possibility it would allow for her to be a good mother to her children: "When my children were with my mother, I knew I was still a mother to them. I was still taking care of them with my job, but my heart got so sore after not even a few years in the backyard [i.e., in live-in service]. I needed my children with me to be a good mother to them. That's when I took the work in Bez Valley, because that way I could come home in the evenings, I could help them with their school work . . . be a really good mother."

So the effort to maintain family life and be good mothers to their children led the women in this study to seek out and remain in live-out domestic work. So successful were they that by the mid-1970s, the "live-out" worker had become an identifiable new category in the structure of paid domestic work (Whisson and Weil 1971; Preston-Whyte 1976). By 1979, when Cock completed the fieldwork for her study in the eastern Cape, only 16 percent of her total sample lived in (Cock 1980, 25), a remarkable statistic given the equation of apartheid relations of servitude with live-in domestic service.[5]

The scrapping of influx control in the 1980s accelerated this trend, with Preston-Whyte reporting on her 1980s data that workers "are less dependent on domestic employers for a place to live" leading to a "trend to non-resident domestic service" (Preston-Whyte 1991, 46). By the 1990s, the freedom of movement and residence implied by the end of apartheid facilitated this live-out movement. But workers also shaped this transformation. While domestic workers under apartheid have been characterized as "ultra-exploited" victims (Cock 1980), they were neither defenseless nor passive. Within apartheid's coercive and constrained forms of urban and labor control, African women domestic workers sought ways to restructure their work so they could maintain autonomous family lives. They did so in ways that suggested their contradictory location as workers who get paid to care for others' families but are constrained in their ability to do the same for their own.

Workers' efforts in this transition to live-out work has been documented in many other contexts as well, but with a focus on workers' desire for self-worth and dignity rather than on workers' seeking control over their family lives. Evelyn Nakano Glenn (1986) highlights the shift among Japanese American workers as a strategy to wrest control from employers and gain an independence and autonomy that allowed them to free themselves from the degrading and dehumanizing conditions of residential domestic service. For Dill, live-out work for African American women was about ameliorating the lack of dignity implied by the degrading nature of live-in domestic service, "provid[ing] workers with a buffer between themselves and their jobs and help[ing] sustain their efforts to assert their sense of self-worth" (1988, 47). In shunning uniforms (Clark-Lewis 1987), refusing to do certain tasks (Romero 1988), and refusing to live in, these workers shored up a sense of dignity.

For South African domestic workers, however, this was an outcome but not the primary motivation for live-out work. Indeed, the nature of the work did not change much. Few workers referenced any changes to the work process itself implied by live-out work, and only one worker explicitly addressed this question. "There is no difference you see," said Joyce Nhlapo. "I am saying for the work you do. You are sweeping outside, cleaning, washing, you are cutting the potatoes. You only have your bag of clothes with you every day. But you are still doing the same work." Said Phuti Masimane, "There is this thing when you are not staying in. It's the same work, but you work better. *Ja* (Yes), you are having your own life, you see."

The nature of the work remained the same for these live-out workers; their feelings of control issued from the autonomy and independence of home life. In this, these workers were closer to Palmer's analysis of the shift to nonresidential work in the United States by the 1920s where workers "could arrange their work schedules around caring for their own homes and children" (1989, 69). For South African domestic workers, this choice to live out impelled by a need to be mothers to their children was captured in the expression of being able to "knock off"—that is, leave work and go home to family. Beauty Mkhize, a full-time live-out domestic worker in Linmeyer, and mother of two, said, "It is bad when you are live-in. . . . There is no one there for [your] children, giving them love. "This is how I was looking for washing and ironing only, to do this work where you can knock off."

Being able to "knock off" expressed the distinction between work time and family time, and these workers' ability to be both mothers and workers. Another worker, for instance, said that she needed to "knock off" because of her need to provide care to her family: "No, I said to her I have got my husband, and my small one can't be without a mother at night. I needed to knock off, not work all day, all night." Similarly, when Selina Vilakazi,[6] the provincial regional organizer for the South African Domestic Service and Allied Workers Union (SADSAWU), was asked if there was more "live-out" work today compared to the past, she responded definitively. "Backyards must be abolished," she said, smashing a fist into the palm of her hand. "*Ja*, because people are still staying in the backyards. Especially from the rural areas; they've got no housing, you see . . . it's much better to live out because then you can knock off."

Rose Nakedi, another full-time live-out worker added, "You have to knock off. Not be a slave. To have your own place. When you come home from work, you know, and your child runs to you and says 'Mama, I did this in school,' then you know you are doing a good job. Like this, there is more control." For Rose, being able to "knock off" meant being able to take care of one's family and be a good mother, and the greater "control" that came with live-out service was about control of when work would end, and family care could begin, rather than control over the work itself.

Situated at the confluence of paid care work for other families and unpaid care work for their own, these workers negotiated the terms of their incorporation into paid domestic work by restructuring the occupation. Even while the apartheid machinery's tying of residence to employment structured paid domestic work as live-in, domestic workers were able to enact strategies that wrested control to privilege the maintenance of their families.

But, while the shift to live-out work allowed African women to better manage their responsibilities as workers and mothers, it did not challenge the structural logics of apartheid that constructed them as a serving class. It also did not mean an end to oppressive working conditions. While live-out work today remains significantly better for workers than live-in in terms of number of hours worked per day (Department Labor 2002), live-out work did not erase servitude.[7] Suzanne Gordon, who worked to professionalize the occupation through the Domestic Workers and Employers Project (DWEP) declared in the 1980s that live-out work offered the kind of dignity to domestic work that not only redeemed it from its reputation of degrading servility but actually made paid domestic work better than many other forms of work: "Those domestic workers who are able to commute daily from their own homes, who are adequately paid and who work an eight-hour day are possibly better off than some cashiers in supermarkets, or many factory workers" (1985, xxv).

But, the live-out domestic workers who related their life histories to me did not understand themselves as better off than other members of the working class. Indeed, they saw live-out work as a choice that placed additional burdens on them. Many who chose live-out work did so to be able to live with and care for their own families even though some still did not get to raise their children themselves. For the many who did, since they did not choose live-out work as a strategy to make their lives easier or their work more tolerable, but rather to retain their own familial lives, life as a live-out domestic worker was demanding, and their experiences were related through narratives of hardship.

With limited provision of housing, sanitation, water, and electricity in post-apartheid South Africa, live-out workers' daily lives were strenuous—at times more strenuous than those who worked as live-in domestics. Complicating these strains, since only a few employers of live-out workers subsidized their transportation costs, the financial burdens of their daily commutes to work were demanding. The time burdens of these commutes defined another axis of vulnerability; live-out workers I followed spent an average of three hours commuting to and from work every day. This time burden made the "second shift"[8] more precarious for this group of workers. Anderson notes this in relation to live-out domestic workers in Europe: "The advantages of live-out work are clear. Less personal control tends to be exercised by the employer over the worker. The worker is less dependent on the employer . . . and also because she has her own accommodation and is not dependent on her employer for her living space. One must beware of painting too rosy a picture, though, for those who live out are often juggling their own family commitments and domestic responsibilities with those attached to their employers' households" (2000, 46).

Among this group of domestic workers, many repeatedly emphasized the "tiredness" issuing from "days when you must be busy from when you wake up to when you go to sleep." "This is life as a domestic worker, if you want to know," said Judi Manamela, lowering her head and slowing her pace. "You just move, move, don't even sit down. You are washing, cleaning, cooking all day long. Even at home, you don't get no peace. No one knows how hard you must work . . . they are thinking you are just this domestic worker."

Judi's sentiments capture the low social status of domestic workers despite the transition to live-out work, which Dill also found among African

American domestics: "The shift to live-out work did provide the worker with greater personal freedom, less isolation from friends and family, and more limited working hours. . . . Yet many of the factors that had contributed to the occupation's low status did not change substantially" (Dill 1988, 35).

A radical transformation of the social status and burdens of paid domestic work was thus elusive for live-out workers. They claimed in the shift to live-out work an incredibly important autonomy from employers and the capacity to maintain an independent familial life, but it did not significantly transform their location as a class of "servants" attending to the needs of mainly white, middle-class households at the expense, sometimes, of their dignity. Workers, however, initiated another restructuring of their work—from full- to part-time—that did attempt to transform their work from one of degrading servitude to one of dignified work.

"Didn't You Hear? We Domestic Workers Only Work Part-Time": The Shift to Part-Time Work

Commentators on the contemporary organization of South African domestic work point to part-time work as an important transformation of the sector post-apartheid. For example, Rob Rees commented that one of the new dynamics of paid domestic work in post-apartheid South Africa was that a "large and growing number of domestic workers are employed on a casual or part-time basis" (1998, 53). Often, this is accompanied by the assumption that the rise in part-time work is a marker of the end of servitude relations. Susan Flint, for example, counterposed the rise in part-time "domestic work" with the decline of "domestic service," arguing that "with domestic service on the decline," there is "an increase in part-time, temporary, and agency workers in domestic employment" (1988, 200).

While there has been a shift to part-time work in South African paid domestic work, it has not ended domestic servitude, nor is it a phenomenon emerging only with the end of apartheid. While national rates of part-time work were around 55 percent of the workforce in 2003,[9] this was not a recent shift. Indeed, the transition to part-time work can be traced back to as early as the 1970s.

In 1972, the government survey, *Statistics of Houses, Domestic Servants, and Flats* (SHDSF)[10] began to document part-time domestic work as a category, suggesting its prevalence at the time. This, together with the *Survey of Household Expenditure* (SHE),[11] confirms that from as early as 1975, the numbers of employing households for full-time and part-time workers were similar. Indeed, a portion of the paid domestic work force was working part-time as early as that, although they did not yet constitute the majority of the workforce. By 1985, however more households were employing a domestic worker part-time rather than full-time, cementing the shift to part-time work as the dominant work arrangement at least a decade prior to the official birth of the "new" South Africa.

Today, newspaper listings under "Domestic Employment Wanted" reveal a greater proportion of workers seeking part-time work, and some workers confirmed that this was the case. The shift to part-time work has also become an important part of the lore of domestic work in Johannesburg. Doris Radebe, a jovial worker with a sly sense of humor, shook with laughter as she cracked a joke playing *fah-fee* on a park bench near Berea one day. "Did you hear about the domestic worker whose husband complained she was not sleeping with him every night? She said, 'Didn't you hear? We domestic workers only work part-time.'"

While the trend toward part-time work has continued, it is not novel to the post-apartheid organization of paid domestic work and represents an attempted restructuring of apartheid servitude by workers themselves beginning at least a few decades prior to the post-apartheid state's efforts.

Workers and Part-Time Work: Autonomy, Control, and Skill through a Work-by-Task Labor Arrangement

Scholars who have considered the shift from the "domestic servant" to the part-time "housekeeper" (Glenn 1986; Hondagneu-Sotelo 1994, 2001; Romero 1988; Clark-Lewis 1987; Ruiz 1987), see it as a worker strategy to modernize the relationship from one between "mistress" and "maid" to one between "employer" and "employee" or "client" and "tradesperson." Romero, for example, argues that in the shift to "day work" among Chicana women in the Southwest, live-out work provided more autonomy over the work process itself, and allowed these workers to modernize the occupation. For her, Chicana workers who chose live-out work struggled to "control the work process and alter the employer-employee relationship to a client-tradesperson relationship in which labor services rather than labor power is sold" (Romero 1992, 15). In this, the shift to "day work" represented a move by workers to structure the work process in ways that provided more control and autonomy and mitigated the degrading conditions of their work.

South African domestic workers similarly referenced the ways in which part-time work was a conscious strategy of wanting to convert what they saw as the "work-by-time" arrangement of full-time work to the "work-by-task" arrangement of part-time work. In this, they enacted a transformation of the structure of the occupation that attempted to regain control over the work process itself. Portia Moleme, for example, had worked in the sector for nearly twenty years. She had developed relationships with some of her employer's friends and family, as well as many other domestic workers. "I knew for a long time, for years, I could see that to work daily is better. There is much more money that way," she recalled. She explained further, when I asked how she eventually made the transition to part-time work, that "it was not easy at first. I took time off from my job to have my baby. Then, in that time, I was talking to many people, other *ousies* [domestic workers], and also one of the friends of the family [employer's]. She wanted someone to work one day to do washing and ironing and cleaning. . . . And, then, one of the other *ousies* on the street where I was working even before, she said to me that she was now leaving the job and it was for a char [part-time housekeeper] for one day."

Portia's experience in the social networks that organize recruitment secured her additional days work. When asked "is part-time better?" she said, "*Ja* [yes], sometimes it is very good. I come, I change, and then I clean and I do the washing and ironing once a week, so four o' clock I am ready to go, and the house is all clean, and I have the clothes on the bed in the pile."

For Portia, the delimitation of the tasks and the ability to claim the product of one's labor at the end of the day was a source of pride and highlighted the importance of a work-by-task structure. She has a fixed regimen of work to accomplish, and the ability to claim the task at the end of the day affords her a sense of control over her work, as she delimits the end of the task as the end of her work. Mabel Mabena, a live-in domestic worker, once complained to me: "You know what I hate? . . . When you finish clean that floor, and then they just drop more juice on it. Then they just stand there and look at you. Like you must clean it. *Hayi* [no]! I already cleaned that floor. I did my job."

In this, Mabel exposed the implications of not having a work-by-task structure. For Mabel, her time was purchased, and as long as she was "on the job" she was required to do whatever was necessary in her role as housekeeper. Some recognized the extent to which full-time live-out workers, as opposed to part-time workers, were not really employed on a work-by-task basis but rather continued on a work-by-time arrangement. Joyce Nhlapo, with her usual insight, said to me: "See, you must look at it like this way. When you are with one family for the whole week [live-out]. Tell me, what are you doing? Every day? Washing? Cleaning? Ironing? You see, this is what I am telling you; you are there to also do other things. They give you this work, that work. You are still their worker. You come every morning, and you must say, 'what today, madam?' "

Joyce highlights that with a work-by-time structure in full-time live-out work, the worker is not in control of their work, having to ask "what today, madam?" as opposed to Portia who comes in and controls her own work. For some workers, the autonomy and control of the work-by-task process of part-time work resulted in an ability to claim the work as skilled. "I like this work because I come in and I know what to do," said one of the part-time workers at a union meeting. "Washing, then I put it up, and do the cleaning—bedrooms, then bathroom, then the kitchen. Then I get the washing from the line and I do the ironing. Then I pack up and then I knock off."

This worker enjoyed the work precisely because she is in control of it: She "know[s] what to do," and she can "pack up" and then "knock off." The employer's instructions do not form part of her narrative of detailing her work routine, and, like Portia, she describes her workday by the tasks she performs, in succession, indicating autonomy and control. Simultaneously, in stating "I know what to do," the worker emphasizes the skill that a work-by-task process implies. There is also a clear delimitation of work from life, with the ubiquitous "and then I knock off." The work-by-task structuring therefore allowed part-time workers to operate as "skilled workers" rather than as under a work-by-time structure in which their personal services are sold.

Worker strategies for part-time work have therefore been attempts to regain control of the work process, to establish a degree of autonomy and skill. In this, they placed limits on middle-class control of working-class labor, signaling a class politics as much as a shift in the structure of the work. Some workers, however, did not see the shift to part-time work as positive. Instead, they understood this shift as an employer strategy of control.

Employers and Part-Time Work: From "Like One of the Family" to "Like a Machine"

Margaret Manamela worked part-time three days a week, and described her entry into this form of work as an employer preference. "I was working very well for them [employers]," she said. "That's why I was so surprised when they came, they sat down, and they said, 'we have decided now we only need you one day a week.'"

Margaret agreed to the new arrangement, and then was assisted by her employer in finding another part-time job with one of their friends. Margaret preferred the part-time work, but complained that it was an employer strategy rather than her own choice, racializing their motivations. "They don't want us black people in their houses any more," she offered, decisively. "You must do your work, then you must go home. Only your hands must work for them. Then, you must leave. . . . It is better for us like that . . . we have our own families . . . They are wanting only a worker one day a week, not many days, because they say they don't have money. It's very bad."

In direct contrast with much of the scholarship regarding the experiences of part-time domestic work, some workers in this study agreed with Margaret and did not regard part-time work as their choice but rather that of employers, a strategy used to dictate the terms of employment. For example, I asked Selina Vilakazi, regional organizer at the union, "Is there a lot more part-time employment today?" "Yes, yes, you see, it's the employers," she said animatedly, as if I had struck on something important with my question. "Yes, you see, they like to pay the hours. They don't like the full-time. . . . It's bad. It's bad for the workers, because you know, you go there, you got to finish the whole house in one day, and tomorrow you are doing next door. You see, it's too much work." Selina's statement summarizes the ways in which many workers understood the shift to part-time work as a strategy by employers to extract and control workers' labor.

First, workers saw it as the attempt by employers to restructure the relationship from one of "like one of the family" to "like a machine" by transforming the work process in ways that created personal distance between themselves and their employees. Joyce Nhlapo offered a neat—more radicalized—summary of many workers' sentiments:

> They say you are like one of their family. You know how they say that, *neh*? You see, they are making you into their child. . . . but, then they are saying, you know what, you work one morning, one afternoon, you see, there is no feeling there. It's, it's like being, cold, you understand me . . . it's too much work for them. You see how they are doing this, when you are too much work to even treat you like you are a person. . . . you are just this machine for cleaning, they rent you for one day, you see.

For Joyce, the coercive control of the "like one of the family" ideology is transformed by employers on their own terms, and workers are instead dehumanized as mere machines. For Joyce and other workers, part-time work, rather than offering autonomy, control, and skill through depersonalized work regimens, was a depersonalization of their labor in ways that they found demeaning. Hondagneu-Sotelo (2001) suggests that immigrant workers in Los Angeles are equally critical of depersonalization by employers. For domestic workers in South Africa, like Elsie Mbatha, this resulted in work intensification that implied coercive control: "Domestic work?! You earn peanuts—even when you do a part-time job. You know what, you can work part-time and earn more. But you work hard. . . . When you do a part-time job maybe you come once or twice a week, or twice a month. That job will be a whole month's job. You must do it in one day. You do the fridge, you do the stove, do the windows, and you must finish it in one day. *Ayikhona!* I'm not a machine" (*Speak*, Feb/April 1986). Another worker at a Department of Labor meeting repeated the metaphor of mechanization, implying dehumanization: "It is too much work . . . one big double-storey in one morning, the whole thing to clean and vacuum, and then also to do the polishing. She [employer] is thinking I am a machine. I am a human being . . . and my bones are tired."

Second, as this worker intimates, workers understood the "mechanized" work process of part-time work as involving work intensification. This was the most commonly expressed element of part-time work mentioned by workers, and many saw it as a coercive employer strategy to extract more labor from them. Not only was the work increased, but the pace accelerated. "You go fast, one day this house, next day that flat. It is very tiring work. You are just working to finish up so quickly, like a cleaning machine," said Margaret Manamela, for example, repeating the metaphor of being treated "like a machine" through part-time work. And, another worker in Lenasia who refused to spend more than five minutes talking to me because of this work speed-up said "I clean this house Monday in the mornings, the master say they got no money for more days. I do everything. It's too much work."

Indeed, this work intensification is noted by Parreñas as well, who reports that, in Rome, "part-time workers generally have more floors to scrub, more clothes to wash and iron than do live-in workers" and "further intensifying the routine of part-time work is the hustle and bustle of running from one job to the next" (2001, 154–55). This was a significant element of the work routines of part-time workers in Johannesburg as well. With an inadequate transportation infrastructure and a city marred by apartheid urban sprawl, part-time workers who had full workweeks spent many, many hours getting from one part of the city to the next, usually with good cheer and tremendous patience, but often bearing by week's end the burden of exhaustion.

Third, this intensified work routine and the constant traveling around entrenched the isolation of those workers who maintained full workweeks. Elizabeth Clark-Lewis in her descriptions of the benefits of "day work" for African American domestic workers argues that "the previously isolated African-American women began to make contact with one another and their newly flexible working conditions, encountering many others like themselves" (1987, 206). Unlike these African American workers, however, the apartheid landscape and work intensification made part-time workers in South Africa yet more isolated and prevented the development of solidarity.

Part-time workers were difficult to find in the public spaces usually frequented by full-time domestics. The routines of part-time work severely restricted their social lives in important ways, as they negotiated many households and their own during a single week. While full-time live-out and live-in workers construct critical spaces of engagement in public parks and on street corners, these spaces became inaccessible to part-time workers due to the intensification of their work. As a result, like Selina Vilakazi, a few workers told me that part-time work was "very bad" and was an employer, not an employee, preference. This is reproduced by analyses of the sector. "Many employers are no longer able to afford domestic workers on a full-time basis, and the tendency is towards employing someone once or twice a week" (Flint 1988, 191).

While these different causal attributions may seem contradictory, there was a crucial difference between workers who claimed that part-time work was a worker choice and those that saw it as an employer preference. For those who saw part-time work as offering control and acknowledging the skill of their work, they had nearly full workweeks. For those who regarded part-time work as "very bad" and a strategy of control by employers, they were invariably those who were struggling to find enough days to fill the week. For them, part-time work represented employment insecurity.

The literature on paid domestic work generally celebrates part-time work in the sector, finding it to be a process of work restructuring initiated and controlled by workers. Of course, the tendency in other sectors is to lament such "casualization" because it is often an employer strategy that generates insecurity for workers. In one of the few sobering instances where the shift to part-time work in domestic work is contextualized in a broader analysis of the labor market, Neva Makgetla suggests that the higher proportion of part-time workers in the domestic versus formal sectors of the economy suggested greater levels of employment insecurity for these workers (*Business Day*, May 21, 2004). Jacqueline Andall noted the same for domestic workers in Italy: "for Black women, this means employment security in the live-in sphere, but vulnerability in the hourly paid sector" (2000, 187).

While nearly half of South African domestic workers work part-time, almost 80 percent worked for only one employer,[12] suggesting a large number of part-time workers who work potentially only one day a week for a single employer. Just over half of all domestic workers worked less than a full workweek (CASE 2001). The insecurity this implies, and reduced earnings, leads to heightened vulnerability for part-time workers. Flint therefore argues that "this change [to part-time work] has made work-seeking even more difficult for thousands of black women, and is, in itself, a more precarious way of earning a living" (1988, 191). For the workers in this study who attributed part-time work to employer control, they struggled to find enough work to fill a week, and this had implications for their capacity to sustain themselves.

Palesa Lebala, for instance, is thirty-six years old and rents a small shack in Thembelihle, an informal settlement in Lenasia, an "Indian" township south of Johannesburg. On Mondays, she wakes at 4 a.m., and walks under the cover of darkness carrying a five-liter plastic barrel to collect water from a local resident's garden tap. When she returns to her shack, she makes some tea and washes up as she gets ready to go to work. She walks for nearly an hour to her employer's house on the other side of Lenasia with another worker because "it's not safe to walk by yourself, you get raped, and they want to kill you for your cell phone," she explains. "For Mrs. Loonat, I wash, and then I iron and I polish and clean the house." On Thursdays, Palesa works for a widowed woman living in a flat in Lenasia, doing the same tasks. And, on Friday, she takes a minibus taxi to Lenasia South, where she does the washing and ironing for a family of four, a job she secured through her aunt in Soweto who had worked for the family as a full-time live-out worker but could not afford to make the journey once the family decided they only needed "help" one day a week. Palesa says, "I am happy to have these jobs. But, it makes me very tired, every day, and now I have got these pains, and there is no money to go to the doctor." "I am very worried because now I have to find two more days," said Palesa. "I want to bring my child here for school, but I need money for rent. Now, I don't have enough work, only three days. It's not enough. I have to wait for one of them [employers] to find me another day. It means I can't leave them till they can see my work and try and find me another day's work."

As Palesa suggests, far from reducing their dependence on their employers through greater autonomy and control as is documented by Romero (1988) and Clark-Lewis (1987) and suggested by the workers who were working close to full-time, part-time workers with only one or two days a week relied heavily on their employers' informal referral networks to fill up additional days. Newspaper advertisements for domestic work seekers are often placed by employers. For example, in a typical ad in a local newspaper, an employer advertises the services of her "houseboy:" "He is hardworking, honest, and reliable and is clean and sober in his habits. With his pleasant disposition and co-operative nature I recommend him extremely highly. He will do part time work but requires accommodation" (*Rosebank Killarney Gazette*, January 6, 2007).

Almost always referencing the personal qualities of their "reliable" and "clean" workers, there is an invoking of relations between "mistresses" and "maids." In late 1996, a local university's weekly newsletter listed an advertisement of a staff member, offering her char's services to other prospective employers. The advertisement said the worker "has worked for me for over 10 years and still does. I've never lost even a single grain of sugar" (UCT *Monday Paper* 15/25, 1996). A letter from the staff of the history department in a subsequent issue sarcastically commended the paper's "special commitment to the upkeep of suburban households through those helpful Victorian age advertisements in which masters and mistresses offer the good services of their scullery maids" (UCT *Monday Paper* 15/27, 1996).

Given this entrenchment of dependence on employers, who become the brokers of their employees' labor, part-time workers who struggled to fill a full workweek saw this work arrangement as "very bad." But, for those workers who were more successful at filling their weeks with work, it was regarded as restructuring of control by workers and as a more effective work arrangement. In the main, workers with more experience in the sector were able to fill up their weeks with part-time work much more easily than workers newly entering paid domestic work, with important implications for the structuring of the sector post-apartheid.

The Generation Gap: Live-in Domestic Service as the Post-Apartheid Form

Popular wisdom in South Africa assumes that older domestic workers who worked as live-in domestic workers under apartheid continue to do so, as the remaining remnants of apartheid servitude, while new entrants into the market secure the more contractual, less servile, part-time and live-out work that establishes the post-apartheid form of the institution as one less marked by relations of servitude. The reality, however, is the exact opposite.

Nationally, in 2000, about a third of domestic workers were live-in (CASE 2001, Markdata 2000). This, in itself, is not an insignificant proportion. But, in Gauteng province, one of the most important paid domestic labor markets, live-in domestic workers slightly outnumbered those who live-out (50.7% versus 49.3%, Markdata 2000). Provinces with the lowest urbanization rates, and therefore less urban housing available for workers, tended to have much lower rates of live-in domestic service than areas with greater urban density.[13] Instead of large markets for paid domestic service, such as Gauteng, becoming increasingly part-time and live-out as new entrants into the market are absorbed, the urbanized centers were absorbing ever-larger numbers of African women work-seekers into live-in domestic service, as older workers leaving the sector increasingly worked live-out and part-time.

Workers with more experience, who invariably tended to be older, were able to negotiate both live-out and part-time work arrangements fairly successfully as their preferred form of work. This was assisted by the possibility that the longer a domestic worker works for an employer, the more likely their needs in terms of child care will change to accommodate a part-time "char" arrangement. Employers often assist workers—as in the ads above—in finding the other part-time jobs required to fill a week once deciding to reduce their workers' hours.

Portia Moleme, for example, had managed to fill her workweek by drawing on an extended network of fellow domestics as resources for securing additional workdays. A local study (CASE 1999) similarly found that experience in the sector was directly correlated with number of employers, which in turn is linked to the terms of employment (i.e., full-time versus part-time) and relative levels of employment security.[14] With age and experience linked, the study found that while domestic workers between the ages of fifty-one and sixty were more likely to work for two employers (compared with those under fifty who worked for one), older domestic workers (sixty-one years or more) were more likely to work for three or more employers.

Similarly, in this study, as domestic workers gained more experience in the sector, they were more successful at finding employers to fill a workweek. As Portia explained, "I like this work now. It is not too bad to find another day for me. I am working too long. I know how to find another day."

In a sector marked by highly informalized recruitment networks (see Hondagneu-Sotelo 1994, 2001), workers with more experience not only choose part-time work but are able to successfully utilize their knowledge of the labor market's informal circuits to ensure that it is a viable work arrangement. At the same time, this is assisted by their years of experience developing relationships with their employers, who become important resources in securing additional jobs.

Younger, more inexperienced entrants into the paid domestic labor market, by contrast, found themselves invariably drawn into live-in domestic service. Not only were these workers mainly rural migrants, and therefore unskilled at negotiating the housing options in Johannesburg, but they remained incapable of negotiating their way out of live-in arrangements in ways older workers were able to and did not have the same long-standing relationships with employers to facilitate part-time work. For example, Selena Simelane is thirty-one years old and has worked as a live-in domestic for a family in the suburb of Observatory for five years. She explains that she took the job specifically because "when I first came, there was no place to sleep. I am looking now. I know more people. Maybe when my child is out of the school, then I can get my house. Maybe even get Saturday work, not work here every day." Selena acknowledges both the aspiration toward a different work arrangement that comes with more experience and the valuable networks that enable the realization of that vision the longer one remains in the sector. In this, Selena represents the post-apartheid form of domestic work, for most live-in workers were new entrants into this sector. Furthermore, new entrants into this labor market were the majority of workers in this sample, suggesting that visions of paid domestic work contracting with the retirement of its apartheid-era veterans misrepresent the extent to which the paid domestic labor market is a replenishing one. There were many more domestic workers in this study who had five years or less of experience in the sector than those who had five years or more. This was confirmed by another study's report that the highest proportion of domestic workers worked for between one and five years for their current employer (CASE 1999). That report also concluded that "respondents who worked for one employer were more likely to have less than five years experience while workers with multiple employers tended to have more experience." This suggests "that domestics for whom domestic work is a relatively new occupation tend to work for one employer but as they gain experience they tend to work for more than one employer" (CASE 1999). For those who began work as domestics during the post-apartheid era, the trend is toward work for one employer, mainly on a live-in basis, or where live-out and part-time, usually under quite precarious conditions of employment and social vulnerability.

Phuti Masimane therefore summarized the nature of domestic work during the post-apartheid era: "The young girls are leaving our homesteads; they are looking for the work in the city. Durban also. But there is only standard one, low education, so they are having the trouble with jobs. And also with houses. You see, this is how they come here by the squatter camps and are working. They don't want to even live by the employers. Sometimes, they are having no choice."

In 1985, Suzanne Gordon explained live-in service as the failure of choice due to apartheid restrictions. "While the present restrictive laws governing the movement of black people apply, together with the severe dearth of housing for blacks," she argued, "there will continue to be considerable numbers of women forced to accept living-in jobs" (xxv). In the post-apartheid era, with large numbers of new entrants into paid domestic work, "having no choice" but to accept live-in work arrangements defines the coercive nature of women's entry into, and negotiations of, paid domestic work. Continued poor levels of education and the inability to sustain rural livelihoods have combined with the slow rate of state-provided housing to mobilize a workforce of low-wage laborers who are, paradoxically, just as likely to be relegated to live-in domestic service as their older apartheid-era veterans once were.

The shift to live-out and part-time work, therefore, while popularly understood as a post-apartheid phenomenon coinciding with democratization and the necessary restructuring of relations of servitude that would presumably accompany it, actually has a longer history and a different set of motivating imperatives. While the shift to live-out work was pursued as a strategy for workers to maintain autonomous familial lives, the shift to part-time work for workers who understood it as their choice offered them greater control over their work, recovering a sense of dignity and skill. But, this is not to suggest a neat categorical distinction between these two transformations and the logics that inspired them. While the emphasis here is on the ways in which workers have themselves shaped the structure and conditions of their work and in so doing participated in the transformation of the occupation, the transmutation of the apartheid state and its strictures, as well as the role of employers, have been defining features of the transformation of paid domestic work over time.

Workers' capacities to restructure the occupation was conditioned and made possible only by the reconfiguration of apartheid urban and labor control policies. Employers have been equally significant in these transformations.

This reinterrogation of the historical shifts in paid domestic work is not to deny the important role of employers and the state in shaping the structure of the occupation over time, but rather to correct continuing popular misconceptions about the sources of these shifts that read workers as passive accoutrements to the wills and imperatives of political orders and employers. It is to forcefully document, at the outset of this much more detailed foray into the contemporary nature of paid domestic work in South Africa, the importance of workers themselves in the historical, current, and, hopefully, future contours of paid domestic work in South Africa.

Part II

Turning "Servants" into Workers

3

Protecting "Vulnerable" Workers?

Workers Embrace and
Reject State Power

In 1990, shortly after Nelson Mandela had been released from prison and a "new" South Africa was imminent, a focus group was held with domestic workers as part of an effort to record women's hopes for democracy. When asked, "How would you want your lives to be changed," the assembled domestic workers connected political emancipation directly with the overturning of their position as paid care workers. "We would certainly like our lives to change," they said. "Like those women that we work for. When they come home, they are with no worry. We stay here in their houses and our children are elsewhere, we can't even check on them. We would therefore like to be free."[1]

One hot Johannesburg summer day, my research assistant and I—weary from the heat—found a young domestic worker, Joyce Nhlapo, perched precariously on the green metal fencing of a public park. She would prove a firebrand. In tight silver pants with high heels, heavy makeup, thickly drawn-in eyebrows, and an expertly manicured set of extensions piled high above her head, she took control of the encounter right away with her signature loud-mouthed confidence. Her comments, laced either with caustic cynicism or sarcastic disdain, were insightful, as she equated political unfreedom with the peculiar location of domestic workers. "There is no freedom for domestic workers," she said. "We are still in prison, locked away in those houses. We are the workers that freedom forgot," she said.

Over the following decade, the post-apartheid democratic state attempted to realize the aspirations of domestic workers and ensure that they would not be the workers that freedom forgot. A range of legislative interventions were thoughtfully crafted and introduced that would, together, represent one of the most extensive efforts at the formalization, modernization, and professionalization of paid domestic work anywhere in the world.

From 1996, just two years after the historic first democratic elections, existing labor legislation included domestic workers for the first time within its definition of *employee*,[2] recoding paid domestic work as a form of employment like any other and recognizing erstwhile "servants" as *workers*. Not only were domestic workers included within a labor rights regime, but labor relations in the sector were formalized with access to a statutory state agency (Commission for Conciliation, Mediation and Arbitration [CCMA]) offering workers efficient access to legal recourse in the case of an unfair labor practice.

With a range of protections already legislated, and access to state agencies to claim their rights ensured, the state then introduced a landmark piece of legislation, Sectoral Determination Seven for the Domestic Worker Sector, in August 2002, which sets out the terms and conditions of employment for workers in a particular sector.[3] For the first time in South African history, it legally compelled all employers of domestic workers to pay a legislated minimum hourly wage, as well as state-stipulated annual increases.[4] Mandatory "contracts' and compulsory pay slips were introduced to formalize the relationship as one between employer and employee and to directly challenge the informal relationships between "mistresses" and "maids." Working hours were regulated, overtime and standby pay stipulated, leave provisions extended, and even permissible and nonpermissible deductions explicitly regulated. As one of the most remarkable moves of the post-apartheid state, affecting one of the largest work forces in the country, and no less than a million households, Sectoral Determination Seven would solidify the post-apartheid state's efforts to transform "servants" into workers and to establish one of the world's most comprehensive regulatory frameworks for paid domestic work.

The determination issued, in part, from a conscious effort to "engender" democracy. As Gay Seidman (1999) showed, what was noteworthy about democratization in South Africa was how quickly, and how crucially, it became explicitly gendered. African feminist discourse was rearticulated very soon after Mandela's release from prison in February 1990 to demand a democracy that would equate national liberation not only with racial equality but with gender equality as well. The Women's National Coalition, formed in April 1992, became a key organizational and ideological vehicle for the realization of "gendered citizenship" (Seidman 1999), leading to South Africa's unique constitutional recognition of and commitments to, women's claims to equal citizenship.

Beyond constitutional encoding, though, women's activism secured the insertion of gender into a whole range of newly emerging democratic institutions, ideologies, and structures of governance (Hassim 2006). Quotas for political representation of women created the possibility that gender could be foregrounded in critical sites of politics and government—from members of Parliament to cabinet ministers. The struggle to ensure that democratization would be crafted in ways sensitive not only to the overhaul of structures of racial oppression but also to gender oppression secured what was to become known as the "national gender machinery" (Hassim 2006).

A Commission for Gender Equality was established out of a constitutional provision to police the equality clause with respect to gender and to advance the cause of gender equality more broadly. Together with the Office on the Status of Women and a Joint Standing Committee on the Improvement of the Quality of Life and Status of Women, the "gender machinery" codified South Africa's remarkable commitment to "engendering democracy."

The efforts of the state for domestic workers must be understood as, in part, inspired by these gendered sensibilities of the emerging statecraft. One of South Africa's most ardent gender advocates argued that the Department of Labour "should be commended" for the determination and the energy it put into implementing landmark legislation for domestic workers (Budlender 2004, 22). Even fervent critics of the post-apartheid state lauded the remarkable commitment to this most marginalized group of working women. "It is usually difficult for me to praise the government, but this is a sizable step in the right direction. . . . Labour Minister Membathisi Mdladlana has done a sterling job," said a commentator (*Sunday Independent*, April 6, 2003).

The landmark determination issued not only from the genuine intent to protect and recognize domestics as workers but also from the effort to recognize and recode their social contribution and value in ways advocated for by the feminists of the 1970s. On announcing the legislation, the labor minister, Membathisi Mdladlana, cited the importance of the determination in recognizing and valuing domestic workers:

> Domestic workers have been at the back of the queue when it comes to respect, decent wages and conditions of employment. Yet they are our mothers, our aunts and our sisters who ensured that their employers could go to work. It is our mothers, aunts and sisters who have contributed to the upbringing of hundreds and thousands of children who are not their own. . . .
> The time has indeed arrived where domestic workers are valued for the

contribution they have made and are making. It is time that domestic workers are afforded their rightful place in the labour market and in society. (*Press Release*, July 10, 2001)

Given this broad interpretation of the extension of citizenship rights, domestic workers were also included within a government social insurance scheme, the Unemployment Insurance Fund (UIF).[5] In this "world's first extension of coverage of the most vulnerable workers, the domestic workers, to the UIF" (*Sunday Times*, June 2, 2004), employers were required to register their workers with the Fund. Registration entitled domestic workers (working more than twenty-four hours a month) to a full range of social security protections, including unemployment insurance and maternity, illness, dependent, and adoption benefits. Important amendments also allowed domestic workers to claim UIF benefits on the death of their employers and introduced the category of "partial unemployment," which allowed part-time domestic workers who lost one of their jobs to claim unemployment insurance.

The state's attempt to transform "servants" into workers, however, went beyond formalizing the employment relationship and ensuring state social insurance coverage. It also sought to professionalize the occupation with, quite likely, the world's first state-sponsored national qualification in domestic work. In "perhaps the biggest single skills development programme to be launched in South Africa" (*Update*, Services Seta, July 2002), a Domestic Workers Skills Development Project was launched to provide certified training for domestic workers toward a national qualification.[6]

The project received funding of R120 million [$20m][7] from the National Skills Fund (the only skills development training scheme in South Africa funded by government rather than employers) as a project in "the national interest" (Services Seta Marketing Company Brief).[8] The project aimed to oversee the state-subsidized training and certification of more than 27,000 domestic workers nationwide, and was launched to much fanfare and acclaim, with "graduation ceremonies all over the country" (*La Femme*, October 23, 2004), enthused the administrator of the Domestic Services Contact Center.

In this full range of interventions, then, the South African democratic state crafted a remarkably wide-ranging and extensive set of legislative protections for the sector. South African domestic workers thus found themselves straddling, within a single lifetime, two fundamentally opposite workplace regimes: one, an apartheid domestic workplace order with its "ultra-exploitation" (Cock 1980) and "servant status"; the other, a post-apartheid order with minimum wages, compulsory contracts, regulated working conditions, social security, and professional training. They became beneficiaries of one of the most commendable efforts to formalize, modernize, and professionalize the erstwhile relationship between "maids" and "madams" into one between employers and employees.

But could these efforts really transform the sector? Under apartheid, the state resisted intruding into the white "normal" family (Hassim 2005), which has been reinforced post-apartheid by global reticence about state intrusion into the "private" spaces of family life. It was ambitious, at best, to expect that more than a million (mainly white) employers isolated in private homes would heed the call of a black government (still constructing its legitimacy and capacity) to restructure relations with their "servants." In a deeper sense, the potential for some ink-filled legislative paper to overturn a century's worth of colonial attitudes that had embedded themselves materially in the most intimate of spaces seemed unrealistic. Not to mention the logistical nightmare presumed by the kind of state regulatory capacity required to oversee at least a million employer-employee dyads. So, it was nothing short of remarkable that almost immediately after the extension of the legislation in 2002, crucial objective improvements were already apparent.

An Unlikely Change: Wages, Working Conditions, Dignity, and Recognition

As the most important marker of the level of "exploitation" of domestic workers, wages improved significantly compared to previous levels directly as a result of this effort at state regulation. In 2003, just a year after the implementation of Sectoral Determination Seven,[9] the percentage of workers earning in the lowest income bracket[10] fell noticeably[11] while the proportion earning in the minimum wage range[12] increased as dramatically.[13] Historically, a majority of workers (more than 50%) had earned in the lowest income bracket,[14] but by September 2003, less than a year after the minimum wage legislation came into effect, that had been reversed for the first time, with a majority of workers earning above that threshold (*Labor Force Survey*, 2003).

Tom Hertz (2004) analyzed the increases using a regression analysis and confirmed "that the wage increases were caused by the regulations" (2004, 1).[15] So did some of the workers' narratives: "I was earning six hundred a month," said one worker. "Then when the Department came to the area to say this is the new minimum wages, my employer agreed she would give me the minimum wage," she continued. The substantial quantitative improvement of wage levels in the sector as a result of the state's intervention was marked and signaled the critical importance of state regulation in protecting workers from the exploitative low wages characteristic of paid domestic work.

At the same time, the labor relations system also formally improved with the state's crafting of inclusion for domestic workers. In the limited sample of this study, 20 percent of workers had a written contract of employment. Similarly, Hertz (2004) showed a remarkable change in just over a year and a half in the proportion of domestic workers nationally reporting a written contract with their employers. While only 7 percent of workers had a written contract of employment in February 2002, with the introduction of mandatory written contracts, that figure had more than tripled to 25 percent by September 2003. Within five years (by September 2007), the percentage covered increased more than fivefold with a third of workers covered by a contract of employment (*Labor Force Survey* 2007).

There was also an incredible response to the registration of domestic workers within the UIF. Nearly half a million workers were registered by their employers at the end of the first four months alone. Two years after the required deadline for registering workers, nearly 84 percent of the targeted group was registered (*Citizen*, April 4, 2005). "The response by South Africans to the inclusion of this most vulnerable domestic sector has been overwhelming. No other country has ever tried it," celebrated the Department of Labor spokesperson (*Independent*, October 14, 2005).[16]

But, for workers, it was not these objective improvements in wages, working conditions, and formal registration for benefits that was the most important marker of the efficacy of the legislation in its attempt to shift servitude relations. Neither was it, interestingly, the depersonalization of the relationship with employers through the formalization of labor relations in the sector. Quite unexpectedly, it was the outlawing of the instant dismissal that was consistently the most significant change for workers.

Consistently invoked as the most important indicator of a shift in servitude relations, especially for those workers whose residence was tied to their employment, the new procedural requirements for dismissal became *the* most potent, and emotional, marker of an improvement in the sector. Where apartheid relations of servitude were most evident in the instant dismissal, imbued with racist overtones of the "disposability" of black African workers (see Cock 1981), workers spoke with tears, one after the other, about the importance of the new procedural requirements for dismissal:

Dorah Matlala, a domestic worker employed full-time live-in, held back tears when I asked what had changed for domestic workers post-apartheid: "It's better because now she can't tell you, you wake up one morning, to just go."

Almost all workers repeated this sentiment:

This is now the biggest change, you see. Before, you wake up, she just says to you "*voetsek*" [derogatory phrase meaning "get lost"]. (Josephine Kekana)

You sleep much better, now. No more, in the morning, you must worry she says she found another *ousie* [domestic worker]. (Selena Simelane)

In apartheid times, you come back from your holiday, neh? And, you just see all your clothes are on the grass. You are so small, she doesn't even come tell you, you must just know now you have no job. (Doris Radebe)

They don't tell you to just go. This is now why this government is making the domestic to be treated better. You know . . . now also you, your child, is getting food tomorrow. (Lebogang Nkuna)

This paradigmatic focus on making unlawful the instant dismissal expressed the important mitigation by the state of one of the most disruptive and inhumane vulnerabilities of paid domestic work under apartheid. But, more than anything, workers pointed to it not as an indication of improved working conditions but as a means of restoring their dignity. Doris Radebe added with visible emotional strain, "to throw out your clothes, to just tell you one morning to go, it was like disrespecting you. Taking away what little dignity you've still got . . . Being a domestic worker is not easy. Yes, it's true you work very hard. But, it's also that you are treated like an animal, like when she tells you to just go, rather than like a human being."

Another crucial but unexpected response by workers was the importance of recognition by the state, and the visibility attendant to it. Invisibility is a mode of control expertly managed by employers to deny not only the very presence but also the personhood of their workers.[17] The democratic state's recognition of domestics, and overturning of at least their political invisibility, was important to workers. Cynthia Phakathi, a full-time live-out worker, invoked this sense of recognition when asked, "What does democracy mean to you?" "I am just a domestic worker. That's all," she said. "But, this democracy is also for us now. That's what Mandela was saying when he made these laws for us . . . even if you live in the back-yards. . . . Life gets very difficult when you are this woman with this [black skin], but now the government is helping us."

State protection became an important idiom in workers' expressions of the meanings of democratic inclusion. A worker at a union office said: "The government is helping us, protecting us, also taking care of us." And Margaret Manamela, a full-time live-in worker, when asked whether she thought the government was protecting domestic workers, was quite artic-ulate about the meanings of democracy for her. "We need to be protected," she resolved. "We get abused even in our own houses. Also in our em-ployer's houses. When we go to the streets, we must hold everything. There is no peace for the domestic workers. The government needs to protect us. This is what the democracy must make for us—peace, so we can grow our children to be successful, like the [employer's] babies we make big."

Workers responded to this sense of protection by the state in remarkable ways. Despite many assumptions about domestic workers' lack of political acumen and failure of will with regard to the assertion of their rights, their political incorporation has been accompanied by the dramatic expression of a mature consciousness through the claiming of rights and accessing of the organs of state.

Mandela's "Maids": Staking Their Claim on Democracy

In their practical claims-making against the apparatuses of the state mobilized in the effort to transform them into "workers"—the CCMA, the UIF, and state-sponsored training—domestic workers forcefully registered themselves as political agents. Not only did they heed the call of the state by utilizing the expanded access to state agencies and capacities, but in the process, they authorized the state as a legitimate body of rules, prac-tices, and agencies, giving concrete expression to expectations of demo-cratic change.

Just a year after the passage of the new Labor Relations Act (holding employers accountable for unfair dismissal for the first time in South Afri-can history), domestic workers accessed the statutory body charged with enforcing the law—the CCMA—in large numbers and without hesitation, becoming in that first year alone the fifth largest category of workers to bring forward complaints to the Commission. In just the first nine months of the CCMA's existence, a local newspaper was reporting that the CCMA had been "inundated with disputes between 'maids' and matriarchs" (*Sat-*

urday Star, July 26, 1997). A daily suggested that the "recent increase in domestic cases being brought before the CCMA shows" that the "relationships between Madam and Eves [Maids][18] in Gauteng seem to be getting sourer by the day" (*The Star*, July 16, 1997). Yet another carried the headline, "Empowered 'Eve' is flexing her legal muscle," in response to the dramatic uptake of CCMA services by domestic workers (*The Daily News*, August 7, 1997). Long lines of domestic workers queued outside the CCMA's offices in downtown Johannesburg, bearing stories of being dismissed with an hour's notice, of having to eat from the dog's bowl, and of sexual abuse, among others.

By 2001, domestic workers accounted for the third largest caseload of any category of worker for the CCMA (*Review of Operations*, 2000–2001), and in the year following the introduction of Sectoral Determination Seven, there was a sharp (52%) increase in the number of disputes referred for the sector (*Business Day*, April 16, 2003), making them second only to retail workers (and by only 1%) in the number of calls received by the CCMA. Not even public figures seemed to escape this infectious claiming of rights, as even a well-known political leader and anti-apartheid activist, Allan Boesak, was taken to the CCMA by his domestic worker.

On a chilly Tuesday morning in July 2004, I visited the CCMA's offices in the inner city of Johannesburg and found workers snaking their way through its inner halls. Many were domestic workers, and most were visibly distressed. Most had come to the CCMA for assistance after being dismissed, and the anxiety of that predicament hung thick in the air. Yet, at the same time, there was a palpable enthusiasm among those who crowded the halls. I approached a young woman whose face betrayed the combination of distress and hope that animated the faces of the other domestics in line. After an initial introduction, I asked her why she was there. "I am here to make this democracy work for [domestic] workers," she said sharply. When asked what that meant, she continued, "This government was one day only for the madams. Now this government is making life very much better for us the workers also, you see. . . . My employer just threw my clothes on the lawn one day, she says she found herself another maid. So I'm coming here to the government. . . . It is very nice that this government is helping us." In registering themselves so forcefully within an agency of the state, domestic workers authorized the state as the broker of their entry into a status as workers with rights.

Furthermore, where constitutional rights to equality and dignity have been violated, domestic workers have creatively and strategically utilized the CCMA for realizing these rights of citizenship—in particular, the right to dignity with respect to HIV testing and sexual harassment. No less than nine separate cases had been heard by the CCMA relating to sexual harassment by 2004, as other avenues for legal recourse were increasingly constrained. For example, a Thokoza domestic, Lizzie Setjeo, filed a sexual harassment complaint with the CCMA (*Mail and Guardian*, August 3, 2000), and other workers reflected a recognition of the state as an arbiter in these matters. "Sexual abuse of domestics is a really most important issue," said Mavis Khubelo, a polished and articulate worker. "They use your bodies in every way they can, and there was no place you could go to get assistance. But, some of the domestics are now taking these cases to the CCMA, and . . . this is how they are exercising their rights in this new democracy."

Similarly, HIV testing as a precondition of employment is widespread, but it became an important public issue in 2002 when Nokuthula Zulu was ordered by her employer to take an HIV test. When she was dismissed following her refusal to take the test, Zulu took up the matter with the CCMA, which ruled in her favor and ordered eight months' compensation. The union that acted on Zulu's behalf invoked an important idiom for domestic workers when it argued that the significance of the ruling was that it restored "dignity" to the dismissed worker (*Cape Argus, Star*, March 20, 2002), while Zulu herself referenced this as well: "I am very happy that justice has been done because I was devastated by the actions of my employer. . . . I loved their child so dearly, but I felt so humiliated at the end."

Similarly, Sophia Ncobo told me, "I am wondering to myself what is this new thing we call freedom. Because when they do not respect you and take you for that HIV test, then they say 'Go, you are dirty, you have this disease, you are like an animal.' That's why it's very good they must go to the government and fight and say this is not right for us to be treated like this even when they are saying there is this freedom." Sophia directly equated the acknowledgment of the state's capacities in the arbitration of rights with domestic workers' aspirations and understandings of political emancipation. In this, the CCMA and the state's legislative efforts have been imbued by domestic workers with content that has rendered it part of the vocabulary and practice of democratic citizenship.

In the same way, domestic workers have harnessed the protective capacities of that other important state agency in the translation of citizenship rights—the Unemployment Insurance Fund (UIF). Just a year after their inclusion by the UIF, more than 10,000 domestic workers had made claims against the Fund (*Sunday Times*, June 2, 2004). In the following two years, nearly 50,000 more had made claims (*The Mercury*, November 15, 2004) totaling almost R6,7m [$1.12m] since their inclusion (*Citizen*, April 4, 2005). So unexpected and sharp had been domestic workers' accessing of this fundamental citizenship entitlement that the Department of Labor celebrated the "good news" that "domestic workers *are* making use of the UIF" (*The Mercury*, November 15, 2004).

Workers similarly clamored to sign up for state-sponsored professionalization programs. Once again, dignity and recognition by the state was the defining feature of domestic workers' embrace of the state effort. At a Services Seta[19] national conference, thirty-five-year-old Olga Majweta from Claremont said about the training project: "I am grateful to our government, it has restored our dignity as domestic workers and I am now recognized for my role in society" (*BuaNews*, October 28, 2004). Recognition by the state of domestic workers became crucial in their appreciation of the state's efforts. Neliswa Tshali, who was declared the best domestic worker in the Eastern Cape, said at a glittering awards ceremony: "The Services Seta has empowered me with skills and knowledge, in a way I've gained back my self-esteem. I now have goals, I want to do what's best for my children, build a better future for them" (*Press Release*, November 11, 2004), again referencing the politics of recognition involved in this.

Presumptions of domestic worker ignorance and incapacity in exercising their entitlements have been proved inaccurate and replaced with an image of domestic workers as eager and capable of engaging the state and claiming some of their rights. But, despite these objective changes in wages and working conditions, the subjective value for workers of being saved from the indignities of an instant dismissal, and the claims-making (literal and figurative) against the state, workers perplexingly continued to argue, over and over and over again, that things were "worse than before."

Recalcitrant Claims: "Worse Than Before"

Despite evidence of slow and limited, but undeniable, objective changes, when asked what democracy had done for domestic workers, they repeatedly, unmistakably, and puzzlingly argued that "nothing has changed" and, indeed, that things were "worse than before." Hazel Sondlo, a generally feisty woman, reflected a sense of defeat when she confessed "not anything did these things make for us. It's much worse than before also, because they are, they [the employers] say there is nothing they can do, this government is making the laws now." Mavis Khubelo explained through gritted teeth with visible pathos what she felt the new legislation had done to improve the lot of domestic workers: "Can you say, nothing? We are still slaves in these places. Do you know how much it hurts for you to vote for a president, and he makes these laws, and then things just get worse. . . . It's just getting worse, every day, you see apartheid coming back, especially here in Killarney. These old people will die and have a funeral not even knowing that apartheid was buried before them."

Unexpectedly, but strikingly, the anger-tinged lamentations that things were "worse than before" became the most powerful and consistent account of domestic workers' experiences of democratization:

> Let me tell you that nothing has changed. It is the same like before, even worse. (Dorah Matlala)

> It has only gotten worse. . . . Worse, I'm saying, because this is now a new government making good things for domestic workers, but it is now getting worse. (Elinah Motseme)

> It is very much worse than before. Nothing has changed. (Phuti Masimane)

> Things are just getting worse for the domestic workers. Where is this better life that was supposed to come when they put apartheid in the ground, eh? (Doris Radebe)

Over and over again, workers repeated this. This despite the unmistakable evidence of some important, albeit partial, changes in terms of wages and working conditions. And these very workers were utilizing the state apparatus for negotiating better conditions of work in dramatic ways. They were actively claiming their rights to unemployment insurance, they inundated the CCMA to claim their rights to a fair dismissal, as well as using it creatively to secure their rights to dignity, and they frenetically signed up for the state's training programs. So, the forceful claim that "nothing" had improved and, further, that things had "gotten worse," seemed inexplicable.

In fact, workers not only expressed a forceful rejection of the state's efforts in their claims that things were "worse than before" but they even denied any knowledge of the state's efforts. Josephine Kekana dropped her gaze and her voice, almost sheepishly, when asked whether she knew what the state had done to assist domestic workers. "I don't know. I don't know what all these new laws are," she said, emphasizing her lack of knowledge. Jonathan Grossman recounts that when he asked a group of domestic workers in Sea Point, a suburb of Cape Town, in 1999 what they would most like to tell the government, "the favoured answer was that there should be a law to protect them" (2004, 9). As Grossman points out, a year prior to his question, a law *had* been passed that included domestic workers—the Basic Conditions of Employment Act—and the very workers he had spoken to had been through an intensive educational program about it.

After Sectoral Determination Seven had been passed, I asked a group of workers after a Department of Labor information workshop what they wanted the government to do for domestic workers. Again, the preferred answer was, as Palesa Lebala said, "the government needs to protect us, the domestic workers, from this exploitation." Usually, when asking workers about what the new laws meant to them, or how they felt about the state's efforts, they would deny any knowledge about such initiatives at the same time as suggesting their knowledge of it in claiming things had "gotten worse." Josephine Kekana, a full-time live-in worker, for example, after saying "I don't know what all these new laws are," went on four minutes later to admit such knowledge: "The government is trying to do all these things for the domestic workers, with the CCMA, and everything. But things for the domestic workers are now even worse than before."

Many (though not all) workers went further still and rejected the state's efforts outright by insisting that their employers not sign them up with the UIF and refusing to sign mandatory contracts of employment (see chapter 4). Department of Labor inspectors, requested by some employers to seek the cooperation of their employees, were baffled. Why did domestic workers so obstinately refuse to acknowledge changes in the institution? Why, at the same time as claiming some of their rights, did they incongruously deny the democratic state's efforts through their recalcitrant claims that things were "worse than before?"

Rights versus Reality: "We Are Still Slaves. Nothing Has Changed."

How do we explain this paradox? Grossman argues that, instead of suggesting workers' ignorance and apathy, domestic workers' seemingly recalcitrant position reflected workers' knowledge "of the social meaning of the law—the knowledge of their own lived experience" (2004, 9) in which the law had little effect. While not as simple as that, Black South African domestic workers, from poor, often rural, backgrounds bestowed rights by democracy certainly confronted white employers who had been bestowed power by decades of apartheid. Miriam Sithole, desperate for a wage increase so she could bring her children to live with her, was earning well below the minimum wage rate when the new legislation took effect. But, she simply did not have the ability to enforce her rights to a minimum wage. "I definitely couldn't just ask for the minimum wage," she said. "I knew she would fire me right there and then. I would have no home, no job. If I had an education, maybe, I could feel better to ask for more, because I could get another job. But, like this, all these white 'madams' with their expensive jobs and houses are only paying five hundred, six hundred [$100 per month]. But, you dare not even ask for more, because then you'll lose everything."

The formal power of the law confronted the informal power of the deeply entrenched race and class inequalities between middle-class white "madams" and their still working-class black "maids." The result was an institution that remained stubbornly resistant to change.

There were important quantitative shifts in wage levels for the sector, but this did not mean an end to exploitative wages.[20] Oppressive and dehumanizing working conditions also continued, despite impressive improvements on some measures. Many workers, for instance, continued to work twelve-hour days, seven days a week, while degrading practices, such as being forced to eat off separate plates and being denied any visitors, were still commonplace.

Sitting outside a makeshift shop with Joyce Nhlapo one day, the woman who in our initial encounter had cast domestics as the "workers that freedom forgot," offered this extraordinary extension of her argument:

What democracy? What new laws? Those laws stop at the master's door. Inside white people's houses, it is still apartheid law. We are their servants, their girls. You have grandchildren, but you are still their "girl." You work like a dog, morning to night, doing everything, everything, you earn peanuts, and then you must eat like a dog—on the dog's plate, out in the yard, with the dog. They don't respect you even, scream at you, swear at you. Even they teach the children to swear at you. The children you make big, they swear at you. They call you "kaffir [racial slur]." You can't bring your children to stay, you can only go home once a year. Your friends can't come into their yard. They must scream for you like an animal from over the fence. Then the master comes and abuses you in your room at night, because you belong to him. We are still slaves. Nothing has changed.

Joyce spat these words out with hurt and anger, her strong emotion issuing from a recognition of the dramatic impotence of state protection to overturn some of the more dehumanizing moments of paid domestic work in South Africa despite dramatic and crucial improvements in wages, working conditions, and formal protection.

Even beyond the workplace, despite inclusion into an elaborate crafting of state protection and recognition, domestic workers' experiences were predominantly one of hardship and exclusion. "I've got no education, there is no other jobs for me," lamented a worker outside a Department of Labor People's Center one day. "I am living in the room and there is no toilet even. I must wash in the bucket outside . . . [even] in the winter. There is no other place to live. My heart is crying. I want this better life I voted for."[21]

Recalcitrant claims that "nothing had changed" therefore reflected domestic workers' location in a matrix of raced, classed, and gendered exclusions that revealed their unfulfilled expectations of democratic inclusion.

Tardiness in state provision for housing meant conscription into live-in service or living in backyard shacks in established townships or in shacks in informal settlements. For the "lucky" ones who rented actual houses, these were the notorious apartheid "matchboxes"[22] in the townships or decrepit homes and flats in the degenerating suburbs surrounding the inner city. Whatever the type of accommodation, almost all workers lived in a single room. The one-roomed flats, houses, and patchwork shacks that I visited could be easily described as "drab, bare, and . . . cheerless," as Cock (1988) once described live-in "servant's quarters" under apartheid.

This failure of decent housing made South African domestic workers uniquely exploitable by employers. The purchase of a small house for a domestic worker is not only a common practice in South Africa (*Cape Argus*, October 19, 2004), but an expensive example of the "maternalism" described by Judith Rollins (1985).[23] Sindiwe Magona (an ex-domestic worker) in her brilliant fictionalized analysis of paid domestic work in South Africa exposes this in her short story "Sophie":

> I sometimes get so angry I think of leaving this woman. But she bought me a house, a beautiful house in Mdantsane. It has a carpet on the floor. It has a real bathroom; a bathroom I can use. How do you leave a *mlungu* [white] woman who has bought a house for you?
>
> I feel the house is cement; because of it I can never leave this woman. Cement is like that. Never put your feet deep into wet cement. If you do, make sure you get it out before the cement dries. My cement has dried and both my feet are in this woman's house. I am stuck—for the rest of my life. (1994, 31)

Adding to their difficulties, two-fifths (40%) of live-out workers in this study did not return home to a bathroom with water and electricity, making arduous daily journeys to collect water and firewood common—the fuel for a profound sense of inequality with employers. "All South Africans, they are living a happy life," complained Josephine Kekana, "but, we domestic workers have to walk to get our food, to get water, to get wood for the fire. . . . Our employers are enjoying our struggle. We are still suffering."

Josephine continued, later, "*ay*, we don't have a life. No, we don't have a life. We just work. . . . They [our employers] have a very nice life. Josephine, she is just working for her children, to survive."

In making a definite distinction between the quality of hers and her employer's lives, Josephine invoked workers' perceptive appreciation of the dramatic inequalities between themselves and employers that placed limits on the efficacy of the state's efforts. These self-positionings were defined and captured, more than anything, by domestic workers' status as intranational migrants.

Migrancy at the Edge of Democracy: "That's Not My Country"

South African domestic workers remain one of the largest and enduring migrant workforces within the country. In a representative survey of domestic workers in Johannesburg, the migrancy of domestic workers proved one of the "defining characteristics" of the sector (Peberdy and Dinat 2005, 1). Not only did more than half (55.7%) of the South African workers not identify Johannesburg as home, but all (100%) of the South African workers surveyed had a home elsewhere. The majority (65%) were born in a rural area, making them distinctively intranational rural-to-urban migrants.

Ntombi Mangena, a full-time live-in worker in Rosettenville, was born in rural Bergville in KwaZulu-Natal, and migrated to Johannesburg after her husband found work in a chemical plant just outside the city. "I left our homestead when I was very young, and I was going with my husband," she explained, "first to Heidelberg, then Johannesburg. It was very difficult those days. Still. We don't have a home like the other people here. They have their families here, and a home, and they can fight for their rights. But, we are not having a life we can call our own. Even a place we can call our own. When you are a domestic worker, this is how you must live. You are not seeing how you are also in this new South Africa. The old days are for you also your days here."

In this remarkable expression of her positioning as a migrant, a domestic worker, and the compromised location in relation to the new democracy which this implied, Ntombi suggests the implications of her function as a migrant worker in framing her political capacities. Despite state efforts at comprehensive inclusion, this group of workers understood themselves as politically incapacitated by their social location as a cheap, migrant labor force.

Many domestic workers, like Ntombi, who came to Johannesburg from rural locations narrated their entry into their urban work life in ways that emphasized the feelings of exclusion this generated. For example, Mabel Mabena, a live-in domestic worker in Killarney from Phokeng in the North West province, described her entry into Johannesburg from the perspective of a migrant worker:

> My cousin came, she gave me monies for the taxi. My mother was even so sick, she was not coming to the town. My small child, she was still the baby, my eyes were just wet, wet, wet . . . I didn't like Rosebank when I was seeing it first time. Killarney also I still don't like it. It's not home for me . . . Killarney, you must just see how these old ladies look at you. "What are you doing here?" They don't talk with their mouths, [with] their eyes, they ask you. You are in their flats, also. But they still ask you with that eyes, "What are you doing here?" Three years, four years, you feel, *eish*, as a domestic worker you never feel like this is your country.

While these narratives of exclusion were pronounced for live-in workers, their sourcing in the experiences of migrancy ensured that even live-out workers described their work and family lives through the trope of marginality and nonbelonging. Hazel Sondlo, for example, travels from a backyard shack in Soweto to Bez Valley, a predominantly working-class neighborhood where she works every day, by a combination of train and taxi. She related the experience of her daily commute, likening it to the journey of migrant laborers. "*Shoh*," she exclaimed with a whistle, "from my house to Bez Valley is far every day. I talk on the train to the other *ousies* [domestic workers]. It's like those long train rides we used to take from *eBhayi* [Port Elizabeth] to *eGoli* [Johannesburg] when our fathers were on the mines. They used to sing. We don't sing. But, it's like going so far away like that."

In a subsequent discussion with Hazel, she offered the starkest expression yet of this association of even live-out domestic work with migrancy. "I'm learning something. This is not our country," she said. "Whose country is it?" I ask. "It's the madam's country," she said sternly and without any further explanation. "Why?" I probe. "I went to vote there—we got black people there. Making the laws," she said quizzingly. "But, maybe we should say it like that—that's their own country. Those big schools for their children. You seen those big soccer fields? Yeah, that's their country. I just work there. That's not my country."

For domestic workers, lifelong and daily migrant journeys "across the boundaries of race and class," as the title of Dill's (1994) book so precisely describes, are defining. For no other group of South African workers are the dramatic inequalities that characterize the socioeconomic landscape so apparent than for domestic workers. Working in affluence by day, retreating to squalor by night, their work for the wealthy and not-so-wealthy barely services their aspiration to a better life. Where residence patterns are still so strongly racially and economically segregated, there is a consciousness of race and class boundaries for domestic workers as they traverse the post-apartheid landscape, in ways that compound for them their social exclusions.

In their physical migrations between the geographical spaces of rural and urban, township and suburb, domestic workers traverse spaces coded with political meaning that reinforce the failed expectations of democratic inclusion and frame a sensibility in which they resist the efficacy of the state's efforts. But, their recalcitrant claims were also about a lot more than the inefficacy of the state's efforts to immediately produce results. Why "worse than before?" Why completely deny any knowledge of the laws? Why reject being registered with the state? The denial of knowledge about the state's efforts, the refusal to impute to the legislative changes any efficacy, and the refusal to comply with some of its requirements reflected instead something much more insightful.

Consider the following critically important statement by Eunice Dhladhla, deputy general secretary of the South African Domestic Service and Allied Workers Union (SADSAWU). Dhladhla, a remarkable veteran of the struggle for domestic workers' rights with a quiet but powerful intellect and at times the gift of a poet's imagination, when asked about the impact of the state's crafting of political inclusion for domestic workers, said:

> I know it will sound a little bit rude, but I have to say it. The apartheid, it is back to square one. Since this labor thing started, I can say since Mem-

bathisi Mdladlana announced on the radios and papers that now the domestic workers are also workers, so we as the labor department, I quote, so "We as the labor department, we are recognizing now domestic workers, and domestic workers are now covered with the Basic Conditions of Employment Act." That is where the problem started. That is where the apartheid started again. It's alive and kicking in the suburbs. Alive and kicking.

For workers themselves to articulate such a strong claim regarding what is quite possibly one of the most important and extensive state efforts to reform paid domestic work anywhere in the world is extremely significant. And, it offers a very different explanation for an unchanged past of servitude relations from state officials and scholars, who claim that the failure of this commendable set of policies to achieve real-world change is variously a failure of state enforcement capacity, employers' racialized colonial attitudes, and worker apathy (see Fish 2006a; King 2007). By locating the source of the problem *in* the state's efforts, as Eunice did, and thereby rejecting them, domestic workers offered a more profound explanation.

"Vulnerable Workers": The Subject of Democratic Statecraft

By arguing that "the problem started" when the state "announced . . . that now domestic workers are also workers," Eunice echoed many other workers. They explained that things were "worse than before" not despite the state's world first efforts to modernize and formalize the institution, but precisely because of it. Sarah Nwanedi, an otherwise quiet, but reflective worker, stared at me piercingly when I asked her why things were "worse than before." "It's because of what the government is now doing," she said slowly and deliberately. Sarah, Eunice, and other workers kept coming back to this. They located the problem in what I call the *democratic statecraft* for the sector—the collection of democratic state policies, practices, agencies, technologies, techniques, and discourses involved in crafting a political status for domestic workers. Not only did the political incorporation of domestic workers become part of the crafting of a democratic state, but it constituted specific political subjects.

The politics of inclusion for domestic workers was centrally connected to the politics of democratic state formation. Labor rights were mobilized as a technology of governance that used the category of worker and the social location of the workplace as sites for the registering of political subjects with rights. On the occasion of the celebration of ten years of democracy, labor minister Membathisi Mdladlana celebrated the land-mark legislative achievements for domestic workers, arguing that "these workers were taken for granted by the previous apartheid regime," and summarized the extensive mobilization of the post-apartheid state appa-ratus for the protection of domestic workers as a project of democratization (*Sunday Times*, June 2, 2004). The inclusion of domestic workers was thus intimately tied to the project of a democratic state in formation, and they were scripted into the narrative of democratization.

Indeed, on the occasion of the first democratic elections, most domestic workers went to the polls to cast their first votes as "maids," in their uni-forms, with their "madams." Even by the third democratic election, "cars came and went bearing the all-too-familiar sight of madams and maids com-ing in together to cast their vote," reported a local daily (*This Day*, April 15, 2004). "Election day in a few of Johannesburg's northern suburbs was char-acterized by scenes of well-groomed employers disembarking from expen-sive motor vehicles followed closely by uniformed domestic workers and their gardeners" (ibid.). Even a government minister at the time, Mac Maha-raj, commented on "the fact that the voters are really segmented into two fronts, the wealthy and their domestic servants" (*This Day*, April 15, 2004). In this, the category of "domestic worker" was inscribed directly into the most iconic moment of democratic practice. In the democratic statecraft that followed, domestic workers continued to be constituted as a category through which the politics of transition were effected.

As one of the most wide-ranging intrusions of the post-apartheid state into the home, the recasting of the relationship between private and public presumed by the various state interventions in the sector saw the state regulation of domestic workers become one of the most dramatic examples of the post-apartheid democratic statecraft. The requirement to register one's domestic worker necessitated millions of predominantly white, middle-class, and to a certain extent female South Africans to directly engage the demo-cratic state and participate in its regulating functions, at the same time as it incorporated within the state apparatus at least a million of the most disad-vantaged black women workers.

In this democratic statecraft, the effort to politically include domestic workers issued from a particular logic, one premised on a particular con-struction of domestics—as "*vulnerable workers*." What workers exposed, and rejected, in their recalcitrant claims that things were "worse than be-fore" was precisely the, quite literally, subject status implied by their con-stitution as "vulnerable." After considering the kind of compromised subject inherent in the state's democratic statecraft, it was not surprising workers rejected it so forcefully.

"Most Vulnerable Workers" and the "Will to Empower"

State efforts issued from the formative declaration of the Fifteen-Point Program of Action of the Ministry of Labor (1999–2004) that the state's mandate was responsibility for "vulnerable workers." "The State carries the responsibility of protecting vulnerable workers to ensure that they have the same basic rights and are afforded their dignity. The Basic Conditions of Employment Act is the principal instrument through which such protection is extended," states the program.

In invoking constitutional principles of rights to equality and dignity, and specifying legal technologies as the "principal instrument" through which protection was to be effected, the state established "worker" as a category for the realization of the rights of citizenship (Kenny 2007; Seidman 2007) and "vulnerable worker" as a particular modus in the logic of its democratic statecraft.[24] And, "vulnerable worker" certainly became and remained the most overt organizing trope of the state's efforts in the sector.

The report into the investigation of a minimum wage and conditions of employment for domestic workers, for instance, tellingly opened with the fact of domestic workers' vulnerability: "Domestic workers represent a particularly vulnerable category of workers" (Department of Labor 2002, 1). Often, it was not just that domestics were "vulnerable," but that they were the "most vulnerable." For example, in announcing "the world's first extension of coverage of the most vulnerable workers, the domestic workers, to the UIF" (*Sunday Times*, June 2, 2004), and in commending "the response by South Africans to the inclusion of this most vulnerable domestic sector" (*Independent*, October 14, 2005), various levels of government repeatedly mobilized this construction of "vulnerable workers." Membathisi Mdladlana, the minister of labor, even personalized this construction: "My mother was a domestic worker, too, so I know their plight and they are amongst the most vulnerable of all workers" (*BuaNews*, October 28, 2004).

Workers heard this repeatedly from the various city and state officials they encountered in the innumerable information workshops held around the city and country, in encounters at the CCMA, and even from training providers. "Domestic workers are the most vulnerable workers, and that's why we are here to inform you of your rights," said a labor department official, for instance, at a union event in Bez Valley. Over and over again, the Ministry of Labor, the Department of Labor, local government, city officials, and training providers rendered domestic workers a category for state "intervention" through their construction as "most vulnerable."

Domestic workers are indeed vulnerable: Their isolation in the private sphere of the family, their subjection to the whims of employers, their lived realities as migrants, and the failure of more collective organization as workers, do indeed make them vulnerable. Domestic workers' vulnerability in the society, labor market, and in the law is apparent. But this national-level construction, as it filtered into various lower-level state agencies, induced a particular modus of state power and an understanding of a certain kind of "subject."

"Vulnerability" as a mode of entry into citizenship rights for domestic workers presumed a victimized subject with compromised capacity.[25] It presumed the protection of a more capacitated actor to act on behalf of, and for the empowerment of, the "vulnerable" category. The most important piece of legislation for the sector therefore summarized that "the state carries the responsibility of protecting vulnerable workers" (Department of Labor 2002). Rights extended on the basis of victimhood, notes Geraldine Pratt, "regionalize identity-in-injury in ways that extend the administrative and management reach of the state" (2004, 103). In various ways, by posing the vulnerability of these workers as the basis for state regulation of the sector, the state imagined workers as lacking the capacity to effect change themselves, and constructed itself as the agent to act on their behalf, thereby extending the state's responsibility and, with it, its powers and reach.

Through their construction as "vulnerable," in essence, the state became the proxy for workers—their articulator, representative, and protector. In the extension of rights to domestic workers, the state took onto itself the onus of identifying what domestic workers' collective interests were. In the investigation into the possibilities of minimum wages and conditions of employment for the sector, no less than sixty-four national hearings and five major commissioned surveys were undertaken by the state. The purpose of this data gathering was not only to produce a profile of domestic work in the country. Rather, in the hearings, telephone surveys, and taxi rank campaigns,[26] the state directly canvassed workers' experiences in order to formulate a vision of the interests of workers, positioning itself through this as the articulator of domestic workers' collective interests.

At the same time, for workers not designated "vulnerable," collective bargaining arrangements are the primary vehicles through which wages, increases, and conditions of employment are negotiated. But, for "vulnerable workers" such as domestic workers, their designation as "vulnerable" required that the setting of minimum wages and conditions of employment were handed over to a state body, the Employment Conditions Commission (ECC). It was this body, composed of members elected by the minister of labor, that held all authority to establish wages and working conditions for the sector. While workers' and employers' comments were solicited during the investigation into the Determination, and following its promulgation, it was the ECC machinery that authorized the actual levels of the minimum wage and the specific content of domestic workers' workplace rights. Workers were therefore removed from the process of establishing the terms of their employment, precisely because of their construction as "vulnerable," leading the state to act on their behalf, as their representative, in determining the conditions of employment for the sector.

Not only was conceptualization of the regulation a state-mandated affair, but the implementation and enforcement of Sectoral Determination Seven was also effected entirely by the state, as the representative and protector of domestic workers. Registrations through the UIF were administered by the state, the enforcement of minimum wages and conditions of employment was coordinated by an army of state inspectors, and ongoing labor relations were regulated by the CCMA. The state, in its various capacities and agencies, therefore effectively positioned itself as the only active agent in the sector.

This was not unpredictable. Scholarly analyses of the sector had, in their genuine efforts to expose the plight of workers, cast them as "ultra-exploited" victims capable only of being saved by state protection. Susan Flint declared, for instance: "Domestic workers are clearly an ultra-exploited group of workers in dire need of statutory protection" (Flint 1988, 197). The state, following this lead, in casting workers as "vulnerable," posited itself as the only source of active change for the sector. While workers were included through participatory policy making in the discussions prior to and during the legislative intervention, the mechanics of the Sectoral Determination, UIF inclusion, and state-sponsored training presumed workers' incapacity to direct the process themselves.

This kind of overzealous extension of the reaches of the state is not necessarily coterminous with state regulation. In postindependence Zimbabwe, for instance, the state chose a very different system for the regulation of paid domestic work. Instead of the state managing the enforcement of a regulatory system, it chose to empower workers to become the main enforcers of their rights, backing the formation of a union that was mandated with the implementation and oversight of regulatory controls in the sector (see Pape 1993). So, within the ambit of state regulation, the South African state could have conceived of ways to implement a rights-based formal labor relations system for domestic workers that more explicitly recognized the capacity of workers to take ownership over the system. Instead, incorporating workers politically in their status as "vulnerable" led to a capture of control by the state in ways that constructed workers as "subject to" the state's regulatory and protective powers.

And so the construction of domestic workers as the "most vulnerable workers" set in motion a state apparatus that acted on behalf of workers presumed incapable of acting for themselves. A Department of Labor official at a "Domestic Worker Celebration" in Sandringham summarized this effectively. "We are saying that the government is here to protect them," he said, with genuine intent, "and there are all these things we now have in government, of the CCMA, and the inspectorate division, and we run information workshops even for the union, we are saying we are doing these things because domestic workers are vulnerable, and it is our responsibility as the government to protect them, and to empower them."

The paternalistic potential underlying the language of "protection" and workers' subjection through their construction as "vulnerable" was evidenced in the daily, routine practices of the state in its relationship with these workers; the paternalism was disturbing at times. Guided by the characterization of domestic workers as "vulnerable," local state officials—almost all men—sometimes gloated in their rendering of domestic workers as lacking any capacity to understand or alter their positioning. At a "Workshop on the Constitutional Rights of Domestic Workers" at Constitution Hill, a Department of Labor inspector chastised workers: "You domestic workers are too scared to implement your own rights. You must not be quiet and just say, 'Yes, Madam.' The problem is also you, the domestic workers, for not asking for your rights."

Repeatedly, state representatives at various state-sponsored events, information workshops, celebrations, and union meetings paternalistically addressed workers as lacking agency, capacity, and knowledge, rendering them as "vulnerable" and therefore passive and ignorant. The inspector's quote above is indicative of the direct translation of the discourse of domestics' "vulnerability" into a certain reading of the political agency of these workers. As one official put it, domestic workers' "vulnerability" ensured that they were "too scared to enforce the rights they now enjoy as workers." The solution to limited compliance on the part of both employers and employees in a certain area was therefore always to organize an "information workshop," reflecting the logic that if "vulnerability" reflected an incapacity to enforce one's rights, this could be overcome by empowering workers with information.

Not surprisingly, workers' frequent gripe with this type of initiative was to fault the organizers for not including employers as well. Joyce Nhlapo, in a focus group after one such event in Lenasia, angrily suggested that "they must go talk to those employers who don't know anything about these laws, not us." When probed further, she explained: "They must bring the employers here also, not just the domestic workers. We are not stupid. We know our rights also."

In this telling statement, Joyce suggested that the state's efforts to "empower" domestic workers with information about their rights betrayed an understanding of workers as passive in their ignorance, which was vigorously rejected. This undermining of workers reflected their being made subject to the state's control. It was actualized cogently during Department of Labor "inspection blitzes." In these campaigns, teams of inspectors would descend unannounced on a given suburb and go door to door investigating compliance of householders with the legislation for domestic workers. Once establishing that a domestic worker was employed in a home, the inspectors would negotiate entry, and they—with me in tow—would be seated by the nervous but usually hospitable employer in their living room. The inspectors would politely and graciously explain the purpose of their visit before beginning to work through their compliance checklist.

Inspectors on every site inspection on which I tagged along denied the capacity and agency of workers by failing to speak to or acknowledge them at all. Not once was a worker ever asked for or consulted. Instead, in every single case, the inspectors self-consciously presented themselves as state representatives, and therefore as proxies of "vulnerable workers." "Do you provide written payslips at the end of the month?" "Do you have a written particulars of employment with your worker?" They would ask the employer these types of questions, checking off their responses mechanically as they went along. Once completing their checklist, the main inspector would assume an air of authority and explain to the employer the areas of noncompliance. A written warning would be issued to rectify the infringement, accompanied by a usually officious reprimand to, for instance, "make sure you fix this before we come back on the date written here to check again. You are an employer and should act as such; I don't want to see this problem again."

In these inspections, there was a literal "standing in" of the state for the worker. The state did not mediate the relationship between employer and employee, as the latter was never present or consulted, but it was understood that the state represented the worker. Furthermore, that all the inspectors I ever encountered were male, barring one (a junior trainee), suggested the masculinist presentation of the state, and a certain paternalism in their acting as representatives of workers' interests in their site inspections with employers.

Indeed, this paternalism was evident even at various local government–organized events with workers, where various Department of Labor and city officials presented themselves not only as representatives of workers' interests but also, in dealing with questions, often slipped into presenting themselves *as* workers. "Life is very difficult for us as domestic workers, because we work long hours, and we earn little pay," said a Department of Labor official, presenting himself as worker.

Through these various processes, state policies and functionaries, while always conscious of the objective to improve the plight of domestic workers, reinforced workers' "subject" status. Workers were understood as requiring the state's action on their behalf; they were not understood as actors themselves.

Thus, an availing of workers as the subject of rights through their discursive construction as "vulnerable workers" made domestics *subject* to a peculiar logic of state power, what Barbara Cruikshank (1999) calls a "will to empower." In this, Cruikshank (1999) captures the schizophrenia inherent in the politics of empowerment. The South African state, negotiating globalization and democratization, was multiply impelled by the competing logics of market-driven rationality, social development, emancipatory visions for engendering democracy, politics as the extension of rights, and the creation of capacities to access them. In that conjuncture, the politics meant to empower domestic workers simultaneously became the expression of the state's "will to power." The democratic statecraft for domestic workers expressed this logic. Activated in state policy and practice, and translated by its functionaries on the ground, it turned state efforts at improving the lives of domestic workers into a mode of state power.

In their narratives of "worse than before," workers' rejection of the state's efforts reflected a rejection of the logics of power presumed by their construction as "vulnerable" by the state. No wonder Eunice Dhladhla said without hesitation that the "problem started" with the state's initiative. Joyce Nhlapo evocatively captured this when I asked her why workers kept saying things were "worse than before." "You don't understand," she replied. "Things *are* worse than before. You are only here for a few years looking at our problems. We are here our whole lives with these problems, and let me tell you it's worse. With this new laws, and this thing where we domestic workers are the ones who are protected by the government, it is making things worse." I probe, but don't get much of a response. Two hours of conversation later, Joyce volunteered a profound thought, switching to an assertive tone in recognition of the significance of her insight: "Let me just tell you, we are not vulnerable. We don't need anyone else with power to come and protect us. I mean, we domestic workers. We are strong. We have been protecting ourselves all these years."

Joyce's thoughts were presciently aware. Rendering workers as the subject of its democratic statecraft through their "vulnerability," the state presumed the historical and continuing structural incapacities of workers to enact practices of power themselves. But, workers were not incapacitated. Indeed, one of the dominant tropes of self-presentation by domestic workers was to suggest their militant capacities. "Lioness of the household," claimed a tribute by one domestic worker to another, published in a workers' newsletter, "you roar forward, you roar." Far from incapacitated, it memorialized the plight of domestic workers by emphasizing "your roaring is heard everywhere everywhere." Directly disclaiming the oft-repeated presentation of domestic workers as passive in their vulnerability, the emphasis on domestic workers' roar reasserts a capacitated and active subject.

So, by claiming things were "worse than before," domestic workers were commenting on, and distancing themselves from, the "vulnerable," passive, and incapacitated subject invoked by the democratic statecraft. They were disowning the extension of the state's power through its initiatives to protect them. And, they were also commenting on the ways in which the democratic statecraft ignored, dismissed, and invalidated the existing capacities and strengths they possessed. As we see in chapter 4, they were commenting on the ways the state's "will to empower" directly challenged workers' existing practices of power as it extended the state's own. And that power inhered, quite surprisingly, in the intimacy of their work.[27]

4

Intimate Work

State Power versus
Workers' Power

"I will not sign that contract!" said Patricia Kubu with determination. "But, if you have a contract, won't your working conditions be regulated?" I intervene. "No, no, no. I don't want to sign that contract," she said, shaking her head with absolute resolve. She was not the only one. On a Department of Labor "inspection blitz," a sincere employer told the inspector exasperatedly that her worker of many years refused to be registered. Later, I met Linda Mkhonto, who recollected how she "negotiated" Saturdays off when the new legislation came into effect:

> First, when the legislation came out, we didn't talk about the laws. . . . I know I should only work eight to five for Monday to Friday, because I know the laws from the union. So, I know I mustn't work Saturdays. So, on Saturday, I don't tell her anything, I just go to my room in the back and pull the blankets over my head. On Monday when I go to work, she says I must be better now, not sick. I don't say anything. Next week, Saturday, I pull the blankets over my head. Monday, she is wondering. But we don't say anything to one another. Next Saturday, I pull the blankets. Now, she tells me she called the CCMA, and I'm supposed to work on Saturday until twelve, one. But, I know my rights. I know I'm not supposed to work. So, next Saturday, I pull the blankets. That Monday, she says maybe I shouldn't work on Saturdays.

This was nothing short of remarkable. Apartheid-era labor relations in the sector were marked by a toxic cocktail of informality, personalized dependence on employers, and the failure of recourse to state institutions. The post-apartheid state's efforts to institute contracts of employment, legislate rights, and provide access to state recourse targeted exactly the problem of paid domestic work under apartheid. So the reticence of many domestic workers in post-apartheid South Africa to embrace the new formalized and depersonalized labor relations system was enigmatic.

Instead of signing a contract that would formalize the relationship with her employer and give her access to statutory protection, Patricia Kubu refused. Instead of contractually defining a forty-five-hour work week with her employer, or taking her case to the statutory agency tasked with her protection, Linda chose to "pull the blankets" over her head. With one of the world's most extensive efforts at the formalization of paid domestic work, South African domestic workers were not only claiming things were "worse than before," some were actively choosing not to embrace some of the state's efforts. They were refusing to sign contracts, refusing to be registered with the state, and choosing to informally negotiate the conditions of their work. How do we explain this?

As argued in chapter 3, in their recalcitrant claims that things were "worse than before," workers discursively disowned the democratic statecraft because it subjected them to the state's "will to empower." They were refusing to recognize the presumptions of their own incapacity attendant to their construction as "vulnerable." So, too, in their recalcitrant actions—refusing to sign contracts, to be registered, to contractually negotiate the terms of employment with their employers—workers refused to authorize the state's effort at formalization because it delegitimated their existing capacities.

It turns out that while the state's efforts assumed paid domestic work is a form of work like any other, and could therefore be formalized and depersonalized like any other, domestic workers are *not* workers like any other. Domestic workers' workplaces are not impersonal organizations that can be easily regulated through a depersonalized industrial relations system. Instead, domestic workers' workplaces are the intimate spaces of family life, and with their work goes all the close, personal, contact, emotions, experiences, and intimacy that is the fabric of families and households.

In this chapter, a sensitive analysis shows how, having been denied any form of state protection under apartheid, South African domestic workers had utilized exactly this intimacy as a way to independently control their work. They carefully cultivated personal relationships with their employers, recovered the intimacy of the "like one of the family" myth, used their employers' dependence on them to informally regulate wages and working conditions, informally negotiated the limits of their employers' control over their labor, and strategically engaged in "emotion work" as a tactic of class combat. In this work culture, they practiced power from the most unlikely of sites—the intimacy of their work.

By trying to modernize paid domestic work from a presumption of workers' "vulnerability," and their resulting incapacities, the state was insensitive to this already existing intimate work culture and to the capacities of workers that it implied. Depersonalization by the state effectively threatened domestic workers' historically cultivated practices of power. No wonder workers challenged state efforts at formalization. These efforts were understood as the extension of the state's power at the expense of their own.

Intimate Work: "I Work in a Family, Not for a Family"

"I make their beds every day. I wash their sheets every day. I wash their underwear every day. I answer their phone and take messages. I am there before they leave for work and argue. I am there when they come home and argue. I know everything about what's going on in their lives," explained Patricia Kubu. With this, she expressed how, as a domestic worker, she was intimately connected to the family she worked for. She knew almost everything about her employers' lives, and confessed that she often knew more about each of the family members than they knew about each other. Indeed, domestic workers recognized that the nature and setting of their work intimately bound them to the families that employed them. "I work *in* a family, not *for* a family," said Joyce Nhlapo with razor-sharp insight, summarizing many workers' understandings of the inextricability of their work from the intimate lives of others.

For those workers involved in child care, the bonds of intimacy ran deep. "I love the children," said Mavis Khubelo one afternoon with sincere emotion: "I can honestly say that I have a deep love for them. Even more than their parents, because I spend more time with them in their home, teaching them, educating them, disciplining them throughout the day. Their parents just come home and play with them, they give them sweets [candy], to make their children like them. That's because they only arrive when all the hard work of parenting is already done."

Mavis captured the affective dimension of paid domestic work. As a domestic worker she was required to, and indeed did, love the children she cared for. Cameron Macdonald (1998), in a meticulous study on nannies, au pairs, and domestic workers, argues that they are hired to act as proxies for mothers in their absence, but never to completely substitute their presence. The result is a peculiar zone of ambivalence, which Macdonald perceptively calls "shadow mother[ing]." Unlike professional care in institutional settings, such as day care, preschool, or hospital-based nursing care, domestic workers work within the intimate spaces of family life. They are a part of families, but are not. They are paid to take care of families, but sometimes come to care for them. They exist in the liminal spaces between work and family, contract and affect—"in the borderlands of family life" (Murray 1998, 149)—and it complicates any assertion that they are workers like any other.

"You can never escape them," said Margaret Manamela. Her married employer had forgotten she came in on Tuesdays to do laundry, and Margaret walked in on him and his mistress. The management of the secret was a source of emotional strain. "I used to get tired from having to hold that secret. Even at night, he was coming into my thoughts. Their problem became my problem," she complained. Sarah Nwanedi's employer, a twenty-eight year old bipolar woman, once confessed to Sarah her suicidal thoughts while sitting at the kitchen table. One day, Sara was emptying her employer's pockets while doing the laundry and found a vile of cyanide that the woman claimed she would use to take her own life. This unsolicited entry into her employer's most intimate psychic life was too much for Sarah. She found another job a month later.

Similarly, Mpumi Kubheka explained the emotional complications of being confided in by her employer's teenage daughter, whom she had raised since age five:

> Lindy and I were sitting in the garden, and I was cleaning the silver. She said she needed my advice. That's how much I was like a mother to her. . . . So, she told me she was a gay, she was having girlfriends. . . . I told her, "Never mind my child, I will keep your secret." I even told her, "Don't worry, I will protect you." But, I couldn't protect her when the parents found out. . . . Twelve years I worked for them and raised their children, but when this thing started in the family, it got to be so bad, and I couldn't protect her.

In this penetrating story, Mpumi captured how the domestic workplace, as many workers keenly pointed out, is a workplace saturated with intimate relations, and the close, personal, affective dimensions of their employing families' lives became intertwined with their work. In every possible way, domestic workers' work within the emotion-laden spaces of family life made their work intimate. They washed underwear, cleaned bed sheets, overheard family arguments, became part of family conflicts, and were often the first ones to discover intimate family secrets. But, as Beauty Mkhize explained, this forced intimacy was ambiguous. "It's a really very much strange thing to work as a domestic worker," she said. "Because you are so close to the people you are working for. When you're inside their house, their life becomes part of your work, and you become part of their life. . . . But, it's very much true, yes, that you are also very much a stranger. They treat you sometimes like you are not there, like they have no feelings for you."

Karen Hansen's (1989) discussion of domestic workers as "distant companions" captured the ambiguities of intimacy in paid domestic work that Beauty was astutely aware of. While domestic workers share an intimacy with their employers, it can be a deeply uncomfortable one, and employers (as well as workers) manage it through various forms of social distancing. Employers strategically manipulate intimacy and affective relations, not only to mask the relationship as one of waged work but also to obfuscate the dramatic inequalities in the domestic employment relationship through tropes, especially of kinship, that suggest equality. Discomfort with the inextricability of domestic workers from their intimate personal lives, however, equally results in various attempts to create and maintain social and physical distance, often through dehumanizing practices. This produces a "dialectic of intimacy and distance" (Bakan and Stasiulis 1997), a curious kind of relationship in which closeness, familiarity, and intimacy coexist with distancing, estrangement, and dehumanization.

These ambiguities of intimacy are among the more potent sources of the peculiar exploitations of paid domestic work, structuring its unique architecture of dependence and exploitation. In the historical context of the failure of state oversight, however, South African domestic workers recovered precisely these ambiguities of intimacy in paid domestic work to navigate a path through the institution's tense mixture of beneficiation and degradation. Indeed, the unavoidable personal and intimate relationships with their employers became a strategic resource for informally negotiating their conditions of work.

Intimacy and the "Like One of the Family" Myth

Employers have always used the inescapably intimate nature of paid domestic work as a practice of power. Judith Rollins (1985), in her classic study of white employers and black domestic workers in the United States, theorized "maternalism" as an employer mode of control to maintain noncontractual, personalized relations of service. In maternalist practices such as handing down old clothes or the giving of gifts, employers denied the distinctions between paid work and personal servitude, invoking deference and additional labor from their workers and reinforcing inequality. The mystifying ideology of being "like one of the family" is the most potent expression of this maternalism.

As many scholars have argued, the "like one of the family" myth operates as an employer ideology of control by delegitimating paid domestic work as real work, erasing the workers' own familial obligations, and thereby extracting further labor and loyalty through the trope of kin and familial obligation. The "like one of the family" myth constructs, deepens, and reproduces the hierarchies of power between domestic workers and their employers (Romero 1992; Wrigley 1995; Bakan and Stasiulis 1997). Cock (1980) demonstrated this to be a powerful myth within South Africa as well, and it continues to be a significant trope enacted by employers of domestic workers in South Africa as a mechanism of labor control.

This "one of the family" trope has been supplemented by the further mobilization of an additional discursive casting of domestic workers as "helpers." Black employers of domestic workers primarily utilized this construction, together with the epithet "auntie" to offer a similar familial coding of domestic workers' employment relationship. The terms *helpers* and *aunties* define the relationship between employer and employee in familial, voluntaristic terms, masking the relationship as one of waged labor, allowing for the extraction of more and unpaid labor on the basis of charitable obligation, rather than as waged employment. It does not allow workers to assert themselves within the relationship as waged workers, and in discursively denying the relationship as one of paid employment, there is a reinforcement of presumptions of servitude.

The invocation of "family" does more, though, than just deny the labor as a form of work. Bound to the sphere of intimacy and affect, invoking "family" strategically utilizes the ambiguities of intimacy as a way to control workers. As Mavis Khubelo insightfully commented: "They know you love their children, that you are part of the family, so they keep saying this. But, you are only a part of their family when it's convenient for them." As Eunice Dhladhla explained, "if you are like one of the family, then I will say this. One day, when I get the phone call, they say my auntie is sick. I will just go to the fridge, I will just get the food, I will just go and get the keys for the car and I will take the car. I will visit my auntie, and bring her food. That is what someone in the family will do. But, can I do that, when I am the domestic worker?"

Workers were very conscious of the manipulative function of the "like one of the family" myth and employers' invocations of personalized relations, often piercing it with interesting parables as Eunice did. But they, too, strategically mobilized this myth, and the intimacy it suggests, as part of a work culture.

Rhacel Parreñas found that Filipina migrant domestic workers strategically utilized the "like one of the family" myth and manipulated intimacy with their employers:

> While I do agree that the myth of being "like one of the family" perpetuates inequalities, I found that domestic workers can also use this myth to manipulate employers and resist the inequalities that this myth perpetuates in the workplace . . . migrant Filipina domestic workers in Rome and Los Angeles embrace the notion of "like one of the family" and the intimacy resulting from this construction. Though intimacy increases the authority of employers in the workplace and concomitantly stresses the decline in status of migrant Filipina domestic workers, the women in my study still use intimacy to de-emphasize servitude. (2001a, 180)

Filipina migrant domestic workers therefore mobilized intimacy as a turn against servitude. It provided material advantages and was a critical part of a strategy to recover a sense of personhood; that is, being treated "like one of the family" equated to being treated like a person. While this was evident among the South African domestic workers I spoke to, the recovery of intimacy was as much a psychological effort (i.e., knowing that their employers saw them as persons) as it was a work culture designed to maximize control over their work.

Selena Simelane, a full-time live-in worker in Observatory, otherwise quite critical of the "maternalism" of her employer, remarked: "I am having no problems here really, because they are a good employer. I am just like one of the family here. . . . When I need to go home to visit because the small child is gone sick, I just say to her, 'Please, I need to go.' And then she says, 'Sure' and she takes me to Park Station even."

Selena directly connected her strategic use of the "like one of the family" myth with her ability to negotiate working time. Dill makes a similar observation regarding African American domestic workers, arguing that "the intimacy which can develop between an employer and employee, along with the lack of job standardization, may increase the employee's leverage in the relationship and give her some latitude within which to negotiate a work plan that meets her own interests and desires" (1994, 85).

In South Africa, the embedding of paid domestic work so deeply in racialized ideologies of servitude shaped a historical organization of paid domestic work that severely restricted workers' capacities to develop more formalized and contractual relations of work. Indeed, in the late 1970s, the apartheid state mobilized employers as proxies of influx control legislation (chapter 1). In this peculiar form of modern servitude, a good relationship with employers defined not only good conditions of work but also one's political status and positioning. As a result, workers mobilized "good relationships" with their employers as a strategy to control their work, in ways that they continued to even under the implementation of a formal system. "In the mornings, now I come down and I sit with her with the tea and bread and jam," explained Dorcus Mofokeng, a domestic worker I first met outside a training facility. "And we talk. She listens to me. Then, she's also old, you see. She doesn't have anyone to listen to her. So I listen and we talk. . . . It is a very good job for me. My employer understands me and my needs, what I want and how I must work, because we have a very good relationship. So, like this, it is a good job for me."

As Dorcus suggests, developing more personal, and therefore less contractual, relations with employers was a strategy through which each worker could negotiate continued, more favorable working conditions. Dorcus was positive regarding her cultivation of intimacy with her employer because she suggests the favorable conditions of employment that result from having an employer with whom she has developed a personal relationship. For Dorcus, having a "very good relationship" with her employer was connected to her evaluation of her work as "a good job." Other workers similarly cultivated greater intimacy with their employers to more effectively manage the working relationship on their own terms.

Pierette Hondagneu-Sotelo draws a distinction between employers' deployments of intimacy and employees'. While the "maternalism" of, for instance, employers' use of the "like one of the family" myth is "a unilateral positioning of the employer as a benefactor who receives personal thanks, recognition, and validation of self from the domestic worker," *personalism*, she argues, is a "bilateral relationship that involve[s] two individuals recognizing each other not solely in terms of their role or office . . . but rather as persons embedded in a unique set of social relations, and with particular aspirations" (2001, 172). Foreign migrant domestic workers in Los Angeles, she argues, sought personal relations and intimacy with their employers as a strategy of personalism. Reacting against what they perceived as a "new sterility" (11), in which busy employers resolved the ambiguities of intimacy by preferring depersonalized relations, the workers in the study, instead, read this as a dehumanization and craved more intimacy with their employers as a way to recover their sense of personhood (Hondagneu-Sotelo 2001).

South African domestic workers' repetitions of the "like one of the family" myth and the mobilization of intimacy through closer, personal ties with their employers were similarly expressions of personalism. But, it was not just a mutual recognition of personhood. It was also a tactic to control their work. Josephine Kekana, a full-time live-in worker, for example, cultivated intimacy with her employer specifically as a way to ensure more effective working conditions for herself:

> I got her interested in the Lotto [national lottery]. . . . She was not interested in it. She said, how you going to win? I told her, no, you see, if you do not play, how you going to win? It's so nice, because we walk to the garage together on Friday, we buy a little bit of something sweet, then we always sit that night, we watch together for the numbers. . . . That time, when she won with three numbers, you must see how we were jumping together. We even hugged each other. She was so happy. . . . It's very important to have that kind of relationship with them. Otherwise, they exploit you even more.

This cultivation of intimacy is important, suggest some scholars, "to cope with the demands of the workplace" (Parreñas 2001, 186) and "ensure better 'patronage' benefits for the domestic worker" (Ozyegin 2001, 142). Josephine did not work at generating a more intimate and personal attachment with her employer merely as a coping mechanism or means to recover her own sense of dignity though. It was primarily because "otherwise, they exploit you even more." Among South African domestic workers, cultivating intimacy with their employers was a means to control their work, an important practice of power for workers, and a tactic in the effort to restructure class relations.

Gül Ozyegin recognizes this for domestic workers in Turkey, arguing that "this worker-employer intimacy is always strategic," and clarifying that "by 'strategic' I want to suggest that such intimacy is a means of pursuing opposed interests rather than an emotional relationship," she argues that "in domestic service [intimacy] functions as a strategic device for covering up and making manageable some of the differences in status and class that structure the relationship" (2001, 143). Domestic workers in South Africa, rather than "covering up and making manageable" class relations, used intimacy as a way to restructure them.

"White people live in big fancy houses with a separate toilet inside the house," said Monica Ntuli one afternoon as she washed dishes in a bucket on the dusty bareness outside her one-room backyard shack. "But, you learn. You smile with them. You talk to them. Because the monies they are earning and giving you will one day build you a house also. I have learned now to laugh and smile with these rich people. I won't ever be rich like them some day, but their money is making a better life for me, and if I must smile to get it, that is what I know I am going to be doing."

So, South African domestic workers—not unlike domestic workers elsewhere—have cultivated intimacy with employers as a work culture. In a similar way, as Monica Ntuli suggests, South African domestics mobilized affect and emotion in their working relationships as part of the manipulations of the unavoidable, but hierarchically structured, forms of intimacy inhering in their work and workplaces.

The Intimate "Emotion Work" of Deference and Dependence

Cynthia Phakhathi, a live-out worker, explained the "emotion work" implied by developing intimacy with her employers: "If you want her to listen to you, you must also listen to her, so that you must also care for her. It's hard work, really. Really. It even makes you tired. One day, I listened to her two hours, three hours, I must just smile. Just smile. Later, I was so tired from just to smile." Cynthia later recollected the utilities of this affective work: "I say for my employer I have to make her feel also like a person. Now, she knows how I'm making her feel also like that. It's much better. She can be, what can I say, that she is also a human being, and can feel also that [Cynthia], no, she can't clean all the windows today, you see. Because she has got that thing in her now, to say she is a person, with the feelings to see what is too much."

Arlie Hochschild (1983) distinguishes "emotion work" from "emotional labor," the latter being the emotional work performed as a requirement of the job,[1] and the former the kinds of unpaid emotional work engaged in by workers to effect greater gains and control over their work. Encouraging intimacy and attachment became part of the "emotion work" of South African domestic workers in the domestic workplace. Demands for deference and dependence, in particular, exposed and mobilized the ambiguities of intimacy in the relationship.

Mpumi Kubheka, a full-time live-in worker in Sandton, was incredibly forthright and revealing about deference as a form of affective work. "I hear the union, the Department of Labor, they say we domestic workers only know one word to say, 'yes,'" she complained with irritation. "They are not realizing how much it pains when you say 'yes,' but if you don't, you will have to tell your babies 'no.' It pains, it does, but you tell yourself it is part of the job. You must just stop being too soft and let the feelings get to you. You have to be tough. It makes you so tired, and sometimes even sick, because this is the most tiring thing you are doing all day."

And, Mavis Khubelo, in her always articulate way, showed how self-conscious a practice of power this was for workers:

> One thing, you must realize with us domestic workers, don't be fooled when they say "Yes, madam" all the time, like little sheep with no teeth. They have lots of very sharp teeth, but you see when you show it, you are giving your power to her, the employer. When you keep it hidden, you are keeping some power for yourself. You must learn to control when you want to show your teeth. And maybe today, if you must struggle to just put on that smile and say 'Yes, madam,' it's because she'll give you fresh food, not stale food, maybe. And maybe you'll make her in a better mood. . . . They give you all kinds of unnecessary work otherwise just to make you feel small.

Nicole Constable argues that "through such behavior, like other forms of deference behavior, a domestic worker expresses both an understanding and a critique of the existing power structure, but she simultaneously conforms to her employer's desires" (1997, 204). Indeed, this use of affect and intimacy in South Africa reinforced the overall structural relations of employment rather than overturning them. But, neither a psychological device to protect against the demeaning aspects of the authority of employers, nor a "cultural critique from which the performer derives pleasure" (Constable 1997, 205), South African domestic workers articulated clearly the ways in which, as a private expression of a collective dynamic, they deployed the affective performativity of deference as a way to informally control their work.

Sophia Ncobo told me in an interesting story just how this worked. "I came home one day," she recalled. "She was just screaming. *Baie, baie woes* [very, very angry]. She screamed at me. I said, to myself, 'Sophia, be quiet.' Don't say anything. She screamed at me, I didn't say anything. I just put my head down like this. I just said, sorry *medem. Een [one] week later*, I was *baie moeg* [very tired]. She came. She told me it's alright, I mustn't work if I'm tired. Then, she said. She said to me she was sorry. For that day when she was screaming at me. You see, you must have feelings for them. Or, they will not have any feelings for you."

In much the same way as they used deference, domestic workers' "emotion work" of dependence manipulated intimacy and affect as a way to control their work. Gift giving by employers, for example, has been exposed as a strategy of power and control by employers (Cock 1980; Rollins 1985; Romero 1992). In apartheid South Africa, where gifts for domestic workers were commonplace, Cock argued that "these gifts have important functions . . . [They] help to reinforce social hierarchy by promoting feelings of loyalty, faithfulness, and gratitude. . . . Thus, the gifts given by employers to their domestic workers help to cement their loyalty and reinforce the hierarchical nature of the relationship between them" (1980, 13).

Cock correctly cautioned that "this is not to deny the often sincere generosity of employers; it is simply to focus on the status-enhancing properties of such gifts which operate to secure the loyalty of the domestic worker within an extremely hierarchical-unequal relationship," but went on to note forcefully that "this kind of paternalism is entirely demeaning for the domestic worker" (1980, 13).

Recent literature recognizes these functions of gifts as part of the demeaning maternalism of employers, but points to the benefits reaped by employees as a result. Parreñas, for instance, argues that gifts "suggest that the intimacy of the family engenders the employers placing a great level of trust in employees, which consequently can result in tangible improvements and greater material benefits in employees' lives" (2001, 188). And Ozyegin (2001) redefines this process not as benevolent maternalism but as patronage because, as she argues, in patron-client relationships, the subordinate party benefits from the relationship.

In post-apartheid South Africa, while gifts—especially of old clothes—seem less common than under apartheid, many domestic workers recognized the function of these gifts for propping up the power of their employers. The domestic worker turned novelist, Sindiwe Magona, used the fictionalized voice of "Sophie" to suggest some workers' conscious recognition of the asymmetrical power implied by gift giving: "The dribs and drabs the white woman sees as charity are nothing but a salve to her conscience, an insult to the maid's dignity, and an assault to her self-esteem. The maid remains in a never-ending position of indebtedness" (1994, 13).

But most of the domestic workers in this study also simultaneously accepted rather than challenged the practice. Many of the workers who accepted gifts of old clothes sold them as second-hand clothing in the informal trading centers of the city or, for internal migrants, in the rural areas when they returned there. But, they did not benefit in simple material terms from these gifts. Rather, the acceptance of gifts represented a politics of dependence within the employer-employee relationship.

Allowing gift giving, and tacitly supporting the dependence it presumed, allowed workers to manipulate the tropes of intimacy, especially trust, as part of a strategy to control their own labor. As Florence Dhlomo explained: "More than twelve years, every year, I take it back to Newcastle with me, the bundle [of clothes]. I sell and make money. She [the employer] is thinking she is giving me her *vrot* [rotten] things because I am her slave. But, I am making a business. One day with that money my child will be important because I am using the money for the school fees to educate them, and then I won't be a slave any more."

With self-conscious insight, Florence suggested the importance of her "emotion work" of dependence in ensuring that she could eventually exit the occupation altogether, the ultimate defiance. Workers also reinforced discursively their dependence on employers in order to alter the conditions of their employment and the structure of their work. Kedibone Maake argued, in an incredible narrative, "we need each other. I tell her also how much I need her and the job. She feels responsible for me also very much. She won't just tell me to go, I know I trust her that way. We have a good relationship that way. I also won't just leave one day. She is also knowing she can trust me. I make her feel like that to trust me so she knows I need the job, and she needs me, and we will not let each other down." ·

Kedibone details her careful manipulation of the affective relations of trust between herself and her employer. Workers engaged in this strategic emotion work of dependence as part of the manipulation of the tenuous relations of intimacy in the domestic workplace, turning a potent practice of employers' power on to itself.

In South Africa, among the most important discursive devices used by employers to enforce this dependence of domestic workers is the construction of employment as a form of charity. For privileged householders, employing a domestic worker is often understood as a charitable opportunity to support another family. Employers propagate the idea that employing a domestic worker is not a necessity, but a choice they make to help out the less fortunate, struggling under the oppression of unemployment. So, for example, a university academic pointed out in a local magazine a logic that has only intensified post-apartheid: "When I was living in a *platteland dorp* [country town] I didn't buy a washing machine because that way I could feed three more people" (*Fair Lady*, October 14, 1987).

By making the job itself the most prized gift, benevolently bestowed by the employer, the job becomes another form of charity, the worker becomes the dependent object, and the relationship as one of waged work is obscured. The dependence required by this ideological device is a strategy of control by employers, and domestic workers responded, not by overturning it, but by recovering and utilizing the passivity of dependence as a Trojan horse in their class combat. Esther Dhlamini explained:

> We are so exploitable because there are no jobs. When you find a job, you have to do anything and everything because you can't afford not to have it. Even if it's just hundred rand [$16.60] a month. It's better than nothing. But, I must also say that the employers they also know this. And it's a good thing to keep them thinking that without their job you will be really finished. You even cry to remind her. You tell her about how you are struggling and your children are suffering. How can she tell you to go if she feels for you?

In this interesting narrative, Esther summarized the reinforcement of dependence as a tactic of control through the explicit use of emotion and the manipulation of affect and feeling. In similar ways, domestics came to informally and socially regulate their work.

Social versus State Regulation: Talking Silently and Other Tales

As part of their "emotion work," South African domestic workers carefully managed the forms of communication in their relationship with their employers and, in doing so, socially regulated their work in the absence of state regulation. Workers rehearsed compelling strategies of negotiating their working conditions and responsibilities through informal games of power. Esther Dhlamini, for example, in describing her relations with her employer under apartheid indicated how she negotiated her work tasks:

> When I first started working for that woman, she went to work and I was busy cleaning. When I got to the bathroom, I see that she left the panties in the bath, because she was thinking that it was my job to wash her panties. That was how little they thought of us, to just leave the panties in the bath like that, not even to ask you. So, I decided I am not going to tell her I don't do this kind of dirty job. That day, I just lifted the panties, just on the tip like this, and I put it around the tap. Then I cleaned the bath. When she came home, she saw what I did with the panties. The next day, she leaves them in the bath again. So, I do the same thing also. I just put them on the, what you say, on the bath, and I clean the bath. Then next day she does the same

thing, and I also do the same thing. She can see I'm not going to clean them, so she doesn't leave them any more in the bath then after that.

Despite the elaboration of an extensive state machinery for managing labor relations, domestic workers post-apartheid continued to relate similarly intriguing stories of informally managing relationships with their employers as a way to "negotiate" the conditions of their employment. Selena Simelane, who, interestingly, also "negotiated" with her employer that she did not do underwear by hanging it over the faucet in the bath, also related the following story:

> Let me tell you this one about the dog. She told me I must feed the dog, that is my job, and I must take them for a walk by the park. . . . I said okay. Then, one Sunday, she put the old newspapers on the kitchen counter. I didn't really know at that time she was talking to me silently, that I must clean the dog's mess. So, I talked silently back to her also. I just left the newspaper there. . . . Then, next week, she takes the Sunday paper again, she leaves it by the dog's food. Again, she is trying to tell me something. This time, I take it, I put the newspaper in the bin. Then next Sunday, there is lots of dog's mess now in the garden. I see her husband he is now cleaning the mess. From that day, it was his job to clean the mess, not my job.

In the absence of a formal, contractual, state-regulated relationship, these workers managed the limits of their work informally, by "silently talking back." Workers expressed that they felt "uncomfortable" (Kedibone Maake) explicitly defining the limits of their work through open communication with their employers and "preferred" to manage the limits of their work in these implicit ways because direct communication "across the of boundaries of race and class" (Dill 1994) were fraught with complications. "White people don't understand us when we talk," said Joyce Nhlapo. "They grow up and they learn not to listen to a *kaffir*. So, you can't. There's no way you can sit down and have a good discussion with her."

But, some workers also offered compelling insights into their motivations that went beyond this: "My employer and I, we have a good relationship. I can come to her and have an open, and honest discussion about my work, and anything else as well. But, it's because we have such a good relationship, it's sometimes very hard to be honest with her," explained Mavis Khubelo. "Like telling her, especially, when you think she is really using you and the friendship you have to make you stay later some days, or . . . things like that." Then Mavis Khubelo said something really interesting: "It's like with your sister or a good friend. Because you are so close, you sometimes can't say what you are really thinking because it's uncomfortable. Like with your sister, when you think there's something wrong, you don't just say it, because there are feelings there."

Because of the intimate dependencies of paid domestic work, domestic workers in the context of the historical failure of state protection and even post-apartheid, informally negotiated their conditions of work, through silence and other games of communication. In this, they attempted to regulate the sector themselves. Similarly, under apartheid, where the capacity of workers to negotiate fair terms of employment were severely constrained, and even post-apartheid, where the employment relationship is still typically negotiated over the backyard fence, workers activated social networks to regulate the sector. Hondagneu-Sotelo (2001) very effectively summarized this social regulation, in the absence of state regulation, which animated the standardization of wages and working conditions in the Los Angeles domestic labor market. Both employers and employees, she argues, relied on network linkages that, in the absence of state regulation, established the conditions of employment and going rate of pay, so to speak, of domestic labor services.

In much the same way, the initial job search and subsequent negotiation of pay and working hours were the primary mechanisms in South Africa that stimulated these networks. But, it issued from the intimate dependencies between "maids" and "madams." Hazel Sondlo explained how domestic workers' networks creatively used employers' dependence on "reliable help" to ensure better terms of employment:

> Her [employer's] sister was looking for help. So, she asked me, and then I said, yes, I know one. Someone who is very reliable. But, I told her [employer] if her sister is not treating her well, giving her what I'm getting also, and working not long hours, then we are both going to pack up our things. Ay, ay, ay. You should have seen the fireworks! I'm telling you. She says no, her sister must be treating my friend very well, because she can't afford for me to leave her. That is how they are so dependent on us, see. Sometimes you can get what you ask for, because it's more expensive for them if you go than if they pay you right.

Workers informally regulated conditions of employment by protecting potential work seekers in their search for an employer, often either securing a "good" employer for family and friends or warning potential workers about a "bad madam" (Florence Dhlomo). In all cases, workers manipulated their employers' dependence on, and trust in, them as a way to secure their position as a labor broker and ensure informal regulation of the sector.

Doris Radebe, for example, a worker in Berea, explained how this process worked in describing her own efforts to find her cousin a job in Johannesburg: "There was this woman next door from where I was working. She was seeing I am a good worker. But I see, no, she is not treating the *ousies* she got very nicely, so I said to my cousin, no wait, you see, we'll find you a better one." Doris' employer's friend eventually asked Doris if she knew of a good worker, and Doris recounted: "I say, yes, a very very good lady. But, then, I told her, she is coming from lots of experience and she is making three fifty, so she must pay more, and she has got her family, so she must go home."

It was because Doris's employer trusted her and depended on her that she was able to position herself as a broker and to protect a fellow domestic worker. The networked relations among domestic workers and their manipulations of intimate relations of trust and dependence therefore became the basis of an informal regulation of pay and working conditions in the sector. Together, these various strategies represented an *intimate work culture*.

An Intimate Work Culture

In these implicit manipulations of the ambiguities of intimacy by domestic workers, they seem to confirm Jacklyn Cock's assertion that they "display few overt signs of dissatisfaction and their voice of complaint is rarely heard" (Cock 1980b, 9). Cock went on to suggest that "this passivity and acquiescence in the social order must be understood to result from the vulnerability and powerlessness of black women in South Africa" (10). In contrast to Cock's understanding of domestic workers as passive victims of domination, Judith Rollins suggests that while domestic workers do not overtly, or publicly, manifest a consciousness of their class exploitation and subordination, they are not passive. She argues that they engage in "ressentiment," which as "a long-term seething, deep-rooted negative feeling . . . attests to domestics' lack of belief in their own inferiority, their sense of injustice about their treatment and position, and the rejection of the legitimacy of their subordination" (1985, 227–31). This private recognition and rejection of their subordination suggests for Rollins the ways in which domestic workers are not merely accepting of their subordination. But, for her, ressentiment at best "protect[s] them from the psychological damage risked by accepting employers' belief system, but [has] not been effective in changing the behaviors themselves" (1985, 231–32).

In contrast to Rollins, Bonnie Thornton Dill (1988) refuses to recognize these strategies as merely psychological, but seeks to understand them as strategies of resistance that attempt to alter relations of class power. She documents the ways in which individual workers seek to inventively manage the employer-employee relationship using similar forms of "emotion work" evident among South African domestic workers—including "confrontation, chicanery, or cajolery"—in order "to define what they would and would not give to their employers in the way of time, commitment, and personal involvement" (1988, 38). Cock (1980) did argue similarly that the subservient deference of domestic workers in South Africa was actually a "mask." But, the extent to which these active strategies paradoxically reproduce and reinforce, rather than overturn, the structural logics of paid domestic work has generated skepticism about their characterization as resistance.

As Constable, quoting Abu-Lughod, argues, to romanticize resistance in these instances is to dismiss workers' behavior as nothing more than "impression management," depicting them as mere "cynical manipulators" (Abu-Lughod 1990, quoted in Constable 1997, 13). Indeed, much of the exposure of domestic workers' "agency" has been the delineation of the social-psychological coping mechanisms developed and deployed by domestic workers to shield them from the demeaning and degrading aspects of their work. Mary Romero (1992) and Leslie Salzinger (1991), in demonstrating the ways in which Chicana and Latina domestic workers in the United States have struggled to actively improve the structure and conditions of their work as the expression of a class struggle, refocused the definition of resistance on the more overt strategies employed by these workers to restructure their employment relationship.

More recent literature has sought to redefine the private expressions among domestic workers of their positioning as instances of a more complex, and not easily delineated, interplay of domination and resistance within the domestic workplace. Drawing on instances of domestic workers' manipulations, negotiations, and redefinition of their relationships with their employers, this emerging literature has redefined the domination versus resistance problematic in order to account for the ways in which domestic workers' private resistances seemingly reproduce their domination.

Constable uses a Foucauldian approach to make a distinction between "public protests . . . explicitly aimed at creating social change and improving work conditions" and "other, more discursive methods" such as language, jokes, and humor used by workers as part of a disciplining apparatus that does not presume a neat distinction between domination and resistance (1997, 13). Parreñas similarly suggests that while migrant Filipina domestic workers in Rome and Los Angeles "have not invested in large-scale efforts of mobilization," they do "take a turn" against their dislocations by means of "immediate struggles" (2001a, 188). But, while Constable argues that these "subtler forms of power" are best understood "as forms of cultural critique or commentary or as personal means of coping with stressful and difficult situations" (1997, 11–13), Parreñas argues that "immediate struggles cannot be equated with coping strategies" (2001a, 188). She believes instead that workers "incorporate immediate struggles in their everyday work routine in an attempt to subvert the authority of employers, improve work conditions, and gain control of their labor" (2001a, 188).

Ozyegin (2001), similarly, makes a compelling case for relocating these strategies as instances of class struggle within patriarchy. Equally skeptical of the domination versus resistance problematic, Ozyegin suggests that the privatized strategies employed by domestic workers, in relation to their employers, is the mutual construction of "a language to discuss and negotiate the labor process and reconcile the diverse experiences of their lives" (151). This, "in their simultaneous efforts to both reinforce and alleviate the consequences of class inequalities and differences in class cultures" (151).

Drawing on these insights, it is clear that in South Africa, the "craftiness," "confrontation" (Coley 1981, 253–69), and strategic uses of intimacy and affect are not simply forms of "unaggressive aggressiveness" (Constable 1997, 9). Nor are they simply a resistance against domination. Indeed, I argue, they represent a specific practice of power—in these instances best designated as a *work culture*. Benson argues that a "work culture" is "the ideology and practice with which workers stake out a relatively autonomous sphere of action on the job" (1983, 185–86). In this work culture, a "realm of informal, customary values and rules mediates the formal authority structure of the workplace and distances workers from its impact" (Benson 1983, 185–86).

While work cultures can merely describe forms of coping or the poetics of workers' management of oppression and misery, Michael Burawoy (1979) recognized the "politics of production" implied by worker's organized cultures against authority. South African domestic workers' strategic manipulations of the ambiguities of intimacy—of kinship, familiarity, closeness, trust, dependence, and emotion—certainly "confront[ed] the limitations and exploit[ed] the possibilities of their jobs" (Benson 1983,

185–86). Work cultures are, however, collective in their origination and transmission. They develop and circulate among the collectivity of the shop-floor. Can domestic workers, relatively isolated in individual workplaces, have a work culture?

Dill originally suggested that her study demonstrated "the ways in which individual acts of resistance, even within the work setting of a private family, can have collective consequences for the overall organization of domestic labor as an occupation" (1988, 33). This is a critically important insight also elaborated by Parreñas, who argues that "the individual acts of immediate struggles" that she documents not only have collective consequences but "are in fact collective acts" because they issue from collective sources: "They do not reside at the level of the individual but are rooted in the collective consciousness of a shared struggle among domestic workers" (2001, 194).

This intimate work culture, collective and active, of South African domestic workers, was challenged by the efforts at depersonalization by the state.

Depersonalization by the State: From Employer Maternalism to State Paternalism

In South Africa, domestic workers—despite the cultivation of a work culture using the ambiguities of intimacy in the relationship—interestingly told me that they preferred more contractual, formal, and depersonalized relations. Astutely aware of the unique precariousness produced by the ambiguities of intimacy in the relationship, most workers expressed a desire for the resolution of those ambiguities through depersonalization. Mavis Khubelo captured this perceptively when she explained that she "would much prefer that we could treat each other like equals, like a normal kind of employment relationship," by which she meant "where we don't have to be uncomfortable with each other because we are so close, but also so far."

Unlike the Latina immigrant workers in Hondagneu-Sotelo's study, South African domestic workers did not necessarily "want more intimacy" as a psychosocial need (2001, 193). In the absence of state regulation, they recovered intimacy as a work culture and informally regulated the sector. Hondagneu-Sotelo (2001) argues that workers' use of social regulation offers them *greater* opportunities for upgrading domestic work than a certain kind of state regulation. "The absence of a neocolonialist, state-operated contractual system of domestic work thus represents an opportunity to see better job conditions" (22), she argues, adding that a formal legislative and regulatory apparatus needs to support, rather than supersede, workers' already existing informal efforts to regulate the occupation themselves.

Instead of the post-apartheid state acknowledging, recognizing, and supporting these existing capacities, however, the democratic statecraft began from the premise that domestic workers lacked the same. Through the encoding of domestic workers as "vulnerable" subjects (chapter 3), depersonalization by the state disregarded workers' historical use of intimacy in the workplace. South African domestic workers recognized that the intimate nature and setting of their work made the complete erasure of intimacy impossible, but they sought to control it. It was this control over the management of intimacy that marked their acceptance or rejection of depersonalization. The democratic state imposed the erasure of intimacy as a solution to the "dilemma" of domestic work. But, workers' historical work culture issuing from the manipulation of intimacy was a practice of power. The state's efforts therefore represented a direct challenge to workers.

Instead of a formal state regulatory apparatus that remained sensitive to the existing efforts by workers to regulate the occupation themselves, the rights-based statecraft in the sector negated workers' existing capacities and was therefore, quite predictably, met by workers with skepticism. In continuing to deploy their historical uses of intimacy, and eschewing some of the contractual formalization of the sector, workers were not rejecting depersonalization, but depersonalization by the state. As Mavis Khubelo said quite insightfully:

> I don't have any problems with signing a contract, like other nannies, because I know it is to protect me from exploitation, from long hours, and from not getting leave. So, I have signed the contract with my employer. But, there is a lot less flexibility this way than before. I mean, what I am saying, trying, I mean, this is now the government involved, and that is a good thing. I'm not saying it's a bad thing. But, I don't know the government is always going to protect me. The government has not been here these many years when I was making negotiations with my employer, and developing a relationship so we can understand what we each want. When I can negotiate with my employer, I know her. This is it, of now bringing in the devil you don't know inside also, you understand?

Understood as imposed from elsewhere, rather than originated by workers themselves, depersonalization by the state using the abstract technologies of rights and regulation was met by workers with a reticence regarding its capacity to protect them. The state initiative was seen as an imposed intrusion into a relationship that workers had been historically managing and controlling through inventive means under their own control.

In the insensitivity to these dynamics of the paid domestic work relationship, and workers' creativity in shaping it to mitigate their exploitations, depersonalization by the state threatened one of workers' most potent practices. While workers preferred depersonalization, depersonalization *by the state* made workers subject to the state's rationalizing vision, denying their capacities, presenting them instead as "vulnerable" and to be protected from elsewhere. "They think they are Gods, really, they command, and we must all obey," remarked Joyce Nhlapo bitingly of the role of the state in this process, implying an understanding of the modes of power presumed by the state's intent to protect them.

As both Joyce and Mavis suggest, by invoking the "vulnerability" of workers, the democratic statecraft represented a practice of state power, transferring control over the employment relationship to itself, inducing a mode of control over workers that they recognized and denied. In some ways, in disregarding domestic workers' intimate work culture, and therefore of workers' hesitations regarding a contractual and formalized employment relationship imposed and managed from outside of that relationship, the state replaced employers' maternalism with their own paternalism—one that recoded workers as dependent on state protection, subject to state control and oversight, rather than employers.

The democratic statecraft therefore unwittingly failed to appreciate the extent to which workers were not passive victims, but creative and assertive. Issuing from informal regulation and the manipulation of intimacy, workers were reluctant and hesitant to turn over control of the relationship with their employers to what was seen as simply the aggrandizement of state power. Judi Manamela, a full-time live-out worker in Robertsham, expressed workers' understandings that these initiatives belonged to the state, and not to workers, and that formalization shifted the balance of power in favor of the former. "The workers, some of them, yes, they are not signing. They don't want to be registered. I know about those," she said, and then explained: "I am seeing they don't want this thing with the government, to sign their forms and contracts, because you are just giving them power to exploit you. Us domestic workers, we are very exploited in these jobs, you must understand. That's why they are not wanting more exploitation with that contract thing of the government."

State officials invariably understood the workers Judi was referring to as ignorant and workers' "failure" to enforce their new rights as both the source of the limited efficacy of the new legislation and a confirmation of the "vulnerable" status of workers that justified such statecraft to begin with. Workers, however, were signaling the extent to which formalization by the state required them to abdicate historically honed practices of power that allowed them some measure of control over their own work. Rather than state practices that acted on behalf of workers, presumed too incapacitated to act for themselves, domestic workers emphasized the necessity of regulation for protection that recognized their already existing capacities. Instead, the state was understood as paternalistically shifting the tenuous balance of power in paid domestic work to itself, rendering workers subjects of state power. The coincidence of these two practices of power—state paternalism and workers' intimate work culture—confounds a simple politics for the sector.

The ambiguities of intimacy in paid domestic work challenge assertions that paid domestic work is a form of work like any other. The intimate nature and setting of the work, the contradictions of intimacy and distance, the discomforts of affect, and the capacity of both workers and employers to feel ambivalence over their levels of feeling and unfeeling toward each other place limits to its formalization as a form of work like any other. Assertions that it can be are usually prescriptive, rather than descriptive, statements. Scholarly analysis and political advocacy suggest that domestic workers *should* be workers like any other, not necessarily that they presently are. They recognize that the intimate relations at the core of paid domestic work structure its exploitative features, and therefore propose that resolving the "dilemma" of paid domestic work requires purging the employment relationship of these affective dimensions. In doing so, it becomes nothing more, and nothing less, than an employment relationship like any other (Rollins 1985; Romero 1988).

But, in South Africa, workers had historically developed and deployed an intimate work culture that not only allowed them to informally regulate the conditions of their work by manipulating the ambiguities of intimacy in the relationship but also represented a specific practice of power. Workers understood depersonalization by the state through their construction as "vulnerable" as an extension of state power at the expense of their own. Their failure to claim depersonalization by the state was a rejection of the statecraft that presumed them subjects of the state's authority, control, and power, rather than practitioners of power themselves.

The collision, then, of state power and the intimacy of the work challenged the possibilities of modernizing paid domestic work so that it is nothing more, or less, than an employment relationship like any other. Any simple politics that begins and ends with the recognition that domestic work is a form of work and should be regulated as such, needs to be made more complex by considering the politics of paid domestic work as an intimate form of labor. Such a politics also needs to confront the multivalent coincidences of race and rule implied by workers' manipulations of intimacy.

On Race and the Intimate in the Postcolony

South African domestic workers' response to the state effort to recognize them as workers suggests the dangers of a politics of inclusion that does not recognize their historically developed uses of intimacy.[2] But, it also betrays the racialized making of the political orders of colony and "postcolony." Ann Stoler (2002) stunningly dissects the intimacies of domestic service in the Dutch East Indies to expose the making of empire, and the constitutive relationships between race and the intimate in colonial rule. Attempting to understand how and why "domains of the intimate figured so prominently in the perceptions and policies of those who ruled," Stoler meticulously unearths "the affective grid of colonial politics" (7).

In a similar way, the tensions of intimacy that framed South African domestic workers' recalcitrant entry into a post-apartheid political status render legible the making of the South African "postcolony" from the domain of the intimate. In the crafting of the public domain of democratic transition out of the private spaces of familial domesticity, the microphysics of postcolonial rule are explicable. The practices of power enacted by the state in its multiple sites of interpolation of workers, the modus and logics of subjection in its democratic statecraft, and the obstinate refusals of domestic workers to inhabit such subjectification illuminate the textured relations of rule in the postcolony.

Mbembe's now-classic *On the Postcolony* (2001) detailed the poetics of power in the postcolony. But, the crucial constitutive forms of power in the domestic domain do not figure prominently in such analyses of the postcolonial. As Stoler reflects on "why microsites of familial and intimate space figure so prominently in the macropolitics of imperial rule" (19), we may similarly speculate on the valence of restructured post-apartheid domestic service for the macropolitics of postcolonial rule. How has the familial become a site of postcolonial governance in this instance (i.e., domestic service), and why? How do the state's efforts to reconstitute erstwhile colonial relations of servitude facilitate the making of this specific form of the postcolonial? How do workers' own practices contest those projects?

Furthermore, the intricate contestation over the restructuring of intimacy in domestic workers' democratic debut is all the more significant in a post-colony whose making is defined by, and premised on, a dramatic reordering of race. For what inheres in domestic service, as Ann Stoler suggests, is a particularly powerful equation of race and intimacy. Imperial power was founded on the crafting of a simultaneity between race as difference and the anxiety of intimacy. Few other institutions disrupt and concretize the tensions of racialized intimacy as much as domestic service. In its physical and affective intimacies, race is both produced and complicated. Stoler focuses on domestic service precisely because of the paradox of race and intimacy in the colonial project of servitude. That paradox achieved its most brutal and incongruous expression in apartheid South Africa. The racial requisite of whiteness was a fanatical separation of races as much as it was a servicing by black bodies within the sites of intimate domesticity. The ambiguities of intimacy in paid domestic work are therefore crucially connected to the manufacture, contestations, and anxieties of race.

In this context, black South African domestic workers' cultivation of intimacy with their white employers under apartheid, and continued practices of the same post-apartheid, is significant beyond the mere management of their work. Few other institutions forced such sustained and affectively loaded interracial encounters between blacks and whites under apartheid as did paid domestic work. Recovering intimacy with white employers under apartheid's manic forms of racist separation represented a potent refiguration of the raced relations of colonial rule by black women, inside white homes. What renderings of racial power inhered in black women workers' attempts to cultivate intimacy with white employers? How were those practices of power a negotiation of the political relations of apartheid rule as much as the logics of servitude? And, what do workers' efforts to retain intimacy with their employers post-apartheid suggest about their negotiation of postcolonial configurations of race and rule? These are the questions future scholarship should engage if we are to truly understand how the relations of rule in the public political orders of our times articulate with the racialized intimacies of the domestic domain.

5

Paid to Care

The Dual-Care Regime

Paid domestic work engenders a cruel irony. While domestic workers are paid to care for the children of others, in doing so, they are constrained in their ability to care for their own. Mabel Mabena, a thirty-nine-year-old live-in domestic worker in Killarney, a middle-class suburb of Johannesburg, does all the cooking and cleaning in her employers' home and takes care of their two children. She started working for the family in 1992, when she was twenty-six years old, having left rural Phokeng in the North West province after her second child was born. "I needed to find work because life was getting very difficult," explained Mabel. Her mother, Kedibone, had undergone surgery for an ovarian cyst and had to discontinue working and return home from Potchefstroom, where she worked as a domestic. "So, when she came home, it was not easy and then we needed extra money for the children, because my second one [child] had just come."

Mabel found a job as a live-in domestic worker through her cousin, who was working just a suburb away. She found herself doing general housework, cooking, and taking care of her family's one-year-old son. Five years later, her employers had a daughter, and Mabel argues that she has been the mother to both children: "I raised those children. I'm looking at them, seeing that I was their mother, giving them all the love from when they were just babies."

At the same time as Mabel has been "the mother" to her employers' children, however, her three children (her third child was born just a few years later) are raised by her mother in a government-subsidized housing scheme in Rustenburg, nearly two hundred kilometers away. Mabel sees her children twice each year: for a week at Easter and two weeks at

Christmas. Mabel complained bitterly about the separation from her children, but also understood her breadwinning as a form of care and an expression of love. "Every time I see them again," she said, "they look so different, so much bigger. It's so hard, your own children, but you are so far away from them . . . but, I send my love every month [remittance], and those monies are taking care of them, just like how my mother took care of us."

Mabel understood the pain of separation between mother and child better than anyone. When she was young, her mother worked as a live-in domestic, doing the household and child care work for three children. As she did so, Mabel and her sisters were raised by her aunt. Mabel eloquently explained the life cycle of care for the women in her family that this implied: "My mother, my sisters, we all have been working together to raise many children. Our families, and the white people's children."

Arlie Hochschild theorizes *global care chains* as the transnational distribution of caring resources through "a series of personal links between people across the globe based on the paid or unpaid work of caring" (2000, 131). These global care chains comprise women supplying caring labor for pay while relying on the, both paid and unpaid, caring labor of others. For Hochschild, this typically entails "an older daughter from a poor family who cares for her siblings while her mother works as a nanny caring for the children of a migrating nanny who, in turn, cares for the child of a family in a rich country" (2000, 131). Hochschild acknowledges that while global care chains typically start in poor countries and end in rich ones, they can also start and end within a national territory. The story of Mabel Mabena is archetypal of these *national care chains*—one in which caring resources are extracted, through patterns of uneven economic and social development, from rural to urban, from black to white, and from the poor to the not-so-poor,[1] within national boundaries.

But, the national care chain in South Africa also structures generational continuities. Evelyn Nakano Glenn (1986) documented the "careers in domestic service" of three generations of Japanese American women, while in Bonnie Thornton Dill's (1988) study, almost half of the African American women in domestic service whom she interviewed had mothers who had done some domestic work during their lifetimes. In South Africa, these generational continuities in paid domestic work are within the same families, with just over half of the workers who shared their life histories confirming that their mothers, too, had worked as domestics. They circulate along a temporal as much as spatial care chain, providing paid care for other families during their working lives and, as they age, providing unpaid labor taking care of their grandchildren as their daughters work as domestics.

Hazel Sondlo, for example, provides child care for her employer's young daughter, while relying on the unpaid care work of her mother, who herself had worked as a domestic worker for sixteen years, in Queenstown. Hazel, always upbeat, reflected on this: "One day, maybe our daughters will not be domestic workers their whole lives. I will celebrate when that day comes. We'll slaughter a cow, big one from the farm . . . No more *amakitchini* [another word for domestic workers, literally translated as "those of the kitchens"]. No more you must be cleaning and cooking and putting that baby on your back, your whole life. . . . Even when you are this old woman, you must be working for your child, when your funeral is calling you."

The state's efforts to turn erstwhile "servants" into workers did not disrupt this logic of care provision. In fact, it situated domestic workers' labor at the intersection of two critical policies that "privatized" care.[2] Labor policy regulated domestic workers as a *privatized* (i.e., market-based and commodified) care solution for those who could afford it (i.e., working- and middle-class, mainly white and urban, families). At the same time, social welfare policy ensured that domestic workers (mainly black, rural, and poor) continued to rely on another version of "privatized" care, this time familial.

Structured by the post-apartheid equation of state, family, and market in the responsibility and provision of care, white, urban, and middle-class women were able to secure a "private" *market* solution to their caring needs, while mainly black, rural, and poor women relied on "private" *familial* provision for their care work. In this distinctive "political economy of care," the inequalities of race, class, and the urban/rural divide were reinforced by the very efforts of the state to craft political inclusion for domestic workers.

The State and Welfare—The Paradox of "Privatization"

Unlike many industrialized countries, where economic restructuring has eroded state welfare provision (Meyer 2000), the politics of transition in South Africa has seen the mass expansion of the social security system. Political liberalization required widespread deracialization of state policies and programs and a strong commitment to social citizenship. In fulfilling these political imperatives and the developmental goals contained therein, the Social Assistance Act of 1992 was passed, which provided for the deracialization and hence extension of social security, primarily social grants, to all South Africans. At the same time, economic liberalization pursued with vigor through the macroeconomic policy framework of Growth, Employment and Redistribution (GEAR), adopted in 1996, imposed fiscal restraints on the realization of the social citizenship commitments of the post-apartheid state. The emerging architecture of reconstructed social citizenship this entailed has led to the coining of a new category of welfare state regime—the developmental state.

The South African developmental state has expanded state commitments to social citizenship. During the 1980s to 1990, the apartheid state had attempted to "arrest if not scale down the extent of its commitment to social welfare" (Lund 1990, quoted in Hassim 2005, 70), with the Directorate of Social Planning issuing a report recommending the privatization of welfare provision and its devolution from national government (Lund 1998). The post-apartheid state's reversal of the contraction and privatization of social security seems quite dramatic, then, given trends in the opposite direction among industrialized countries. Compared to most other middle-income countries, South Africa now has a substantial system of cash social assistance (Lund 1993; Van der Berg 1997; Kruger 1998). In its provision of pension, disability, and child support grants to millions of poor and vulnerable South Africans, the social grants system remains one of the most extensive programs of the post-apartheid state. Furthermore, the social insurance system, based on citizens' participation in the labor market, was extended to new categories of workers and provides for assistance through unemployment, maternity, and illness benefits, as well as for compensation in the case of occupational injuries or diseases. Indeed, South Africa is now described as "probably the developing world's largest and most generous welfare state" (*Business Day*, May 4, 2005).

So it is all the more dramatic that within the expansion of this developmental welfare state, the "national care chain" in which domestic workers circulate has remained singularly undisturbed. To understand why requires engaging the paradox of state "privatization" of care. Despite the expansion of state commitments to welfare in general, a restrained vision with regard to care as welfare ensured that it was still understood as a primarily familial, primarily female, responsibility.

The White Paper for Social Welfare (WPSW)[3] that organizes the state's social citizenship framework invokes the discourse of care as a principle of citizenship repeatedly, claiming its goal as the construction of a "just and caring society" (Preamble), and strives to create a welfare system "which facilitates the development of human capacity and self-reliance within a caring and enabling socio-economic environment" (chapter 2). But, crucially, the responsibility and provision of care *as an entitlement of social citizenship* is specifically avoided.

Instead of public responsibility for care, the WPSW urges "national collective responsibility," thus recoding "public" responsibility and privatizing it within communities, families, and women. As Shireen Hassim insightfully summarizes, "the emphasis on the cultural value of caring in government policy frameworks—such as the White Paper for Social Welfare—in effect shifts the burden of caring for the young, the sick, and the elderly onto women (and increasingly onto children as well), without financial compensation for their time, and without effective support by the state" (2004, 14).

Instead of state responsibility and provision, "public" responsibility is substituted with "community care." As Lund et al. note, "a double equation is at work which assumes that community care is equal to care by families which is equal to unpaid care by mostly women" (1996, 115). Even where the state has minimally socialized care responsibility, as in efforts to direct public works programs toward home-based care and early childhood development, it is tied to a strategy of job creation rather than a strategy of resolving the gendered citizenship implied by the failure to provide adequate care for children. Therefore, in invoking a reconstituted understanding of the socialization of care, it has actually emphasized "private" family responsibility and provision.

The implications of this privatized care regime is most evident in its implications for domestic workers, who remain at the intersection of competing modalities for "privatized" care provision within families: of their employers, and of their own.

The "Privatized" Market Provision of Care *by* Domestic Workers

There is no reliable data regarding the way South African households source assistance for their reproductive labor through the market, or what has come to be known as "domestic outsourcing" (Bittman et al. 1999, 249). But, based on a cumulative analysis of the disparate data available on cleaning and child care, it is clear that private paid domestic workers remain a critical solution to the care burdens of many South African households.

An analysis of the *Census of Laundry, Cleaning, and Dyeing Services* (1975, 1988)[4] shows that from 1966 to 1988, the number of laundry and cleaning services increased at a regular rate, especially between 1975 and 1988. Between 1988 and 1995, however, there was a decrease from a reported 1,181 establishments nationwide to 864, to levels below what was available as laundry and cleaning services in 1975, and representing an average annual decrease of 4.4 percent in the number of establishments in this sector of "domestic outsourcing" (Statistics South Africa 1995 [www.statssa.gov.za]). Confirming this trend, *South African Labor Statistics* (1991)[5] reports that from 1970 to 1990, there was an overall and steady decline in the number of workers employed in laundry and dry-cleaning services. While that trend has reversed more recently (Bureau for Market Research 2004),[6] the existing and recently expanding establishments in Gauteng are used predominantly by black households and not white (working- and middle-class) families. The Bureau for Market Research in 2004 found that of all the expenditure by households on laundry and dry-cleaning services in Gauteng, 86 percent was by black households.[7] Indeed of all the household expenditure items comparing the relative share of black and white households, laundry services was the biggest difference between racial groups, demonstrating that such services rely overwhelmingly and disproportionately on black households' clientage, and begging the question: Who does this cleaning work for white households if it's not provided by the commercial market?

There is the possibility that white households purchase labor-saving technologies to "in-source" their domestic labor and do it themselves. Rather than relying on commercial laundries for instance, these white households may be using washing machines within their homes. But, there is no necessary relationship between increases in household purchases of labor-saving devices and the continued responsibility for domestic work within the family. Research from the 1970s showed that the percentage of the white population owning washing machines and vacuum cleaners had increased, but that this made little difference to the extent to which households performed their own domestic labor. "The introduction of labour-saving appliances into the household in the United States and Britain, was a direct result of the shortage of servants . . . the invention of labour-saving appliances solved the 'problem' caused by the scarcity of servants, and made housework much easier and quicker. But, in South Africa, though, the introduction of labour-saving devices has occurred along with the use of servants," argues Jennifer Shindler (1980, 29).

In this study, many workers' employers had washing machines, for instance, but refused to allow their workers to use them. "She has two washing machines," said Palesa Lebala. "But, she doesn't let me use it. She thinks black people can't use those machines, that I'll break them." Undergirded by racist understandings of skill and capacity, labor-saving appliances therefore did not substitute for paid domestic work.

Instead of replacing private paid domestic workers with labor-saving devices, it is possible that households rely on contract cleaning services. There is some evidence that in provinces such as KwaZulu-Natal and the Western Cape there is a greater reliance on contract cleaning services (Department of Labor 2002). But, it is recognized that, despite these small shifts toward commercial provision, domestic workers continue to remain the primary solution middle classes employ for paid household work. "Despite the above changes [of contract cleaning and garden services making inroads in certain provinces] in the domestic labour market, there remain a large number of women today who on a daily, weekly or monthly basis perform low-paid and relatively low-skilled domestic tasks in private households in a direct employee-employer relationship with the person or people living in that household" (Department of Labor 2002, 10).

Similarly, with regards to child care, Beth Goldblatt (2005) notes there is no "sociometrics," or comprehensive data, on child care provision in South Africa. Kruger and Motala (1997) note that unpublished research from the 1995 *October Household Survey* suggests only one-fifth (21%) of under six-year-olds have access to a preschool, day nursery, or day care center. The study most relied on for an indication of the extent of child care provision in South Africa reported that only one-third of white children under the age of seven had access to child care—including both center-based (e.g., nursery schools, day nurseries, preschools, and schools) and home-based care by day mothers (Padayachie et al. 1994). Given such low rates of private (commercial) day care provision, Goldblatt argues "a particular South African phenomenon . . . is the large number of Black domestic workers who care for the children of White parents" (2005, 19). Domestic workers clearly remain a very important means of servicing the child care needs of South African white, working-, and middle-class families.

To summarize, we know there has been an overall historical decline in reliance on laundry services (and continued reliance by black rather than white households on the existing services), and most white children remain unserviced by commercial private child care. We also know that there are close to one million households in the country that employ domestic workers, and that the number of women employed in the sector has been increasing since 1995 (Posel and Casale 2005). The *October Household Survey* (Statistics South Africa 1991) furthermore reported that 58 percent of all South African households employed a domestic worker, while the *Survey of Houses, Sectional Title Units and Domestic Workers* (Statistics South Africa 1996) reported a similar 60.4 percent of households employing at least one domestic worker. At that stage both covered only urban areas, but considering the number of poor households covered that would not be in a position to hire a domestic worker, this suggests an extremely high reliance on domestic workers in middle-class households.

At the same time, *Income and Expenditure Surveys* show that domestic workers are an *increasing* proportion of household expenditure (Statistics South Africa 1995, 2000). It is apparent, based on these data, that the paid domestic work sector is one of the most important sources of "domestic outsourcing" for many of the more privileged South African households. In this, domestic workers provide a private (market) solution to these families' domestic responsibilities.

Cleaning and child care remained the most important activities performed by domestic workers for pay in this transferal of the family's care work to the private market of paid domestic work. Indeed, this sample of Johannesburg workers reflected the national picture, where general cleaning, washing, and ironing were the main tasks performed by domestics, followed by child care. Only a relatively small proportion of domestic workers took care of the ill (5%) and elderly (3%) (Department of Labor 2000). Importantly, in Johannesburg, the primary tasks of cleaning and child care were performed simultaneously. Only two workers performed child care exclusively. In both cases, the women were relatively well educated and each had negotiated the terms of their work because they felt very strongly that they were "nannies" and not "maids." Mavis Khubelo, a worker in Killarney argued, "I was very clear when we sat down that day, and I said, I am not a maid. . . . I know all these employers in this building, they say you are a 'childminder,' but you are the maid, because you must cook and do the washing. I explained to her, and I said I am a 'nanny,' and I am taking care of the children, but I am not going to be your 'maid.'"

Some definitions of care work make the same distinction Mavis did between housework and child care, and reserve "care work" for the latter. Indeed Pierette Hondagneu-Sotelo's (2001) book *Doméstica*, subtitled "Cleaning and Caring in the Shadows of Affluence," assumes, perhaps unintentionally, the mutual exclusivity of cleaning work from caring work. A distinction is often made between "caring for" (physical labor) and "caring about" (emotional labor) (Hooyman and Gonyea 1995; Lynch and McLaughlin 1995), in which "caring for" usually includes "catering for the material and other general well-being of the one receiving care," including cooking, cleaning, and washing (Lynch and McLaughlin 1995, 256). Many care theorists restrict the definition of *caring*, however, to activities that meet a need only when those needs "cannot possibly be met by the person in need herself" (Bubeck 1995, 129; see also Schwarzenberg 1987; Tronto 1998).

This distinction between necessary and unnecessary care is unhelpful given the importance of the semantic and conceptual breakthrough of the concept of "care" from the Marxist concept of "reproductive labor." The terminology of "reproduction" not only rendered women's work within the home secondary to production, but it did not reflect the nonmaterial aspects of the unpaid domestic labor performed by women. The strength of the conceptual shift to *care work* lies precisely in its location of women's domestic labor within the full spectrum of women's caring work performed both within and outside the home (hence analyses of the institutional locations of care work), and in its noninstrumentalism regarding the functions of such work. But, the distinction between necessary and unnecessary care privileges the intimate work implied by "care work," ignoring the original content of the Marxist insight that women's work within the home is, by necessity, that which is involved in "social reproduction." In recognizing this, Berenice Fisher and Joan Tronto offer a working definition of care work, which, while problematic in some ways, is broad and encompasses the affective and material concerns of the "care" and Marxist perspectives, respectively: "On the most general level, we suggest that caring be viewed as a species activity that includes everything that we do to maintain, continue, and repair our 'world' so that we can live in it as well as possible. That world includes our bodies, our selves, and our environment, all of which we seek to interweave in a complex, life-sustaining web" (1990, 40).

Whatever definition is used, it is clear that domestic workers are, in all their assigned tasks, involved in care work, though cleaning and child care are necessarily very different activities. In South Africa, the primary tasks of housework and child care are the main activities of domestic workers, provided in their employers' homes, for pay. For mainly white, working- and middle-class urban families, these functions were therefore provided by the "private" market, but within their homes. In the conceptual framework deployed here, the distinction between this "private" market solution and that of, for instance, a private day care center, or of purchasing meals, or using a contract cleaning service, is that in the case of paid domestic work, the *responsibility* for provision is in the market, but the *provision* itself takes place within the home.

Domestic workers recognized that the two main principles that structured this "private" market solution to care were *affordability* and *accessibility*. Sophia Ncobo, a sixty-year-old lifelong live-in domestic worker chuckled as she related this fictionalized story:

> Linda was a very sad woman. You see, her family was disappearing. She woke up and her husband was gone, and she couldn't find him. She thought the *tokoloshe* [mythical impish creature] came and took him away. Then, the next day, her son was gone. So then, she went to the garden and looked under the stone. He wasn't there. So Linda went to the doctor. She was crying. And, the doctor was looking at her saying "You need: a domestic worker" [*big laugh*]. Really, he said you must go to the street, and buy the domestic worker. Linda was still sad. She was having no money. The money was gone with her husband. The doctor said, no, they are very cheap. And there's lots of them you can choose from. You can get a fat one, a small one, one with two hands, one with five hands. It is very easy. . . . . Her whole family was happy again. That's the end of my story [*laughs*].

I had asked Sophia to make me a tale of a domestic worker, and she provided one of the most entertaining moments in the field for me. On the street corner that Sunday afternoon, and in her loaded storytelling, Sophia captured the "privatized" market solution offered by domestic workers to their employers and conveyed the consciousness of this process among domestics themselves. The accessibility and affordability of their care work was a theme related by many domestics and were at the heart of the commodified solution to care they offered their employers.

Beauty Mkhize, a twenty-three-year-old full-time live-out domestic worker in Linmeyer, answered the question "Why did you become a domestic worker?" as follows: "We are very many girls here looking for jobs. They [employers] have money to pay for us to do the washing, the ironing. My sister was saying Christmas time, you must come to *eGoli* [Johannesburg], the people there have got work for us to do their washing." And Doris Radebe, a worker in Berea, echoed this. "Oh, I was so worried when I first came here," she said. "Worries, worries, day and night. Because there was every day so many of them [women looking for work] walking up and down, here in Yeoville. And they wanted little money. Especially the Zimbabweans. There was this flood, and I was thinking 'ah, Doris, you are not going to get a good employer, there are too many of them [work-seekers].' "

For many, there was the expression of the eventuality of the life cycle of commodified care work by virtue of their structural positioning as uneducated black women. Margaret Manamela, for example, argues that "when you are wearing this black skin, God is your only father. I got Standard 2 [finished up to fourth grade], and there is no other work for me. . . . My mother died in the white man's house, she died with cleaning until her legs broke. I am going to die with these broken legs." Monica Seepe, too, recognized the racialization of her accessibility and affordability as a privatized market solution to her employer's care needs: "I feel them sorry [white people]. They have no troubles like us. Worries, you see. They do not have this disease [HIV/AIDS]. Killing their children. We have these troubles. . . . These white people have money. They just buy things. They just get the domestic worker to come. They have a trouble in the morning, they just call you over the fence. The troubles are going away with that black woman there taking care of everything. Even you go shopping for them. Even you clean her panties. What worries is there for you, [if] there is someone in the bathroom there cleaning your bras and panties."

In continuously referencing the "buying" of their care work and recognizing that such commodification was structured by the affordability and accessibility of poorly educated black women, domestic workers recognized the extent to which they provided a privatized market solution for the care work of their employing families.

While the raced and classed channeling of these women into paid domestic work was structured by continuing apartheid inequalities, the democratic statecraft of inclusion was designed to ensure their affordability and accessibility as a "private" market solution to mainly white, urban, working- and middle-class families.

Domestic Workers' Rights and the Privatization of Care: Structuring Accessibility and Affordability

The State carries the responsibility of protecting vulnerable workers to ensure that they have the same basic rights and are afforded their dignity. The Basic Conditions of Employment Act is the principal instrument through which such protection is extended.

Fifteen-Point Program of Action of the Ministry of Labor
1999—2004

In the democratic statecraft, domestic workers were singled out as one of the categories of "vulnerable workers" deserving particular attention with respect to the equality of rights, and the affording of dignity, as is required by the Constitution. But, in the content of the investigation into, and eventual promulgation of Sectoral Determination Seven, specifically laying out the special protections for the paid domestic work sector, the overriding emphasis was on the maintenance of jobs in the context of high unemployment.

In setting a minimum wage, in considering the administrative obligations of the regulation of the sector, and in considering working conditions, legislative inclusion for domestic workers was negotiated with an overwhelming emphasis on the retention of jobs given the deepening crisis of unemployment in the country. But, in framing inclusion for domestic workers in this way, the Sectoral Determination ensured that the state produced a particular equation between family, state, and market in the political economy of care.

I quote, at length, an excerpt from the official report of the *Investigation into Minimum Wages and Conditions of Employment of Domestic Workers* that neatly summarizes the state's position with regard to the sector:

> In many other sectors, employers can respond to wage cuts by decreasing the number of workers employed and trying to increase the productivity of the remaining workers to achieve the same output. Because domestic workers are usually employed singly, this is not an option for employers of domestic workers. The choice is rather between employing a domestic worker to do the work, household members doing the work themselves, or contracting with other commercial service providers such as crèches, laundries, caterers, fast food outlets and contract cleaners. . . . In many cases the third option will prove more expensive than retaining a domestic worker, even at an increased wage. (Department of Labor 2002, 77)

In this summary statement of the state's position with respect to ensuring that domestic workers enjoy "the same basic rights" as other workers, and "are afforded their dignity," a number of themes that saturate state discourse on the sector are evident.

First, employees and their rights are eclipsed by a concern with employer accessibility; that is, ensuring access of a supply of workers for employers. The Department of Labor (2002, 76) is clear that "while employment in formal sector jobs has declined over the past few years, informal sector employment has grown." Using the *Labor Force Survey*, the percentage increase from 1995 to 2003 for women domestic workers was almost 40 percent

(Statistics South Africa 2003). The state used this as a basis for not only claiming that it is a sector with possibilities for job creation—"at present, domestic work provides employment opportunities for a large number of women who would experience difficulty finding work elsewhere" (Department of Labor 2002)—but also for co-opting this existing labor supply to specify the appropriate distribution of care between family, state, and market.

In contextualizing the political inclusion of domestic workers in the macroeconomics of unemployment, the state presented the "privatization" of care through the market provision of domestic workers as the resolution to the continued labor market participation of both employers and employees. In this, the state used the accessibility of a supply of labor in the context of the coercive political economy of chronic unemployment to ensure a supply of caring labor to employers, and it presented such a solution in recognition of the difficulties of family provision of care for employing households: "some employers indicated they would not be able to continue their own outside work without the assistance of the domestic workers" (Department of Labor 2002, 76). The equation rendered is one in which the only legitimate alternatives presented are the family or the market.

Where commercial market-based forms of care have been largely ill developed due to the availability for decades of a cheaper alternative in the form of private domestic workers, and where the family is presented as a solution that does not compete with the affordability of paid domestic work, the option of private domestic work for pay is presented as effectively the most "rational" one. In effect, the formalization of this option limits further the development of alternative market-based forms (after all, the state reminds us that it would be difficult for commercial market operators to rival the cheapness of domestic workers) and constrains the possibilities of the restructuring of patriarchal family forms to ensure the viability of paid domestic work as a source of care provision. Most significantly, the state has, in the democratic statecraft for domestic workers, extracted itself from the equation of family, state, and market in the responsibility and provision of care. By establishing the continued accessibility of private domestic work, the state kept the responsibility for the provision of care within families and positioned itself as a regulator—rather than provider—of care resources.

Second, the dominant concern in the setting of the minimum wage was undoubtedly employer affordability; that is, ensuring the affordability to employers of domestic care workers. Ryklief and Bethanie (2002) correctly questioned whether the low levels of the eventual minimum wage determination (in 2002, approximately R840 [$140] per month) made the legislative incorporation of domestic workers into a rights regime a "license to exploit." Employer affordability was probably the most important determining factor in the eventual determination. The state argued that this was because families face particular strictures in negotiating the purchase of care: "Determining the affordability of employing a domestic worker is complex. Households are not business units that generate profits. They cannot 'close down' if they go bankrupt," reported the investigation into minimum wages for the sector (Department of Labor 2002, 81). But, the state reinforced the prescription that families and households, by virtue of the logics of household management, have to bear the responsibility for and purchase care. In stressing affordability, the demand-side requirements for a source of affordable care was privileged over the necessary requirement to structure a system of inclusion for those who constitute the supply.

Furthermore, in stressing affordability, private household workers were punted as the most affordable of the state's listing of options for care. In explicitly structuring the protections for domestic workers in ways that secured that very affordability, the state prescribed for families the economic logics of (private) market responsibility and (private) family provision of care.

This "privatization" of care constructed through the political technologies of inclusion for domestic workers was extended through the full range of instruments employed by the state in its engagement with the sector. Together, they constructed a privatized care regime that removed the state from any responsibility for and provision of care, and instead emphasized family and market.

The Domestic Workers Celebrations held in every region of Johannesburg in 2004 in celebration of National Women's Day were a potent expression of this market and familial, and in turn gendered, construction of care by the state. Local government chose to celebrate National Women's Day by celebrating women who "Keep the Home Fires Burning" and then choosing to celebrate domestic workers as the most important exemplars of that category. The campaign, and its rendering of the equivalence of woman, domestic worker, and caregiver within the home, was important in a number of ways. In celebration speeches, for instance, domestic workers were constantly reminded that their work as domestic workers was equivalent to "keeping the home fires burning," with an emphasis on their dual role in the homes of their employers and in their own. So much was this theme repeated that when I asked one domestic worker what she learned from the day's events about her rights as a worker, she remarked triumphantly: "We need to be celebrated, because we are working in the homes to keep the whole of South Africa fed and clothed and taken care of."

At a similar event held at Constitution Hill, one domestic worker remarked over lunch, "We are the ones who make all the homes good. . . . Without us, there will be no black families. Without us, no white families will survive." So, in the local government's "Keeping the Home Fires Burning" campaign, where domestic workers were celebrated for their caretaking in both their own and their employers' families, the state sought to "celebrate" domestic workers for their circulation in a "national care chain," in which they are unpaid care workers in their own families and are mobilized as commodities to provide care for the families of others. In this, there was a "celebration" of the location of domestic workers in a privatized care regime on both ends of the race-class divide, rather than an effort to overturn it.

No wonder when I mentioned the event to Eunice Dhladhla, whose quiet thoughtfulness masked a remarkably keen intellect, she silently ruminated on the word *celebration* and then expressed strong disagreement with the word choice. "I think it's better that they say they 'salute' domestic workers, not 'celebrate' them," she said, explaining that workers forced to leave their own children behind to take care of others was no cause for celebration. Instead, it was a challenge, and workers had no choice but to endure and, like comrades in struggle, deserved to be saluted instead. Eunice was so confident in her assessment, she communicated this to the organizers, and the next event bore T-shirts emblazoned with "We salute domestic workers!" Despite Eunice's efforts, the imagination betrayed by the state's original formulation suggested forcefully that the formal inclusion of erstwhile "servants" into the rights regime of the category "worker" was not accompanied by an effort to disrupt the privatization of care they represent; indeed, it went along with and confirmed it.

On the other end of the nexus of race and class, social welfare policy also reinforced the privatization of care for domestic workers, but in the family rather than the market. In this dual-care regime, domestic workers provided a (private) market solution to the care needs of their employers, while they themselves relied on a (private) family solution to the care of their own families.

The "Privatized" Family Provision of Care *for* Domestic Workers

Much of the literature references the irony of paid domestic work with which this chapter began—that, in providing care to other families, domestic workers are unable to provide care to their own. As Elsa Chaney puts this in Peruvian parlance, "One of the ironies of the child-care question is the fact that poor women are engaged to look after affluent women's children, while their own are (as some put it) *botados* or thrown out on the streets" (1985, 45).

Far from being left without care (*botados*) or with deficient care as Hochschild (2003) is concerned about, research shows the many and diverse strategies domestic workers use to ensure the provision of care to their families. Some engage family resources, including older relatives or siblings, mobilizing an "extended circle of kin" (Glenn 1986, 228; Katzman 1978), others utilize community resources such as neighbors (Ozyegin 2001), and some Filipina domestic workers even hire domestic workers themselves to care for their children and home in the Philippines (Hondagneu-Sotelo and Avila 1997; Parreñas 2000). In these national and global care chains, domestic workers almost always rely on private (family and market) sources of care work.

In the South African "national care chain," domestic workers, in the main, relied on feminized kinship for the provision of care. In this study, workers had an average of five dependents, confirmed by Murphy's (2000) survey showing an average 5.53 dependents for domestic workers nationally. Only one worker had access to an affordable commercial child care center, and none of the remaining women had access to nonfamilial sources of support for housework. Their various care solutions reflected the combined imprint of the structure of their employment and their spatial location. Ozyegin (2001) notes in Turkey how squatter women who are domestics are forced to rely on different care resources, often neighbors, compared to doorkeepers' wives who are also domestic workers but are located in a different residential and employment nexus. Similarly, in South Africa, domestics' spatial and employment configurations conditioned their caregiving capacities and the extent to which they bore responsibility for caregiving themselves or were forced to displace it along the chain to other family providers. But, in all cases, it remained privatized within the family, provided by women, mostly unpaid, and involving, in many cases, women who at some point in their life cycles had been paid domestic workers.

Full-Time Live-in

For live-in domestic workers, there was the inevitable failure to sustain family life in Johannesburg, and the majority of live-in workers circulated in chains that were transgeographic between urban and rural. In these cases, their children lived in rural areas and township locales in more impoverished provinces, usually cared for by a female relative. For these workers, whose life story is typified by Mabel Mabena's, with whom this chapter opened, their role in the care of their families remained primarily monetary. Remittances allowed some measure of support for the unpaid care on which they relied, provided mainly by the grandmothers of their children. While Chaney (1985) quotes a piece of Peruvian folk wisdom that says maids always send their children off to their home province to be raised by relatives and shows this to be largely untrue for domestics in Lima, this pattern described the reality for many domestics in Johannesburg.

For the remaining live-in domestics who did not have children raised by female kin in their homesteads, they were able to care for their young infants at their place of residence/employment, often preparing to send them to live with kin in the rural areas once the child was old enough (usually once they could walk. The provision of care for young infants by domestic workers while maintaining a full-time job of rigorous housework has led to that most interesting of South African images—of a domestic worker with a baby tied to her back using no more than a sheet, blanket, or towel, and a diaper pin.[8] For a few workers, when the child became a toddler, the ability to care for them while working became more onerous, and the provision of care for the child was passed along the chain to female kin elsewhere. As one worker explained, "When he was walking, then I send him to his grandmother."

Yet a few more live-in domestic workers who were able to care for their children at their place of residence/employment, raised school-age children in a perverse form of the "maternalism" that characterizes employer-employee relations (Rollins 1985). Here, the employer usually provided for the school fees of the child and, in some cases, for clothes, food, and educational materials. Selena Simelane, a live-in domestic worker in Observatory, understood this process well. Her employers had asked her to bring her daughter to live with them, and now pay for Lindiwe Simelane's private school education, uniforms, books, food, and clothes. Selena explained insightfully the covert power implied by this arrangement: "They won't pay you enough that you can send your own child to that private school, you see. When I ask for extra money for school uniforms, they say they haven't got money. But, then they are taking Lindiwe to buy that private uniform. If you are raising your own child with your money, what is there, what makes them feel like they are better than you . . . ?"

A local play, *Skin Deep,* directed by Bongani Linda, explored the raced peculiarities of white employers financially supporting and, at times, displacing as parents the children of the women they employ. These employers of full-time live-in workers utilized the tenuous capacities for caregiving of their workers to entrench their own power. Further research into this enigmatic practice is desperately needed.

Full-time Live-out

For full-time live-out domestic workers, the relative stability of their employment allowed some measure of caregiving capacity in Johannesburg. Some of these workers had secured government-subsidized houses, while most of the remainder were able to rent out backyard shacks within the established townships, or vacant "servants quarters" in the backyards of their employers' suburban homes. Eleven of these workers had their children and spouses living with them,[9] and only one relied on a private, low-cost day nursery for child care. The remainder were like Monica Seepe, who lived in a backyard shack in Daveyton. She explained how it was not only the structure of employment that affected the arrangement of care for these workers but also the availability of care along the chain that shaped their employment options:

> It is very difficult for me, because there is no one in Newcastle for the children. My sister died last year of the disease [HIV/AIDS], and then no one wanted to take them, because they think you are dirty if your family died of that disease. So then I brought them to Daveyton. Also, for the schools here. I was not able to go and register them, especially for Grade O. . . . It was making me cry to not take the job in Midrand [live-in]. She said she was going to pay me one thou [R1000/$166], but I was worried where would they [the children] live. Those days I was crying . . . but now I found this job here. I stay in Daveyton, and the children they are with me.

For workers like Monica, maintaining their families in Johannesburg, while working, had different care requirements. The care chains they relied on to ensure the maintenance of their families was more geographically limited and relied on older siblings and a different conception of kin. "These women, you must know, they are strong in another way," said Joyce

Nhlapo, herself a full-time live-in domestic, offering her characteristic insight on this aspect of the care obligations of full-time live-out workers. "These ones who have no one at home," she continued, "they must rely on this neighbor here, in the township, and that woman there. She must say, 'Keep my child here today,' and then 'Come, you make the food on your stove today.' You see, and this other woman she has her own children, to feed, but there's nothing she can do. You understand, they are like chicken in that fenced box."

In these arrangements, neighbors and friends—in an example of what De Fiore (2002) calls "fictive kinship"—are mobilized as additional links in the chain. Having to provide paid care during the day required the displacement of workers' own care to these "other mothers" (De Fiore 2002), usually neighbors, who functioned as kin in their absence. Chaney (1985) also documents the importance of neighbors for Peruvian domestic workers in Lima. As Ozyegin notes of squatter women working as domestics in Turkey, for the private (family) provision of care, "the concept of neighborliness is very important in daily life and governs the moral economy of these communities" (2001, 157). Cynthia Phakathi, a full-time domestic worker living in a township backyard shack with her remaining school-age child, explained this pattern for South African domestics: "There was no electricity, and leaving in the morning was painful. But, we would all help each other very much. Yes, this neighbor next door, I remember her, she was such a difficult one, she was, she was taking them two times, three times, in the week. When they came from school, she was giving them food and when it was very cold, some jerseys [sweaters]."

Part-Time Live-out

The third major category of workers, part-time and live-out domestic workers, resided primarily in informal "squatter" settlements or in township houses or backyard shacks. This residence pattern limited the ability to maintain family in the city.[10] For the older part-time workers who were more established, there were no younger children to take care of, and their small "matchbox" homes or shacks required little maintenance. For younger workers, often in small makeshift shacks, they also relied on distant unpaid family provision of care, mostly by sisters and grandmothers, or, if they had their children with them, on older siblings. One domestic worker who worked fifteen-hour days and lived in an informal settlement left her two youngest children during the day in the care of her sister, who worked the evening shift at a food retail outlet, and in the evenings relied on her fifteen-year-old daughter to look after the children, collect firewood, and cook the evening meal.

Notably, these workers, lacking water, sanitation, and electricity, found their days split between unpaid care work in the mornings and evenings fetching water and firewood, and paid care during the day for their employers. Palesa Lebala, for example, rented a two meter by two meter shack with another domestic worker in Thembelihle, the informal settlement in Lenasia where she worked part-time for two employers. She had an arduous routine of housework, spending her mornings walking to collect firewood in order to have fuel for cooking and heating, and walking twice weekly in unsafe conditions to collect water surreptitiously from a local resident's garden tap. Despite the post-apartheid state's expansion of service delivery and social welfare, women like Palesa remained without access to housing, electricity, or water or to any benefits to support child care. The requirements of social reproduction without the provision of basic services ensured that she was required to fund, through remittances, her displaced child care work, and fund, through her own unpaid labor, the work of her day-to-day social reproduction.

Domestic workers, therefore, relied—to different degrees—on feminized familial and unpaid care work arrangements in the "national care chain" for the provision of child care. For these workers, this reliance on family for care was engendered by the social welfare policy of the post-apartheid state, which does not socialize the responsibility for care but instead reinforces, for poor women, its privatization within families.

The Child Support Grant versus State Responsibility for, and Provision of, Child Care

The failure of any alternatives for domestic workers with respect to their care obligations, especially child care, seems perverse in a developmental state so committed to the expansion of social citizenship. Despite an overwhelming discursive focus on care, state social welfare policy actually resolved the care problematic by understanding socialization as the devolution of state responsibility to "communities." Socialization of care as state responsibility for, and provision of, child care was specifically avoided. This is most evident in the flagship program of the state's social citizenship program with respect to care, the Child Support Grant (CSG)—a social grant issued by the Department of Social Welfare and Development to caregivers for the care of children.

The most important source of financial support for domestic workers' care responsibilities was the minimal entitlement of the CSG. In this study, 67 percent of domestic workers asked had children who were receiving the grant.[11] For these workers, the grant was extremely important. "I get the child maintenance from government. It helps us a lot," said Portia Moleme. "How?" I probe. "With food, and the children's school fees. I get the grant and I send it to the grandmother. They go to school, so they have a future now," Portia explained with relief. Similarly, Margaret Manamela explained that she received the grant of R160 ($26) per month for each of her two children and used it for "food and clothes and school." "Because it's very expensive, and without this grant we would not be surviving," she said.

As one of the largest social assistance programs of the post-apartheid state, the Child Support Grant (CSG) was implemented in 1998 to replace the apartheid-era State Maintenance Grant (SMG). The SMG was introduced in South Africa in the 1920s as a social welfare measure effectively intended to support the nuclear family, providing temporary assistance for women during periods of family breakdown.[12] Distributed along racial lines, whites were the major beneficiaries of these grants initially, with Indian and Colored families becoming the main recipients during the 1970s and 1980s when the state's reformist efforts reconstructed the citizenship status of these groups. Black Africans, however, were mainly excluded from the grant throughout the apartheid era, mainly through administrative exclusions because "homeland" administrations did not administer the grant. Toward the 1990s, the apartheid state attempted to contract welfare provision, so that in 1997, only about 150,000 mostly Colored, and some white, families were receiving the SMG (Leatt 2004).

Political liberalization required the overhaul of the racially differentiated SMG, and the so-named Lund Committee was set up to investigate the possibilities for reform of social security in respect to children. The Committee did not have an enviable task, having to simultaneously manage concerns for equity and imposed fiscal constraints. It recommended the phasing out of the SMG and its replacement by a Child Support Grant (CSG), which was accepted and implemented by government in 1998. In 2005, the CSG covered all eligible children under the age of fourteen, with plans to extend coverage to eligible children under the age of eighteen. By 2003, 2.6 million children were receiving the grant (Leatt 2004), and by 2004, nearly 4.3 million children were covered.

The CSG was implemented as a priority of the developmental welfare state's commitment to political liberalization and equality and to realizing the commitment to social citizenship enshrined in the Constitution. But the

CSG also bore the imprint of economic liberalization, as the Committee report noted: "The Committee started its work knowing that whatever recommendations are made, there will be losers. When the Constitution and macro-economic policy combine the need for equity with a commitment to curbing social spending, no 'win-win' situation is possible."[13] In April 2008, the grant level was very low—R210 [$35] per month per child, disbursed to the "primary caregiver." It was an indication of the relative poverty of domestics' households that, despite its extremely low monetary value, the grant proved (in some cases) absolutely essential for the basic survival of extended households. As Portia Moleme, working in Killarney part-time and live-out, but with children raised by her mother in a small township in the Free State, explained: "Without this money, we will be starving and dying."

But, for domestic workers, the CSG provided only minimal state assistance for their care obligations. Most important, it did nothing to disrupt the pattern of feminized familial responsibility and provision of care. One domestic worker, Precious Mohapi, whose mother was raising four of her five children, provided an articulate expression of this: "My mother, she is old. She gets the pension grant from the government. We get the maintenance for the children. She has to look after my ones [children] in Limpopo, because there is no one else. . . . She worked very hard. We are just all working. These grants are not coming to take these troubles away from us."

As Precious recognized, the CSG, contrary to what its position as a major state aid for child support may suggest, does not interfere with the logic of the "national care chain." Precious' mother is still responsible for the unpaid provision of care within the family, and this solution is for the lack of any other alternative, "because there is no one else." For domestic workers, the CSG only minimally socializes the responsibility for care and does not affect the privatized (familial) and feminized provision of care. The failure of the state to fully socialize the responsibility for and provision of care has resulted in a reinforcement of the "national care chain" and the CSG has become a critical part of a particular post-apartheid political economy of care. For domestic workers, the CSG reinforced the privatization of their care obligations in a number of ways.

First, the program is understood primarily as a development policy that addresses poverty alleviation. When introduced, the CSG was described by the Minister for Welfare and Population Development, Geraldine Fraser-Moleketi, as "an innovative anti-poverty programme" (*Press Release*, March 31, 1998), and in a parliamentary bulletin as a grant "which will act as a poverty alleviation mechanism" (October 27, 1997). The CSG, while necessary and extremely important in the fight against poverty (which is how workers explained its function), is not designed for, nor does it function to address, inequalities in domestics' care work and the tenuous position of the caregivers they rely on.

Second, the policy pronouncements on the CSG do not recognize the unpaid child care work done by the grandmothers and sisters of domestic workers, nor is the grant meant to offer any social recognition and state support for this role. Instead, the CSG is tasked specifically—for other commendable reasons—to "follow the child." But, this ensures that the CSG remains a child-centered policy, rather than one targeting care or the provider of it. The result is that, despite the availability of the grant, the "national care chain" has not been disrupted, failing to provide domestic workers with alternatives to familial unpaid provision of care. "No, my children are still with my sister. She is getting the grant for them," said one worker at a child care training center in the city. As she enrolled for a private program to be accredited as a child care provider, her own children were cared for by her sister because no other alternative for care was available and because the grant "is not enough money for me to bring them to live with me. Things in Jo'burg are too expensive."

The CSG, as a strategy focused on poverty alleviation rather than care equalization, targets caregivers as one of the rural (or urban) poor, rather than specifically in their caring roles. The CSG reinforces the structural location of female family providers of informal care by providing some measure of financial relief for their extraneous economic afflictions but not targeting their actual responsibility for care. For all of the domestic workers who received the grant, the cash assistance did not provide for alternative choices with respect to their care obligations. While it alleviated the desperate poverty of many extended households, it did not disrupt the logic of child care provision within the family.

As much as the CSG provided only limited socialized responsibility of care, it went along with a legislative apparatus that further emphasized the private familial responsibility for care through private maintenance from fathers. Indeed, as Hassim notes, "the changes in the state maintenance grant went along with the proposed privatization of maintenance" (2005, 26). For domestic workers, such private maintenance rarely materialized and confirmed that in investing in the infrastructure of private maintenance, women's responsibility for care remained untouched. Cynthia Phakathi, for example, with her limited means had been struggling to receive maintenance from the fathers of her two children. "I went to the courts, two times I went in April, I was speaking to the case worker. She said I must now come in

June," she explained. "Then, in June," she continued, "he was sitting there telling that he has got no job, he cannot pay. It was hurting me, because he said he can't afford it. They said that day he must give R50 [$8.33] every month. I have never seen that fifty, not even today."

Together with the CSG, private maintenance "privatized" care within the family (among women), for this group of workers. Workers understood the grant, in particular, as it was intended—as a poverty alleviation strategy rather than as a means of providing women support for child care and for finding alternatives to care provision within the family. Joyce Nhlapo, whose mother (a retired domestic worker), cares for her two children and the orphan of her sister who died of HIV/AIDS, understood this well. She reflected on what it meant that her mother received a grant to provide food and clothes for her children, but no compensation for her care work. Joyce argued that the grant did not resolve the problem of having to displace her care work on her unpaid mother, while her employers had the facility to employ someone to do the same work. "Can I say, bring a domestic worker and they will be doing what I do for these people?" she lamented, pointing out that the state's minimal child support grant did not allow her to offer the same care solution to her children that she represented for her employers. Specifically, the issue Joyce raises is the implications of the privatized market solution to which their employers have access versus the privatized family solution that they are forced to rely on. In this, a dual-care regime is constructed.

The Dual-Care Regime

Nancy Fraser (1989), together with other feminists, argues that a dual social citizenship regime in the United States is tied together by assumptions about the gendered division of labor. The masculine system (such as unemployment insurance) is tied to participation in waged labor, is focused on the individual, is less demeaning, and involves less surveillance and control. Recipients are positioned as rights bearers, as deserving, and as consumers who have the right to determine how they allocate the cash that they receive. On the other hand, the feminine system is designed to compensate for family failure, is focused on the household, and financed out of tax revenues rather as a contributory plan. Recipients are positioned as dependents and clients and are closely scrutinized, while benefits are low and have the effect of maintaining dependency. A different, but equally gendered and classed, citizenship regime is evident for domestic workers in South Africa.

The CSG is not a universal grant available to all caregivers as a recognition of the work involved in child care and the need to displace these burdens from women, especially those who are rural, poor, and African. Instead, the CSG, despite the recommendations of the Lund Committee, involves a complex means test. In 2007, in order to qualify, the primary caregiver and their spouse should not have a combined monthly income of more than R1100 ($184) per month if they live in rural areas or in informal housing in urban areas, and R800 per month ($134) for those living in formal housing in urban areas. Clearly, "the threshold levels are very low" (Leatt 2004, 16), and they had not been increased since their introduction in 1998, making the CSG effectively, and increasingly, a grant for only the poorest households. It is an indication of the levels of poverty and unemployment in the country that even with such extremely low thresholds, in 2004, 4.3 million children were getting the grant through just over 3 million caregivers. The means test remains problematic not only in the possible stigmatization of recipient households in public discourse,[14] but also in its implications for the political economy of care.

A few workers were conscious of the politics of care implied by their reliance on state support grants for poverty, rather than child care relief, while their employers benefited from their labor for the same purpose. Mabel Dhlamini, a rural domestic worker from Nongoma in KwaZulu-Natal who raised the three children of her employer, was bitter about the unequal opportunities for child care provision that brought her and her employer together: "I always think, my children being so far away, getting only my grant money every month from me. That envelope is all my love in it, that's all they get. . . . I am the mother to these [employer's] children. And they pay me nothing really, because they are eating my money to make these [employer's] children grow big."

In these national care chains, domestic workers (mainly rural, African, and poor) rely on minimal state support to provide basic care to their children, while a supply of domestic workers to middle-class (mainly white and urban) families ensures cheap, affordable, and good quality care. The Department of Social Development and Welfare's approach to child care is one of "privatization" in the family (i.e., to support family responsibility and family provision of child care, with minimal state assistance), intended to alleviate poverty rather than the burdens of care work on women. At the same time, the Department of Labor's approach to care is one of "privatization" in the market. While these are very different forms of privatization, their equivalence in terms of the politics of care is indicated by this simultaneous usage.

Ann Blum suggests looking at paid domestic work through the "twin lenses of social welfare policy and legislation on labor" (2004, 71). When the analysis of paid domestic work is considered in tandem with the state's approach to welfare, the sectoral determination for domestic workers and the CSG reinforce a two-tiered system of privatized child care provision. One, a social welfare benefit for poor (mainly) rural African women care-givers through the CSG; the other a market provision for middle- (and some working-) class (mainly) urban white women through paid domestic work. In the resulting "national care chain" that is constructed out of this differential "privatization of care," based on race and class as much as gen-der, domestic workers rely on this minimal state benefit that does not at-tack the logic of family provision of care at the same time as they are mo-bilized to provide a privatized solution to the care burden of their employers. The failure of the state to assert public responsibility for care becomes therefore one of the mechanisms through which the "national care chain" is entrenched by the democratic statecraft's efforts to turn "servants" into workers.

Part III
Workers' Struggles

6

Demobilizing Domestic Workers

In 1996, an ironic paradox marked domestic workers' entry into a democratic order. They were extended the right, for the first time in their history, to organize into trade unions. But, in that same year, the national union they had built through the repressive years of apartheid, collapsed. Beginning in the nineteenth century, domestic workers in South Africa publicly organized as an expression of a class politics into gangs, associations, and unions. By the 1980s, their mobilization as workers had grown to such strength that they could no longer be characterized as unorganizable. When the landmark legislation to extend rights to domestic workers was passed, it should have witnessed the strengthening of union efforts within the sector: Democratization saw the end of an era of authoritarianism and limits on political organization, and domestic workers' political capacities had been supported by statutory protection. Yet, instead of an activation of domestic workers' political organizing through the availability of state institutions to support their political activities, there was instead a dramatic "collective demobilization" (Kenny 2004).[1]

The demobilization of domestic workers at the very moment when their rights to organize were enshrined in law was not just an ironic coincidence. This chapter shows how the democratic statecraft of inclusion for domestic workers was partially responsible for their demobilization and depoliticization. Paradoxically, the political effort to turn "servants" into workers dramatically blunted domestic workers' public politics as workers.

Unorganizable? Gangs, Associations, and Domestic Workers' Unions

In 1989, Florrie de Villiers, the first general secretary of the South African Domestic Workers Union (SADWU), captured the prevailing wisdom on the possibilities of domestic worker organizing. "Most people saw organizing a domestic workers' union as impossible," she wrote (De Villiers 1989, 175) That domestic workers are "unorganizable" (Ford 2004)—an "occupational oddity that defies organization" (Smith 2000, 47)—is arguably among the most common and enduring themes in the study of the sector. Domestic workers labor in isolation, behind closed doors, subject to employer and social ideologies that refuse to recognize domestic work as real work, and dependent on employers in ways that do not allow for the assertion of a collective identity. "Isolation, dependence, [and] invisibility" summarized Gaitskell et al. (1984, 87) define for commentators the implausibility of a public politics among domestic workers in South Africa. As de Villiers suggests, the limits on domestic worker organizing have been widely rehearsed. But, contrary to popular wisdom, domestic workers in South Africa have not been passive victims of the structural features of their work. Instead, they have had a long history of mobilizing, organizing, and activating a class politics.

In Johannesburg, organized activity among domestic workers can be traced back to the earliest history of the city itself, the 1890s, to a "secret society" consisting mainly of, at first, Zulu "houseboys"—the *izigebengu* or Ninevites (Van Onselen 1982). In a brilliant account of this early history, Charles Van Onselen argues that while the Ninevites ultimately became merely criminal, the gang had originally been formed by black men, predominantly domestic workers, "to protect their interests 'without recourse to a law court'" (1982, 55). Later, the group inspired a similar gang on the Witwatersrand—the *Amalaita*—as they came to be known, which represented one of the most remarkable early instances of domestic workers collectively organizing, albeit as criminal gangsters.

The Amalaita, a "movement of young black domestic servants," as Van Onselen (1982, 59) documents, were recruited largely from among the "houseboys" on the Witwatersrand, and their activity suggested the earliest expression of organized activity among domestic workers. It was, according to Van Onselen, "a movement which sought to give its members who labored in alienated colonial isolation a sense of purpose and dignity" (1982, 59). While not resembling any traditional model of worker organization, the Amalaita as a group of well-known and much-feared gangsters nonetheless reflected a class politics. "The Amalaita should be seen as the 'houseboys" liberation army fighting to reassert its decolorized manhood during one of the first major waves of South African proletarianization," asserts Van Onselen (1982, 59).

As that process of proletarianization unfolded, and the black working class expanded, domestic workers expressed their public class politics in ways that resembled more closely traditional modes of worker organization. From 1925, domestic workers joined the Industrial and Commercial Workers' Union (ICU), and domestic workers became unionized, albeit under the auspices of a more generalized proletarian movement. Similarly, when workers were organized by the National Liberation League from 1937, it was less as an expression of domestic workers' specific mobilization as a class. Among the first efforts to do exactly that was the Bantu Girls Domestic Servants Association set up by Lucy Twala, which sought to protect the interests of ex-boarding school "girls" who had been trained for domestic service (Gaitskell 1984, 128). But, the initiative failed.

At around the same time, in 1938, another effort at unionization, the African Domestic Servants League, was launched by a man named Mvula. The League was a curious venture. Its committee consisted primarily of dedicated unionists: Self Mampuru, an adviser on trade unions; Dan Tloome, a trade unionist who served as the vice-president of the Council of Non-European Trade Unions and treasurer of the ANC; Nkagaleng Nkadimeng, trade unionist and assistant secretary of the Transvaal African National Congress (ANC); and Albert Segwai, secretary of the League, and of the Progressive Trade Union Group (Hirson 1990). But, despite the League's committee, representing an important collection of men involved and active in the trade union movement, the League seemed to function less as a union and more as an agent of employers to secure "reliable and trustworthy" as well as "better trained and more responsible" servants (Hirson 1990). In the famous line from one of their posters, the League's slogan, "Cheeky Servants Must Go!" summarized their orientation (Hirson 1990).

Its main organizer, J. G. Coka, who resuscitated the League after Mvula's death, seems to have been one of the reasons accounting for the League's peculiar politics—of organizing domestic workers into a unionlike structure but utilizing the structure for opposite ends. In a letter to employers, Coka betrayed his vision of domestic workers and the purposes of the League: "Those of you who know what disappointments lie in the path of working with Africans will appreciate the obstacles that have stood in our way. With their childish ideas and no sense of responsibility, envies and indifferences, it becomes a herculean task to organize them effectively" (Letter from J. G. Coka to employers, African Domestic Servants League, November 1939).[2]

Between Coka's vision, and Segwai's purported misappropriation of funds, the League failed, and while it was an unsuccessful initial attempt at domestic worker unionizing, it did succeed in recruiting workers who believed "that here was a new instrument for obtaining their rights" (Hirson 1990, 61). As Hirson notes, this makes the League, and all other early efforts at domestic worker organizing, "amongst the very first" unions, and as a result, a significant part of the history of trade unionism and the black working class in South Africa (1990, 61). This early history also suggests the split that would come to animate later organizing efforts by domestic workers in the context of apartheid: of, on the one hand, worker-initiated radical unions and, on the other, organizing efforts by concerned parties external to the sector advocating a different content for domestic workers' politics.

"And Then Came SADWU"

By the 1970s, this distinction in domestic worker organizing had precipitated the most successful unionizing effort by domestic workers in South Africa's history: the South African Domestic Workers Union (SADWU). With trade unions and other forms of political organizing severely constrained by the apartheid regime for decades, it was only in the late 1970s that domestic workers began organizing so forcefully. Eventually launched in 1986, SADWU grew to become the largest of the domestic workers' unions in the country's history. Vital and vibrant, it had no less than 85,000 signed-up members at its peak (*The Shopsteward*, Feb/March 1993, 17), was widely regarded as strong and active, and decisively exploded the myth that domestic workers, especially in South Africa under apartheid, were "unorganizable."

In 1989, the SADWU Newsletter published a poem by a domestic worker. "And then came SADWU," the poem celebrated. "Why SADWU? Because she gave us back / our names / our dignity / our loved ones / Because she called me comrade." As the poem powerfully summarized, SADWU's formation was a turning point in the organizational but also subjective life of thousands of domestics.

While the union was formed by the merger of five unions,[3] it represented the convergence of two different streams of domestic worker organizing to that point: one, employer-initiated (white liberal), and the other, worker-initiated and controlled.

On the one hand, the South African Domestic Workers Association (SADWA) emerged from the white liberal Domestic Workers and Employers Project (DWEP). Coordinated by Sue Gordon and Leah Tutu, the DWEP began in Johannesburg in 1972 with Centers of Concern—physical meeting places organizationally linked with each other—that brought domestic workers and their employers together in the effort to foster greater understanding between them. The DWEP's aim was "to bring about an improvement in the position of domestic workers by helping to create a better understanding between a worker and an employer, by revising working and wage conditions of domestic workers, and trying to improve their status and personal image" (Gaitskell et al. 1984, 103–4). In the Centers, DWEP offered workers sewing and cooking classes and sought to create a space where workers could come together as an antidote to their isolation and loneliness.

While the DWEP was a significant initiative, with dozens of Centers around the country and visible projects, it could not sustain itself. As a white liberal organization, DWEP was criticized for being dominated by white women employers rather than by the women workers they sought to assist. In 1980, DWEP came under attack after its members supported the Cape Provincial Council in a legislative initiative that would have required employers to keep a duplicate key of their employee's rooms, to be made available to the police as requested. Amid increasing awareness of the importance of worker-controlled representation, in February 1981, SADWA was formed in Durban by workers who had been involved with DWEP but who sought to construct something for themselves—an exclusively employees' association.

Almost immediately, workers began to articulate their demands. In 1982, SADWA sent a memorandum to the Department of Manpower demanding legal protection for domestic and farm workers. Receiving only an acknowledgment of the receipt a year later, SADWA sent a delegation to Pretoria in December 1984 with the same demands (*Daily News*, September 19, 1985). Relentless as SADWA was, it was located and organized from the place of employment—which was invariably the white suburbs—and attempted change through diplomacy.

When SADWU was formed in 1986, it merged SADWA with a different orientation to domestic workers' expression of a class politics—that of the Domestic Workers Association (DWA). Initiated by workers and controlled by them, the DWA was deeply skeptical of the DWEP approach, arguing that it "provided tea and sympathy rather than treating the roots of the domestic workers' problems" (Maggie Oewies, *Herald*, October 19, 1980). Gaitskell et al. (1984) argued that the DWA's approach was partly due to its location among a different constituency—live-out workers in the townships rather than live-in workers in the suburbs.

The merger of these two streams into SADWU in 1986 witnessed a strengthening of the movement and the inauguration of an era of radical and active union politics by domestic workers. While SADWU was always weak compared to other sections of the organized working class (e.g., mine workers, shop workers, and clothing and textile workers), it was vital and strong relative to domestic worker unionization elsewhere. Affiliated to the Congress of South African Trade Unions (COSATU), SADWU was significant in that it organized domestic workers under the banner of a broader politics of the working class. Florrie de Villiers remembered the launch of SADWU in the unexpected interest by domestic workers in joining the union: "About seventeen hundred people attended the launching of the National Domestic Workers' Union in Cape Town on 29–30 November 1986. There were supposed to be two thousand but roadblocks prevented many people from getting there. We now have a membership of fifty thousand" (1989, 176).

From its launch, SADWU demonstrated a sophistication that belied domestic workers' status as the country's least educated workforce and confirmed their strength as the largest single category of employment:

It is now time we domestic workers make our voices heard. It is time to come together to make our demands for a decent life heard. There are more domestic workers than there are mine workers in South Africa. If we could unite the 800,000 domestic workers who are all over the country's homes we can win what other workers have won in mines, factories, and shops. We domestic workers have the same problems. We all suffer from bad wages, long hours and bad conditions of work. We are like slaves. This is why we need a union of domestic workers.[4]

At the launch, SADWA president Violet Mothlasedi said: "Employers must wake up. . . . We want recognition for our contribution—recognition that domestic workers are not just super human robots who don't mind working seven days a week, 12 hours or more a day for very little pay, away from their husbands and children."[5] It was a message that tens of thousands of workers responded to.

Emboldened by this response, SADWU launched a legislation campaign on June 1, 1989. It made comprehensive recommendations for the recognition of domestic workers as workers by extending protective labor legislation and for the passage of a national minimum (living) wage. SADWU supported its demands with important shows of strength including marches, petitions, and protests. When, in 1991, the National Manpower Commission set up a committee in response to the union's demands, "it was clear the unions had won a major victory" (*Speak*, 1992, 38:10).

Despite this victory and the entry into a democratic era, the union began to shrink and lose vitality. In 1996, with a much-reduced membership of 25,000 and torn apart by internal leadership wrangles and allegations of mismanagement, the union—with the strong support of the COSATU office bearers—dissolved itself.

And Then Came SADSAWU . . .

In 2001, however, in a transformed political landscape under a stable democratic regime, veteran members of the dissolved SADWU established a successor union, the South African Domestic Service and Allied Workers Union (SADSAWU). While various other unions—including a National Congress of Trade Unions (NACTU) affiliate and the Professional and Transport Workers Union (PTWU)—continued to organize domestic workers in Johannesburg and its surrounds, SADSAWU had remained the only national union specifically organizing domestic workers. This generated high expectations for SADSAWU's capacity to emulate the success of SADWU.

The political environment was certainly favorable. Just a year after the launch of SADSAWU, the government introduced its landmark legislation recognizing domestic work as real work, giving domestic workers specific rights as workers, and introducing a national minimum wage (see chapter 3). This recognition of domestic workers as political agents by the state should have predicted a reactivation of domestic workers' politics and an assertion of their political capacities. Paradoxically, despite democratization and an extensive state initiative for the political empowerment of domestic workers, SADSAWU—the most important representative of domestic workers— atrophied dramatically, and domestic workers faced a dramatic "collective demobilization" (Kenny 2004).

Compared to SADWU's relative growth and strength during the 1980s, between 2002 and 2005 SADSAWU lacked any visible vitality. Membership records at the Johannesburg office in 2004 indicated a total union membership nationally of no more than 9,000. With consistently declining union density in the sector, did this represent a blunting of domestic workers' political capacities instead of an assertion of their political agency in a democratic political formation?

Democratization and the Depoliticization of Domestic Workers

This "collective demobilization" of domestic workers in post-apartheid South Africa is reminiscent of the fate of other sections of the organized working class following the transition to democracy and has been analyzed by South African labor studies scholars. Gay Seidman (1994) demonstrated that the authoritarian state in South Africa (and Brazil) shaped the character of the militant labor movement because it reinforced exclusion at the levels of both work and community, at the same time as it denied oppositional party politics. Democratization has therefore necessarily presumed a different relationship between organized labor and the state. The availability of legitimate institutional channels for managing industrial relations (Adler and Webster 2000), a formal alliance between the state and labor (Adler and Webster 2000), the siphoning of unions' human resources (von Holdt 2003), and workers' own political subjectivities in response to changes in the state and capitalism (Kenny 2004, 2007), have been shown to have conditioned a shift in organized labor's (unions') relationships to the state. A reconfigured, less conflictual labor movement has thus been necessitated by the transition to a democratic state. But, looking at workers' relationships to the state offers another level at which to consider the contradictory demobilization of organized workers following their political incorporation.

In the democratic statecraft for the sector, the availing of workers for protection through their construction as "vulnerable" positioned the state as the articulator, representative, and protector of workers' collective interests (chapter 3). This displaced the union from that role and had specific implications for domestic workers' collective mobilization. As shown in chapter 3, through domestic workers' imputed "vulnerability," the state positioned itself as the arbiter of their interests, in ways that obfuscated the union.

In the investigation into the possibilities of minimum wages and conditions of employment for the sector, for instance, the union was included but simultaneously bypassed. Stakeholders were invited to offer submissions in the initial phase, to which COSATU responded with an important submission, and union representatives were consulted during all phases of the research. But, the state's "will to empower" positioned unions as the beneficiaries of the state's efforts as protectors of the sector rather than as the representative of workers' collective interests. National and provincial workshops that brought together "role players" as part of the investigations into Sectoral Determination Seven consistently deemphasized the role of the union as representatives of workers and advocates for their collective interests. A union official who participated in a workshop in Pretoria, for example, described her participation as follows: "They [the government] really are trying to help us very much. I remember in that meeting, we explained what we needed from them to help us do our work better. They were very supportive, really. So, we work together in that way. We help them too to make sure this sectoral determination gets enforced."

And another, who was asked specifically what position regarding the Sectoral Determination the unions were advancing in their meetings with the labor department, said: "We tell them we are suffering in the backyards, and we discuss how we can work together to stop this suffering. They ask us what they can do for us, and we discuss training centers, and workshops with the employers."

In the meetings leading up to the promulgation of Sectoral Determination Seven, therefore, union officials were rendered the subjects of the state's protective impulse and responded in ways that negated their role as representatives of workers' collective interests. In the national hearings, surveys, and taxi rank campaigns, the union was bypassed as the articulator of workers' interests as the state positioned itself in that role. Similarly, in the process through which the Sectoral Determination was promulgated, the union was excised almost completely as a representative and advocate of domestic workers' collective interests. Understood as "vulnerable" and poorly organized, the Employment Conditions Commission substituted state fiat for the processes of collective bargaining between employers and employees that would traditionally negotiate the wages and working conditions of the sector but which was not feasible given the structural constraints of the sector. There was therefore a facilitated substitution of employer and employee associations by state agencies.

In an important example of this state positioning of itself as articulator and representative of worker interests, the efforts to include domestic workers within the Unemployment Insurance Fund (UIF) suggested a promiscuity between the state's competing interests for the sector. A Gender Monitoring and Advocacy Coalition for the inclusion of domestic workers into the Unemployment Insurance Fund (GMAC-UIF) was set up by one agency of the state, the governmental Commission for Gender Equality, and utilized a coalition that included SADSAWU as merely one among many interested parties rather than as the only worker-controlled representational body. The coalition then petitioned another agency of the state, Parliament, for the inclusion of domestic workers within the UIF. Significantly, petitioning Parliament as part of the Commission-led coalition, SADSAWU was reduced to an auxiliary voice to the primary positioning by a state body of itself as the advocate for workers' interests. This analysis betrays a more worker-centered mode of analysis than that deployed by Fish (2006a, b).

Systematically, the democratic statecraft that substituted the state for the union delegitimated the political capacities of workers, and unwittingly demobilized the union. With the elaboration of formal institutionalized channels for the resolution of labor disputes, workers have for the first time access to an unparalleled state-mandated system of protecting their conditions of employment. A necessary result has been the reformulation of the role of the union as a militant advocate for workers' interests. Instead, the union functions in an auxiliary, supportive role to the state, which has simultaneously depoliticized the union and ensured more effective state oversight of workers' interests in relation to wages and working conditions.

The state's elaboration of an extensive apparatus to manage the labor relations of the sector, most notably the Commission for Conciliation, Mediation, and Arbitration (CCMA), made state agencies the primary spaces for workers to claim their rights in ways that redefined the role of the union as the advocate of workers' rights. This was captured most convincingly and succinctly by a worker outside the CCMA one day: "I don't need the union. They eat your money, when you can come to the CCMA now and they do even more for you to solve your problem, because they are the government. They got the power." With a state agency dedicated to resolving labor relations issues for workers, workers invariably did not see any role for the union as their advocate in these processes. As Lebogang Nkuna added, "The government is protecting us. Only the employers are trying to keep us down. We just have to go to the CCMA, and they'll solve the problem."

In a context in which the state functions as the protector and advocate of workers, workers questioned the utility of the union. In part, as a result, SADSAWU, rather than being activated by the extensive democratic statecraft around domestic workers and becoming the model of an active citizenship, has instead been reduced in numbers and stripped of its political function as a union. This happened, in part, as a compound effect of the union's existing weaknesses.

SADSAWU's predecessor, SADWU, was marred by internal leadership wrangles, financial mismanagement, and a series of other dysfunctions that tainted the unionizing possibilities in the sector. SADSAWU bears this legacy, in combination with a state proactively committed to the sector. The result has been a reconstruction of the union's function to deal almost exclusively with matters of labor relations, on behalf of the state, rather than on behalf of workers. On an average day, SADSAWU's dingy office in downtown Johannesburg functions merely as a clearinghouse and referral center for various agencies of government. Members visit or call with an employment-related problem and are referred to the appropriate agency of government, converting the union into an intermediary between the worker and the state. Eunice Dhladhla, deputy general secretary of SADSAWU, based in the Johannesburg branch, explained the main function of the union, highlighting its political deactivation:

> The Department of Labor gave us the go-ahead that if there are these cases, we can write letters to the Labor Department, asking the inspectors to go and inspect what kind of house, and inspecting—Does she comply with the laws? Does she get the minimum wage? As Mdladlana says, it's R800 [$133][6] if the person is starting to work for you. Does he/she work the right hours? So, the inspectors go out and find out does that certain employer comply with the laws. So, that's what we are doing. If there is someone who was raped or underpaid, we just write a letter to the labor department and give them the address to go and inspect. . . . They write back to us and say we've received your letter, and we are sending the inspector immediately.

With the state positioned as the representative and advocate of workers' interests, the union functions as part of the extended state machinery dedicated to effective implementation of Sectoral Determination Seven and the maintenance of orderly labor relations within the sector. This effectively procedural function is, in some ways, a necessary function of the shifting relations bound to be produced by a movement of organized workers in conversation with a democratic state so willing and eager to assist in reforming the sector. At the same time, as has been remarked of the labor movement more generally (Adler and Webster 2000), the union's reconstructed role has resulted in a facilitating role for the state and a revisioned advocacy and political role for the union.

Nowhere was this more clear than in an analysis of union meetings and union organizing workshops during 2004 and 2005. Held on weekends, union meetings were a stark indication of both the demobilization of workers and the depoliticization of the union. With barely more than a half-dozen workers at any membership meeting, workers used the opportunity to express their grievances—directed not at the union and membership but instead at the Department of Labor representative who was invariably invited, and who used the meeting as a de facto forum for dealing with individual labor relations issues.

More dramatic was the format of union organizing workshops seeking to recruit new members. Usually starting with a prayer, then a revolutionary song, the agenda was remarkably consistent: The invited Department of Labor official(s) would spend the remaining meeting time explaining the new legislation, fielding questions on individual employment matters from the group, and distributing Department literature and booklets. The meeting would close with another revolutionary song and the passing around of union subscription forms. In all of the union organizing workshops I attended, the role of the union never extended beyond information dissemination on behalf of the Department of Labor. The obfuscation of the political function of the union in these meetings and workshops was so dramatic that, even down to the people involved, there would be almost no difference in form or content between a Department of Labor versus a union meeting, except in the opening and closing song. The union's erstwhile militance had been distilled into a few minutes of poetic, but ephemeral, song.

This fledgling relationship between the state and union was dramatic but also more complex. While the state clearly positioned itself in relation to workers in ways that made the union redundant rather than more effective, there was necessarily a different relationship to be drawn between an authoritarian state assaulting worker rights, and a democratic state committed to enhancing them. Eunice expressed the consciousness of the union that a democratic state requires cooperative rather than adversarial relations:

> Since it was Labor Department . . . Not like before, when it was [Department of] Manpower . . . we've got a very good relationship with them. Like you see, we've got a lot of documents from them. When there is something new, we go and collect the government gazettes, everything. So, when workers come it's easy for us to go and give those books to them . . . so we are working hand in hand. Very nice.

> When we were in the union in SADWA in the 1980s, we would write letters to the employers, but they would tell us "you unions, can't you see that these

workers will be dismissed because you are demanding 300, as I'm paying my worker 150. So, now these workers would be out of jobs if you are carrying on like this." And at that time it wasn't easy, because it was the [Department of] Manpower. No one was on our side. The only law that was protecting us was, what do you call it, Section 21? When you write a letter to them, Manpower, they would just tear that letter, and no one can help you. But, since it was Labor, when you go there, or take the worker with you, something will happen.

In directly comparing the past, SADWA under the Department of Manpower, to SADSAWU under the Department of Labor, Eunice suggested the necessity of reconstructed relationships in a different political formation. The union's reconstituted relationship with the state has followed the trajectory of organized labor more broadly as a result of the necessities of democratization, from an advocacy role to a simple "education" function.

SADWU's campaigning during the 1980s and into the 1990s continued to represent a tradition of "social movement unionism" (Seidman 1994) in which the union extended its political advocacy to sociopolitical issues beyond the workplace. For SADWU, one of the most distinctive elements of this was its political struggle for child care as deeply connected to the predicament of domestic workers. Margaret Nhlapo, an organizer for SADWU in the 1980s, for example, said: "It is very, very difficult. This is the one thing that causes a lot of heartache amongst our members. Our own children are running in the street while we must smile at our employer's children. In the cities we may redress this by calling for crèches, for time-off."

More specifically, SADWU threw its weight behind the COSATU Resolution on Child Care that cut to the heart of the domestic workers' location in a particular political economy of care:

Noting that . . . the bosses, state and tradition has always made childcare the private, exclusive responsibility of women,

Believing . . . that childcare is a social responsibility. That this responsibility should be shared by the bosses, the state and parents.[7]

At the same time, SADWU campaigned as vigorously for housing for its members as it did for comprehensive legislation to cover the employment relationship. "SADWU should campaign for houses to make our members independent of the employer," said Margaret Nhlapo in 1993, adding that "even when domestic workers are covered by the new laws, they will still be oppressed because of that backyard room" (*The Shopsteward*, Feb/Mar 1993, 17).

Not only was the range of issues SADWU dealt with much broader than the workplace, but their organizing was creative, vigorous, and militant. They used inventive strategies such as picketing "bad madams," which even made national newspaper headlines. "The move to embarrass the 'madams,'" reported the *Sunday Times* in 1994, "follows a picket by about 100 domestic workers outside a house in Jan Hofmeyr last Saturday, in solidarity with Miss Esther Msuthwana who was dismissed by Mrs. Lorraine de Beer" (August 4). The strategy proved quite effective, followed by littering suburban electricity boxes with notices to keep employers aware of the presence of the union as a guardian of workers' interests. And, SADWU was quite militant. Margaret remarked on this in commenting on a minimum wage campaign SADWU had organized in 1989: "We were very proud that so many workers came. They braved the weather and came. They had the spirit. And some were very militant" (*Speak*, 1990, 25:4). Indeed, SADWU had even organized a major protest march during the 1990s in which workers took over the streets of downtown Johannesburg with their brooms and mops, wielding them in a decisive display of force. "For the second time in just over a year, domestic workers in the Witwatersrand took to the streets of Johannesburg this week, demanding recognition for their union," reported a local daily (*The Star*, July 22, 1990). "Hoisting brooms, brushes, buckets and other cleaning equipment," it continued, "about 5 000 domestic workers marched from Saratoga Avenue near Berea to the Johannesburg regional offices of the Department of Manpower in President Street."

SADSAWU failed to emulate the politicized militancy of SADWU, in part, as a reflection of the shift from an authoritarian to a democratic state. The result is that, at a time when domestic workers have been incorporated politically in a democratic context where political capacities should be enhanced, SADSAWU has been stripped of its political content. In a telling statement, Selinah Vilakazi, Gauteng regional organizer at SADSAWU, when asked what the union does for workers, replied, "We educate them. We give them education that now they've got their rights."

In this summary statement, Selinah captured the reduction of the union's once-militant unionism to a mere education function. The deflated purpose of the union seems ironic given domestic workers' incorporation as political agents in post-apartheid South Africa. Instead of activating them politically, domestic workers' inclusion has paradoxically depoliticized them. The result has been a privatization for workers of their politics, with different implications for the activation of domestic workers as political agents.

The "Scorpion" and the Privatization of Politics

For SADSAWU and organized domestic workers, their political incorporation did not activate their existing political capacities. This resulted in the contradictory effect of domestic workers privatizing their politics in a market-based union substitute, "the *Scorpion*." Not to be confused with the former elite division of the National Prosecuting Authority with the same name, Scorpion is a private legal management service that targets the poor and offers an insurance-type scheme in which very low monthly premiums guarantee private legal assistance when needed. More than one-third of the workers interviewed belonged to the Scorpion legal service, and most as a substitute for membership of a union. As Nthabiseng Moshoeshoe said, "when you are joining the union, you must understand you are giving your money away each month, and for what? I know when I need the help, if my employer says I must go, or something, I will get the lawyer from the Scorpion."

As a generalized legal insurance policy, workers turned in the thousands to "the Scorpion," literally transferring their political capacities to the market. Selinah Vilakazi, regional organizer for the union, drew the connection between the union's demobilization and the Scorpion's mobilization of workers: "It's very hard (for those who are not union members) because they go to CCMA, but they don't know the procedures. It's very hard for them. But they are so stubborn. They join the Scorpion, which doesn't help them . . . now, our membership is declining. It's because the Scorpion is there, and they are grabbing the workers to come to them. The others, they go to CCMA without joining the union. It's so difficult when they are not represented."

Some workers reflected consciously on the direct relationship between the deactivation of workers' public class politics and their turn to private, market-based solutions: "You see, the union, who is it working for, I'm asking you?" inquired Dorcus Mofokeng. "You see, if you pay them, they must work for you. But, who are they working for? I see they are working with the employers, working with the government, with you also. They work too much for all these people, then you say, who are they working for?" Petunia Sono added: "The government is helping the domestic workers, with the CCMA and those things also. Then the Scorpions they also help you make sure if you are dismissed, then you can go there, you can also tell your story and get your severance [pay]."

Workers remained skeptical of the capacity of unions as an agent of representation, in part, as a result of the availability of state institutions and agencies that so effectively guarantees protection of worker rights in labor disputes. With an extensive state-managed labor relations system for domestics, workers joined the Scorpion legal service because it offered them representation in the context of a protective and supportive state. Seeing the state's new labor relations system for domestic workers as protective context, the necessity of the kind of collective representation offered by unionization was deactivated, and they turned to the Scorpion as an instance of a privatized politics.

But, inasmuch as the turn to the Scorpion service suggested the protective benefits of state legislation in workers' minds, it referenced the continued practical limitations on workers' now-guaranteed constitutional rights to freedom of association. In a context where employers remain terrified of the possibilities of worker unionization, workers suggested that their turn to the Scorpion was a "safer" option. "*Hayi!* [No!]," exclaimed Miriam Mamatela. "Shuh, if I join the union, she will dismiss me tomorrow! [The Scorpion?] That way, it's better." And another worker outside a Scorpion office one day said: "I can't even say union with my madam. She will tell me to pack up and go. . . . With the Scorpion, she is not afraid that I am going to ask for higher wages, because the Scorpion it is only there for you when you are dismissed, to help you to get a lawyer to fight against your dismissal."

Historical fear of domestic worker unionization among employers, therefore, limited the possibilities post-apartheid of domestic workers' unionization. These comments also suggested the limited range of representation offered by the Scorpion legal service. In exchange for very low monthly fees, the Scorpion service could be utilized effectively only upon dismissal. While many workers utilized the union during this period of crisis (i.e., following dismissal) as well, many Scorpion members indicated their own awareness of the limits of this form of representation. Mpumelelo Ndala said:

> Definitely, I have thought about the Scorpion, whether I must join, and what they can do for me if I pay them. My friends where I am working, they are all the members. But, they also complain, you see . . . because when you want to get more money, you can't go to them, really. If she is paying you the minimum wage, let's just say, but you think that it is not enough because you are working there many years, and you do even the shopping for the family . . . then you can't go to the Scorpion. Maybe only when she fires you, then you can go to them, to go to the courts. It's only very much for when you lose your job, not for while you are having this job.

Workers' turning to the Scorpion service in such large numbers was therefore both confirmation of the efficacy of state protection in providing a formalized industrial relations system that guarantees workers access to agencies that guarantee their rights *and*, paradoxically, a reflection of workers' evaluations of the extent to which they can mobilize publicly as workers in a collective class politics. For inasmuch as the Scorpion is a privatized (market) solution, it is also a privatized (individual) solution, reflecting an individualizing logic in workers' efforts to secure better and more protected conditions of employment.

Privatizing Politics, Reproducing Class

Widely understood as a politically unorganized class of workers, the post-apartheid state's efforts to turn "servants" into workers would have presumably activated these workers' political capacities. In an ironic contradiction, an active historical tradition of a public class politics among domestic workers has been muted by the terms of these workers' inclusion. Politically incorporated as "vulnerable," the democratic statecraft has positioned itself as the articulator and representative of workers' interests, as well as its protective agent, in ways that have substituted the state for the union and demobilized domestics. Stripped of much of its political content, the union has been transformed into an auxiliary of the state. Paradoxically, some domestic workers have instead privatized their politics in the market-based "Scorpion."

The combined constraints of this muting of domestic workers' class politics limits the possibilities for their political advocacy against the class hierarchies and inequalities at the root of paid domestic work. The democratic statecraft has therefore, quite ironically, stunted domestic workers' capacity for an activated politics that challenges the logics of their function in, and location as, a reproducing class.

7

"Like the Heart in the Body"

Manyanos and Mother-Workers

On a warm Sunday afternoon, I asked Sophia Ncobo—a domestic worker of more than forty years—what was the most important part of her life. She replied without hesitation, "my children. I am still the mother to my children. They are the most important to me, to have a good life."

Sophia's three children were raised by her mother in a township outside Port Elizabeth while Sophia worked as a live-in domestic worker raising the two children of her employer in Troyeville, a suburb of Johannesburg. This disconnect between the immediate mothering for pay in her working life and the "mothering from a distance" (Parreñas 2001b, 361) of her own children in her private life inspired a certain valuation of motherhood for Sophia. "It is hardest when you think you are working to make sure your children don't have to live in hardship and suffering," she said. "To be the mother that you can give them that opportunity is the most important thing to me. To protect them, and make things better for my children. There is nothing else important to me."

Like most of the domestic workers in this study, this expressed importance of motherhood found collective expression in Sophia's membership of the religious *manyano*. "I joined a long time ago," narrated Sophia. "The Methodist manyano. It was a place for the women who were married. . . . I joined when things were very bad . . . we were all domestic workers, and it was this place, where, in the time when you were there . . . you were talking about your problems and how you must keep up the morals . . . the manyano has always been like the heart in the body."

The *manyano*[1]—or mother's prayer union—is a distinctive church-based organization of married mothers who, through regular weekly meetings, involve themselves primarily in praying and preaching. The name, manyano, is believed to derive from *ukumanyai*, an isiXhosa word meaning "to unite" (Moss 1999). These church groups remain one of the most remarkable and enduring aspects of domestic workers' associational lives in Johannesburg. Reportedly referenced as "the 'heartbeat' of local churches in Southern Africa" (Moss 1999, 109), they are "the oldest, largest, and most enduring and cohesive not only of all black African women's organizations, but of all African organizations in South Africa" (Brandel-Syrier 1962, 97). This significant movement has always been associated, in particular, with domestic workers.

Usually hidden behind closed doors, domestic workers' invisibility is forcefully disrupted on manyano meeting days when they can be seen along the pavements of white suburbia in their distinctive uniforms.[2] Just over half the women in this study belonged to a manyano (54%), and all who did, like Sophia Ncobo, regarded it as among the most important aspects of their lives. While overall membership rates for manyanos had started to decline by the 1990s (Theilen 2005, 91), manyano membership continued to remain a powerful and enduring force in the associational lives of the domestic workers in this study. Florence Dhlomo, a forty-nine-year-old mother of three, working live-in for a family in Killarney, also summarized the importance of manyano membership for this group of workers: "I have been in the manyano many years. We are the women's group . . . we are all women . . . and [most are] domestic workers also. Because we need God. Especially in our lives . . . see, now that's how this manyano it becomes important to me . . . all of us here the domestic workers."

As "the most visible and widespread of all women's voluntary associations in the region" (Epprecht 1993, 202), manyanos bear a special relationship to paid domestic work. Historically, and even today, manyano "membership consists predominantly of live-in domestic workers" (Theilen 2005, 88).[3] The result has been a powerful and enduring relationship between manyanos and domestic workers in South Africa. This intimate relationship is evidenced by the correspondence of the structure of the working week for domestic workers during apartheid and the schedule of manyano activities. Thursday afternoons, or "Sheila's Day"—in response to domestic workers' naming of the day—became both the widespread "day" off for domestic workers[4] and the entrenched meeting time for manyanos.

So important is the manyano in the lives of domestic workers, specifically, and black African women more generally, that Deborah Gaitskell argues "those interested in exploring the history of African women's lives, or indeed social change and . . . political mobilisation of different African communities, cannot afford to ignore what was happening in the . . . world of the manyano" (1990, 271). Certainly, given the presumed failure of domestic workers to organize successfully as workers, it is interesting that South African domestic workers are so remarkably organizable as mothers in the manyanos.

The importance of the manyanos to domestic workers is indicative of the overwhelming role of religion in South African domestic workers' lives. Many detailed ethnographies of domestic service recognize the, often primary, importance of religion in the associational lives of domestic workers (Barnes 1993; Gill 1994; Constable 1997; Yeoh and Huang 1998; Parreñas 2001). For African American domestic workers, too, the church has been demonstrated to be pervasively important; Bonnie Thornton Dill for example, notes that for this group of workers, "their participation in various social groupings, particularly in the church, and their reputations as decent, law-abiding, hard-working citizens offset the low status of domestic work" (1988, 49). Similarly, for Elizabeth Clark-Lewis, the churches were the pivotal institutions around which African American domestic workers organized their work and family lives: "After the family, the church was the most important means of individual and community expression" (1987, 200). In fact, church participation became the basis for a restructuring of the occupation for African American domestic workers: "Not being able to attend regular services on Sundays and generally feeling left out of the continuing life of their churches became for these women a potent symbol of the restrictions of live-in labor" (Clark-Lewis 1987, 203), and as Phyllis Palmer therefore concludes, "workers preferred part-time and day work because they could have Sundays off" for church (1989, 69). In studies of contemporary migrant domestic work, the significance of religious attachments for Filipina domestic workers in North America, Europe, and East Asia have been documented as well (Constable 1997; Yeoh and Huang 1998; Parreñas 2001a).

In attempting to explain the idiomatic and practical significance of religion for these workers, however, religion is often understood as a privatized and escapist solution to domestics' daily struggles in ways that deactivate workers politically. Julia De Souza's attribution of this presumed "magical thinking" of Brazilian domestic workers to a "marginal type of world view" issuing from their background in precapitalist subsistence economies is an extreme example of this (1980, 46). Others have made an effort to interrogate the role of religion in the lives of domestic workers, but often reproduce the idea that it functions as no more than an emotional salve. Nicole Constable, for instance, argues that Filipina maids in Hong Kong invoke religion as "an aid in controlling negative feelings towards employers" (1997, 192)—effectively, a coping mechanism—while Brenda Yeoh and Shirlena Huang argue that for Filipina maids in Singapore, going to church is "primarily to seek solace in a habitual refuge" (1998, 597).

For those who have tried to understand religion as part of the associational lives of domestic workers, it is analyzed as a social space for communal gathering, developing a sense of identity through community, and accessing social support. Cock (1989), for example, discussed domestic workers' religious activities under "social life" and as an aspect of their leisure pursuits. Rhacel Parreñas (2001a) offers a more analytical perspective, arguing that the church's significance for Filipina migrant domestics in Rome is as a "private domain" (204) that assists in coping with the "dislocation of nonbelonging" (197). Here, social services organized by the church allow workers' associational lives to draw on forms of social support. Indeed, for Yeoh and Huang, the church comes to organize a collective identity for workers as they "forge a sense of identity and comradeship with compatriots" through regularized church services and activities (1998, 597). Lesley Gill's study of domestic workers in La Paz concurs with this reading that religion offers these workers an important space to construct identity and a sense of belonging by providing "an institutional base for developing important social relationships. It also provides the rituals to validate these emerging bonds, which help to create a shared sense of community" (1994, 131). In South Africa, McNeil (1989), too, has suggested that the significance of religion for domestic workers lies in its provision of a source of social interaction and the practical social support attendant to this.[5]

Religion is clearly an important part of the associational life of domestic workers, providing a coping infrastructure, identity, and social support. But, for South African domestic workers, why does religious activity coalesce into content so strongly organized around these mothers' prayer unions and their identities as mothers? To begin answering this question, a brief look at the history of the manyanos and the scholarship attempting to understand it is first necessary.

The Anti-Politics or "Private Politics" of Manyanos?

In 1905, in the earliest written record of such an event, a manyano gathering took place at Verdrict in Natal (Attwell 1997). On the Witwatersrand, the manyano movement began in 1907 with the establishment of the Wesleyan Methodist prayer union at Potchefstroom by Mrs. S. Gqosho (Gaitskell 1990). This was the culmination of a process of revivalism in the mission churches (Anglican, Methodist, and American Board Mission) during the late nineteenth century that had spread across the country. Already in the 1880s in the eastern Cape, missionary wives were organizing groups of African women into regular meetings "of shared 'testimony,' exposition of biblical verses and extemporaneous prayers" that came to define the manyanos (Gaitskell 1990, 255). In the former Natal province, Transkei, and Transvaal, women's revivalist prayer meetings characterized by singing, prayer, and preaching had also begun, "help[ing] women in their new responsibilities as Christian wives and mothers" and representing the informal forerunners of the more structured manyano movement (Gaitskell 1990, 255–56). By the turn of the century, African women were gathering across the country in their distinctive manyano uniforms "safeguarding female chastity, marital fidelity, and maternal and domestic responsibilities" (Gaitskell 1990, 251).

With its origins partially located in concerns around the sexual "purity" of young unmarried African women and in the praying for families (Gaitskell 1982), the manyano movement in the first half of the twentieth century located womanhood in Christian constructions of motherhood and family values, and in the domestic sphere, with missionary injections of what Gaitskell (1990) calls "devout domesticity." Weekly manyano meetings evolved into revivalistic praying sessions, becoming the stronghold of married African women, and growing in strength. On the Witwatersrand, specifically, the movement gathered momentum quickly—from 7 members in 1907 at its formation, to 800 in 1913, to nearly 10,000 by World War II (Gaitskell 1990). Johannesburg alone had a membership of nearly 3,500 by the mid 1940s, and by the 1970s, South Africa had a total manyano membership of 34,000 (the largest on the continent) (Gaitskell 1990, 269).

Throughout this period of manyano popularity and growth, the prayer unions adopted and preached a conception of womanhood tied centrally to domesticity and traditional family structures. Cynthia Phakathi, a full-time live-out domestic worker, for instance, explained, "They teach us to be good women [in the manyano], and to our husbands, and all the family. We learn not to drink . . . and we tell stories on how to keep your house."

At the same time, manyanos locate hardship in "other-worldly" sources rather than in structures of oppression, advocating collective prayer rather than collective action. Mabel Mabena, a live-in domestic worker and member of the Rosebank Methodist Manyano, for example, explained, "you suffer because God wants you to suffer. When you want to end your suffering, you must pray to God. You must become good, and you must pray." Furthermore, manyanos have remained within the logic of racial separatism rather than offering a challenge to it.[6]

It seems understandable then that manyanos are sometimes considered conservative ideological mechanisms for reproducing relations of subordination for African women. As Gaitskell notes, respected ANC women's leader of the 1950s, Lilian Ngoyi, publicly attacked the manyanos for their conservatism and apolitical orientation as she observed them in their common practice of weeping, noting that she "felt there was something very wrong, for after weeping nothing would be done. They all waited for some power from God" (Ngoyi, quoted in Gaitskell 1990, 270). Belinda Bozzoli too, saw the manyanos as a conservative, and even antifeminist, project given that their constructions of motherhood sought to "conserve and consolidate the family and the woman's position within it" (1983, 165). And in Lyn Holness's personal account, she suggests the apoliticism of manyanos by arguing that "the Manyano movement has had neither a theological nor a socio-political thrust . . . neither has it had a transformative goal, other than to equip its members to deal with their specific situations" (1997, 23). Not simply apolitical, women's involvement in manyanos may be a substitute for overt political action and therefore antipolitical. Consider the following words offered by aging Sophia Ncobo: "With our uniforms, we are God's servants. . . . It keeps us away from all the trouble at that time, the what do you call them, the [political] organisations. They were saying freedom, but they were killing the people. My sister's boy was also in jail. In the manyano, we didn't make trouble. We were praying."

Despite Sophia's rendering of manyano prayer as antithetical to political organizing as a mechanism for change, historians have increasingly uncovered the role of manyanos in the political mobilizations against the segregationist and apartheid regimes. Manyano women were important instigators of the 1913 anti-pass demonstrations in Bloemfontein (Wells 1991), in "one of the most impressive examples of Christian women's involvement in local political affairs" (Sundkler and Steed 2000, 412). A few years later, manyano women participated in the Thaba Nchu protest, regarded as "a landmark in women's resistance" (Sundkler and Steed 2000, 412). The 1929 Potchefstroom protest against residential permits was probably influenced by the manyano movement (Gaitskell 1990), and William Beinart notes "it seems to have been the manyano that provided the initial organisational core for the women's movement during the boycott" in Herschel in the 1920s (1987, 239).

In the 1940s, manyano women defended women's rights to brew beer, in 1954 resisted expropriation of African-owned property and forced removals, and in 1955 protested against the implementation of inferior education for Africans (Kuumba 2002). In 1985, the Methodist manyano of the Cape district issued an unambiguous statement of their politicization by condemning the apartheid regime, calling it a "heretical system of separation" maintained by the "tyrannical arrogance" of the regime. They stated: "We appeal for the end of apartheid in its entirety, for a unitary system of education for all South Africans, and the immediate release of all detainees." Of course, they concluded their statement with: "Despite all this, we continue to pray for the Government" (*Argus*, November 23, 1985).

But the political importance of the manyanos goes well beyond the role they played in facilitating formal protests and/or organized resistance. Claims that manyanos have and may be seen as antipolitical are complicated by a closer reading of the interpretive meanings domestic workers attach to their involvement in the manyanos. Marc Epprecht (1993) argues in a study of the equivalent *kopano* movement in Lesotho, that the political valence of these mother's prayer unions lies in what they tell us about their members' understandings of their social and political positionings, suggesting a "private politics." Barbara Moss (1999) in a discussion of the equivalent *ruwadzano* movement in Zimbabwe, suggests that the focus on marriage and reproduction intimated women's economic insecurity, which increased the importance of traditional constructions of womanhood for status. As Gaitskell notes about these mother's prayer unions under apartheid, their popularity reflected the context of political and social change in which these women's roles as mothers were threatened: "Undeniably . . . part of the appeal of the new message and the community it fostered was the priority and support it offered to motherhood in a time of economic and social upheaval" (1990, 252; see also Gaitskell 1983).

In its content, the manyano movement under apartheid offered a commentary on the way black women understood the state as threatening their social and familial roles through widespread disruption of African family forms. Their response, through the manyanos, while seemingly conservative and apolitical in its defense of womanhood tied to motherhood, was, as Gaitskell (1983) perceptively suggests, a commentary on the political constraints on their lives. Given the assault of the state on the black African family, family life became, for black women, "something to struggle *for*, rather than against." When manyano women in 1913 in Bloemfontein went to prison rather than show their passes confirming employment by whites "they were fighting to remain at home as housewives" (Gaitskell 1983, 225), rather than be coerced into low-waged employment for whites. It was in this context of state attack against African livelihoods through the forced disintegration of black African familial life that domestic workers' seemingly conservative participation in a movement that preached a return to domesticity may have signaled something else.

In post-apartheid South Africa, domestic workers, through their participation in the manyanos, make legible their positioning—in particular—as compromised mothers and dehumanized workers. In their sustained embrace of the familial-centered motherhood preached by the manyanos, domestic workers express the continued fragility of sustaining stable families through the tenuous political economy of care in which they circulate as migrants. Their turn to the manyanos identifies, and responds to, one of the most acute sources of pain for domestic workers in a post-apartheid social and political order—their inability to remain present mothers to their children. In constructing an autonomous space in the manyanos organized around familial life, domestic workers not only comment on the logics of their position as compromised mothers. They also restore an independent sense of self that suggests, and responds to, their position as dehumanized workers.

Compromised Mothers: Reconstructing Motherhood

The presumed failure of domestic workers to organize collectively as workers is not often supplemented by an analysis of their mobilization as mothers.[7] Others have recognized the importance of motherhood for domestic workers. For example, Geraldine Pratt (2004) mentions a similar valuing of motherhood among Filipina domestic workers in Canada, and Mary Romero documents a similar process for Chicana workers in the United States. "Since the status of motherhood is much higher than that of domestic worker," she argues, "identifying with the traditional family role served to minimize the stigma attached to the work role. . . . [This] was part of these women's strategy for coping with the stigma of being a domestic worker. In essence, they maintained a social identity based on the family rather than on the work role. . . . Since the status attached to being a mother and wife is much higher than that assigned to the domestic, women defined their work as adding to the fulfillment of their traditional female role" (1988, 88).

In South Africa, domestic worker's motherism is so forceful that, in a 1995 submission to the Constitutional Assembly, domestic workers referenced their position as compromised mothers in mapping their expectations of constitutional incorporation:

> We are victims of (the) past. After all our work and our pain, some of us have not got enough to give our children. Some of us have got nothing to give our children. That is why we are speaking—so that we can try to make sure that the new constitution will help us to give them a future. . . .
>
> We say that the new constitution must be like a guide to the future that we are building also. We know about working for everything we get. We know also about being patient. But we want to see that we are being patient and working for a future where our children will really enjoy their rights— and everything it does must help us along the path to that future.[8]

In this set of expectations of a transformed political order, domestic workers suggested the significance to them of their position as mothers. Similarly, when the South African Domestic Workers Union (SADWU) was launched in 1986, the general secretary of the union located domestic workers' political aspirations in their positioning as mothers for their children:

> To all Domestic Workers:—
> The future of our children depends on constructive and active participation in our struggle towards liberation. Comrades, don't waste time and energy, join SADWU now and fight along with all other progressive thinking people. (Florrie de Villiers, *SADWU Newsletter*, 1986)

Domestic workers' long-standing participation in, and continued reliance on, manyanos reflects and extends this historical mobilization of their identities as mothers. The significance of motherhood as a potent trope for domestic workers seems obvious. More than any other category of workers or women, they face the irony that, as they work to take care of others' children, they are constrained in their ability to do the same for their own (see chapter 5). Despite efforts to transform them into "workers," domestic workers spoke heart-wrenchingly of the pain they experienced being so intimately invested in the familial lives of others while being agonizingly separated from their own. Especially for live-in domestic workers, constrained in maintaining any independent space of familial life, the manyano and its valorization of domesticity and motherhood made legible their pain and attempted to resolve it.

As continuing migrants between urban and rural, the immediacy of the familial lives of their employers, and the distance of their own (especially live-in domestic work), rehearsed apartheid-era exclusions and the inability to maintain autonomous family lives. Hazel Sondlo summarized very insightfully and emotively in consecutive interviews the continued compromised position of domestic workers with regard to the maintenance of a distinct and separate private life:

> When you were a "girl" in those days [i.e., apartheid] and nothing more, then you were small like a child, even when you are a mother with your own big children. But, that was not for the government . . . [for them,] you were this small girl with no husband, no children, you must go get a pass to work far from your family. . . .
>
> If you are asking me to tell you the honest, to tell you just what life is like, understand this. There is no difference from when we were "*kaffirs*," I'm not lying to you. . . . You have no family to these people that take you from the streets and make you a slave to their family. You are nothing to them. A piece of shit. Your boyfriend comes, he must scream for you from the street, from behind the fence. . . . Your child comes, they make this child their child. . . .
>
> No other person in this country has this thing like this, you must show me. We are the only ones who must live no life like this.

Continued laboring as mothers for other families, while unable to be physically present in the caring for their own, engendered the pain of being compromised mothers. Rose Nakedi continued,

> this black government of ours does not care for its black people. . . . I am in this place [for that reason]. No one in the government is making it different for us. . . . I am working for my family, for my children. Not for me. This is hard work, it is not nice work. I say it is for my children, to be a doctor and a teacher one day. . . . They must have a family one day and live with them, not go once a year when it's Christmas time to see your children grown so big without you. . . . To be like the white people, I want them to live with their children and make their children big with everything they need.

As Rose suggests, for domestic workers, the structure of the occupation exacerbated this restriction of their familial and private autonomy—racialized exclusions uninterrupted by the formal regulation of the sector post-apartheid. For live-in workers, this dislocation was especially pronounced. Phuti Masimane, a retired worker, summarized her experiences under apartheid as a live-in domestic with, "You was having no life. Your life was belonging to your 'madam' and the children [of the employer]."

The "total institution" of live-in domestic service (cf. Cock 1980) continues to constrain the development of any autonomous space for workers post-apartheid. The structure of the working week that leaves little to no time off to cultivate non-workplace ties and affiliations restricts the capacity of workers to develop spaces independent of their working lives. For live-in domestic workers, their physical inseparability from their workplace is particularly constraining; while for live-out workers, the rigors of paid labor during the day and unpaid labor at night leaves little space for independence and autonomy.

Domestic workers' manyano activity issues directly from this constrained ability to maintain a home life distinct from their work, and the consequences of this for their ability to function as mothers. In response, the manyanos reconstruct inclusion both practically and symbolically.

In the pragmatic inclusions offered by the manyanos, domestic workers respond to the constraints they experience. Weekly manyano meetings offer domestic workers the ability to construct an autonomous space from their workplaces. The historical relationship between domestic workers' day off of work and their manyano meetings is evidence of the symbolic value of the manyano as a space separate and distinct from work. So important is this construction of an autonomous space, and its implications for the dependency domestics endure as workers, that one of the most heated issues for many domestics is not being given time off to attend manyano meetings. "The worst thing, I can tell you, the worst is when I can't go to manyano," said Phumla Fikile. "Because they are needing me to iron the washing. My heart pains to stand with the ironing-board and to miss the group."

It is the significance of manyano meetings as an autonomous space from work that makes the failure to attend because of the intrusive demands of the workplace so egregious for workers. This is an aspect of the lives of domestic workers that has not changed since the days of apartheid as Christine Kgapola narrated of her experiences, during apartheid, of not being able to attend church meetings because of her employer's demands on her time: "You feel so lonely, you feel like you are lost. They will get up very late and you will never be able to go to church. When you've finished to do the bathroom and all those beds maybe it'll be about one o'clock. You won't be able to go to church any more. You feel bad . . . You can cry, but it won't help you. They don't feel that pain you've got, wanting to go to church, they don't feel it" (Gordon 1985, 213).

Mercia Willsworth, too, reported that, at that time, one of the main grievances of employees whose jobs involved them in weekend duties was, "we
can't go to church" (1979, 282). This remained one of the grievances of
domestic workers in this study. Margaret "Maggie" Manamela, a fifty-
eight-year-old domestic live-in worker in Berea summed up the sentiments
of manyano women in this regard with clarity and insight: "I work for them
the whole day, and in the night time. That's why it makes me angry. Last
week they told me I must stay to do washing because [of] the boy's rugby
game. . . . I was getting mad. Manyano time is not their time . . . Not time
for 'Maggie' [referring to her employer's renaming of her], but for Margaret Manamela."

In its symbolic function, the valuing of motherhood that underpins the
manyanos offers a reading of these workers' sense of the impositions on
their family and personal lives of their work. Both the performative and
narrative aspects of manyano activity suggest this. The forerunner to the
manyanos, *isililo*, literally translates as "wailing" (Gaitskell 1982), and
the content of a prayer meeting would often require crying late into the
night, a symbolic manifestation of these women's lamentations of the pain
of their lives. Gaitskell documents that "accounts from the 1950s stress
an atmosphere of weeping, sighing and mutual loud commiseration as
women spoke about their troubles regarding children, family, sickness,
and death, as well as their struggle for survival" (1990, 262). She therefore
suggests that the movement "seems to reflect in part the increasing help-
lessness and powerlessness many African women felt in the face of . . .
the social and economic forces which exacerbated their problems as
mothers" (1982, 343). Mabel Dhlamini, not a manyano member, had rec-
ollections of manyano meetings in Nongoma where she grew up that suggested the performative aspects of the manyano and the reflection this
offered on these women's struggles: "They cry, whole night long. I am not
even telling you things that are not right. So loud, they would just cry and
cry and cry. . . . You must think they must be really suffering to cry and cry
like that."

Post-apartheid, domestic workers' continued reliance on the manyanos
as an associational form, and on its performative wailing, expresses their
continuing struggles and dislocation, as well as the pain of being compromised in their capacity to mother. In its narrative content, the manyano's
valorization of the ideology of motherhood that forms its core suggests the
continued and combined effects of familial disruption experienced by domestic workers. Over and over, when they related the importance of the manyanos, it was for the manyanos' validation of a construction of motherhood

175

denied by the political economy of migrancy. Rose Nakedi directly referenced the significance of the manyanos for this group of women as located
in their concerns around appropriate motherhood: "You see, we have to
teach the children the right things. Even when you are not there with your
children, when you are good Christian women then your children also
learn the right things."

Where political regimes deny and structure motherhood capacities as
explicitly as did apartheid, it is not surprising that domestic workers found
manyanos' reconstruction of the meanings of motherhood appealing. As
Parreñas theorizes, a migrant Filipina domestic worker bases her subjective responses "on her dislocations and not on the abstract relations that
mold these dislocations. . . . These responses are acts of resistance against
the dislocations engendered by her positioning in the social processes of
migration and global restructuring" (2001, 251). Post-apartheid, domestic
workers' continued reliance on manyanos as spaces to reconstruct the value
of motherhood, and the autonomous familial lives it suggests, comments
on the coercive economy of care in which they are located, which directly
compromises their capacities as mothers. In response, they value the autonomous space of the manyano and code into it a valuation of motherhood.
The stabilization of the meanings of motherhood within the manyano, not
surprisingly, has resonated powerfully with domestic workers. They deal
with the traumas induced by being compromised mothers through a spiritual
life. Nthabiseng Motsemme, in evaluating a similar privileging of the church
in narratives of emancipation for black South African women, argues that
"in this instance the church plays a contradictory role where it is both born
out of domination and yet provides a space for positive affirmation for
black women in their daily lives" as "a powerful alternative imaginary
space of spiritual time, which becomes an important psychic reservoir for
oppressive [oppressed] women to negotiate and make sense of their trau-
matising present realities" (2002, 665). A similar trauma commented on by
domestic workers through their manyano activity was their dehumanization as workers.

Dehumanized Workers: Reconstructing Personhood

One of the most emotive aspects of paid domestic work conveyed by
workers in this study was of the denial of their personhood. Post-apartheid
democratization has not yet resulted in the conferring of dignity on domestic workers in their relations of employment. Joyce Nhlapo, with her char-

acteristic radical political consciousness, bitingly explained one afternoon on a park bench: "It's worse. You see, for my mother, she was just nobody. For Verwoerd [former prime minister and architect of apartheid], she was nobody. Now Mandela . . . I am a somebody. You understand me? See, this is it. Now . . . I must go into their house and be a nobody. So it's worse. You understand?"

In this incredible narrative, Joyce captures the contradiction of the denial of personhood in the context of domestic workers' incorporation into a political order presuming legal personhood and equality. Workers in this study repeatedly related the ways in which this degradation of the self did not accord with the presumptions of selfhood attendant to the technologies of citizenship within which they had been incorporated by the democratic statecraft after 1994. Most often, this denial of personhood was related to the structure of live-in domestic service, which, in blurring the boundaries between the worker and the person, constrained the development of an independent identity for workers. Mpumelelo Ndala, a thirty-year-old live-in worker in Bez Valley, expressed the dilemmas for personhood of live-in domestic service with, "in the backyard, you are not yourself. I don't know who you are. You are the maid."

Especially for migrant workers, distanced from all that constructs their sense of themselves, the isolation of live-in domestic service produced feelings of disconnectedness from a sense of self—there was a deflation of the conception of self that came with being separated from the stable markers of one's identity. Florence Dhlomo, a domestic worker in Killarney who does not return home to Newcastle for more than a month at a time, summarized the implications of migrant domestic work for maintaining a sense of identity: "To talk about, it's too difficult," she said. "There is worry. Lots, and then you cry [because] everything is so far away. There is nothing. Here, it's only you work . . . so hard. There's no laughter here, or feelings for you, as a person, or to be happy."

Florence captured the loss of an independent identity attendant to the physical laboring and emotional requisites of paid domestic work, where emotive content that defines a sense of humanity and personhood is stripped away. This is compounded by the notorious practice in South Africa of employers denying the personhood of their domestic workers by "renaming" them.[9] Many domestic workers in this study, like "Maggie" quoted earlier, were still subjected to this intensely degrading practice. Mpumelelo Ndala explained, "She can't say my name, she calls me 'Maria'." "Is that your name?" I ask. "No, It's not my real name. My Christian name is Martha . . . but, here, I'm Maria."

Among domestic workers who worked for Indian and other African families, a recurrent complaint surfaced of being referenced by generic terms that did not acknowledge their individuality:

They call you *"ousie"* [a common generic term for domestic worker]. They don't even care about you. (Joyce Nhlapo)

I hate it when she says *"ousie."* Yesterday, I see her telling *medem* Shaida [employer's neighbor] that she, her *"ousie"* will come to wash. Then she comes call me. *Uh-uh!* [No] I don't like that. (Palesa Lebala)

They call for me, they say "Auntie! Auntie." They call for me . . . I have to look behind me, who are they calling? . . . My name is not "auntie." (Nthabiseng Moshoeshoe)

Besides stripping domestic workers of a definitive marker of individual identity, a name, employers engaged in other practices of dehumanization that denied workers' personhood. Of these, domestic workers most referenced the failure of employers to distinguish their humanity, especially in relation to animals. "The dog eats from their plates, but I must sit on the *stoep* [patio] with my *bord* [plate]," complained Precious Mohapi. Judith Mokoena similarly complained: "She doesn't give me proper food. She opens from the freezer the stale food. When I go to the shops, she tells me to buy that fancy food for the dogs. She gives them better food. I'm not even better than the dog."

Often mentioned by workers, the denial of personhood by employers was also evidenced in obscuring their visibility as persons. A union official explained this: "There is this thing, you are not even there. You are invisible. He [male employer] is going to get in to the bath, then he remembers the towel. So, he just walks. Right there. Naked. Just walks by you with his naked[ness], like there is nobody there." Other workers related stories of employers having private conversations in front of them as if they were not there, and failing to greet them as if they were a mere object in the room, rather than a person.

The pervasive sexual exploitation and assaults of domestic workers remained one of the most brutal manifestations of this denial of personhood, in which workers were converted into mere objects, their physical bodies claimed as property by their male employers and for sexual experimentation by their employers' sons (see also Motsei 1990). Workers reported this in worrying numbers, and at least one connected it explicitly to the ways in which it signaled a denial of personhood: "There was a worker who was pregnant and she didn't know whose child it was—the employer or his son. Because they both raped her. She couldn't even go tell anyone, because the whole thing killed her as a person. They just saw her as a body that they can own."

Through these various exclusionary devices, paid domestic work continues to undermine the personhood and personal dignity of domestic workers. The manyanos offered an antidote to this by conveying personhood. More than anything, this is captured in the significance of the uniform in the manyano. The extent to which domestic workers covet the donning of their uniforms may seem perplexing. Epprecht notes the seemingly inexplicable but "notorious loyalty" of Basotho women to their *kopano [manyano equivalent in Lesotho]* uniforms,[10] allegedly even denying their children school fees or clothes in order to buy them (1993, 209). Suzanne Gordon, too, in relating the life story of Miriam Ngulube, a domestic worker during apartheid, notes the significance of the manyano, with particular reference to the importance of the uniform: "Mother's Union meetings are the solace of her life. Dressed in her immaculate black and white uniform with a small-brimmed white hat, she enters transiently the life of community with other similarly-clad women" (1985, 70).

Post-apartheid, talking about their manyano uniforms was one of only a few instances where domestic workers spoke about themselves with pride and self-respect. "Thursdays, we would wear our uniforms. They were beautiful. And, it felt so good. It made you feel so good," said Phuti Masimane. Esther Dhlamini smiled warmly as she recollected, "I used to crochet the belt for our uniforms. Have you seen them? You put on your uniform, and you are looking so wonderful and feeling so nice."

In the symbolic significance of the uniform as conveying personhood and dignity, manyano activity among domestic workers reflected their attempts to redefine their humanity and individuality in the face of workplace relations that undermined these. Lyn Holness's personal experience with her parent's domestic worker attests to this recovery of personhood through the manyano uniform as symbolic of its role in the lives of domestic workers:

> Amongst my earliest memories are those of sitting, as a young child, in the room of Elizabeth Nompi Ngobo, my parents' domestic worker, and watching with fascination as she dressed for Manyano. Fastidiously washed and lavishly perfumed for the occasion, Elizabeth would don her distinctive black, red and white uniform . . . and excitedly set off to join

179

her friends for their weekly Thursday afternoon Manyano meeting. Elizabeth, the white family's domestic worker, had been transformed into Ms E N Ngobo, Manyano woman in uniform, person in her own right. (1997, 21)

This reclamation of a sense of personal identity and dignity through manyano membership is argued by some to represent a powerful "private politics" (Epprecht 1993). This sense is conveyed in Gaitskell's quoting of a missionary's reaction to African women's subversion of the dominant order through their manyano uniforms: "I am sure a lot of the delicious feelings of Woman's rights give spices to the occasion. You should see those Officers sitting up front, in their white caps and blouses and pink ribbon badges" (1990, 265). As this missionary begins to recognize, manyano activity suggests a recovery by domestic workers of not only an independent but also an assertive self—an independent will to refuse dehumanizing conditions of service and to collectively mobilize an alternative construction of the self. Rather than a self tied to degrading service, it is premised on a reconstructed moral vision of personhood different to that presumed by their location as compromised mothers and dehumanized workers.

In domestic workers' reclamation of a self organized around motherhood, they suggest the continuing post-apartheid assault on their capacities to maintain an independent sense of personhood located in the self-enhancing and identity-defining structures of intimate family life. Under apartheid, manyanos were a political tradition developed by African women in a context where they were dislocated from structures of power.[11] That the manyanos continue to function in this way for domestic workers despite a new state so actively committed to politically including them is indicative of the extent to which domestic workers' political capacities have not necessarily been activated by the legal recognition of their status as workers. Instead, that legal recognition merely confirms and deepens their location in the post-apartheid political economy of care as a class of mother-workers.

Domestic Workers—A Class of Mother-Workers?

Lesley Gill, analyzing Bolivian domestic workers' religious commitments, summarizes their associational lives through religion in a very useful way:

Women are more than mothers and wives who provide reproductive labor for families in the private sphere, and workers who struggle to overcome the constraints of their reproductive responsibilities in the public sphere. They also participate in the vibrant social life of Bolivia's most cosmopolitan city by taking part in a broad array of activities that involve churches, schools, and numerous leisurely pursuits. It is in these arenas, as well as in the home and the workplace, where women—rich and poor, Aymara, chola, and white [ethnicities]—create and refashion the images of ethnicity, class, and gender. By so doing, they convey a particular image of themselves and cultivate status, an aspect of class that encompasses continuous claims to honor and importance. (1994, 9)

As Gill suggests here, domestic workers experience and live their realities in ways that suggest their classed location as "servants." In South Africa, domestic workers are a class distinguished by their unique positioning as mother-workers.[12] On the one hand, domestic workers are among a unique group of working women engaged in "mother-work," as they care for others' children. On the other hand, the reason for their engagement in this work is their subjective valuation of the importance of motherhood. Their relationship to waged work as a laboring class is connected to their understandings of mothering and care, and their classed subjectivities are thus completely inflected by their commitments as mothers.

"Who cares for your child?" I asked Mabel Mabena, a live-in worker whose two children were cared for by their grandmother in another province.

"I do," she responded.

Mabel only saw her children once a year for two weeks over Christmas, so I was baffled by the response. "Who takes care of them? I mean, every day," I probed.

"I do," she repeated emphatically.

Later, she explained, "I take care of my children. That is why I am working here looking after the madam's children. I put my love in the envelope every month, and that way, they have clothes, they have food. I am taking care of my children with my work, so one day they can have a better life."

Equating care with provisioning, and provisioning with love, Mabel's waged labor, as for so many other domestic workers, was about mothering. Bridget Kenny (2004) makes insightful arguments about South African retail workers' similar invocations of providing as an expression of motherhood (and fatherhood)—that is, of care. For domestic workers, there is the additional twist, however, that the labor of mothering others' children became an expression of mothering their own. Their classed location as working women was a literal labor of love, as their care work for others' families took care of their own. Understanding breadwinning as a form of care, and money as an expression of love, domestic workers unseated some of their employers' very different understandings of care. For the domestic workers who related their lives in this study, caring for a child was still about being attentive to their needs, but the definition of what kind of attention and what kind of needs allowed them to understand breadwinning as care. So Sarah Nwanedi explained: "I love my children very much, and I make sure they are well taken care of. That's how this money I'm sending takes care of them."

In this understanding of themselves, which finds expression in their manyano activity, South African domestic workers cultivate a sense of themselves as capacitated and active. Florence Dhlomo, when asked what emotion best described her experiences as a member of the manyano, said without hesitation, "empowered." For these mother-workers, experiencing the vulnerabilities of their private and public care work, this sense of empowerment issued precisely from the manyanos' stabilization of the meanings of motherhood and its validation of their understandings of care. Even if separated from their children for all but one or two weeks a year, many still felt powerfully connected to their identities as mothers because of their role in taking care of them through their waged work. The manyanos therefore were, and remain, particularly resonant for this class of mother-workers.

The curious paradox of domestic workers' manyano activity, however, is that their collective demobilization as workers is actually presumed by their collective mobilization as mothers. Constable, in recognizing the importance of religion in the lives of Filipina domestic workers in Hong Kong, argues that it promotes tolerance and passivity: "[D]omestic workers also advocate religious solutions to their difficulties as a substitute for attempting to enact change" (1997, 192). Clearly, while the manyanos make legible domestic workers' location as compromised mothers and dehumanized workers, the response offered arguably retards their collective mobilization publicly and as workers.

Because it is organized outside the realm of public politics and constitutes an imaginary of belonging outside of formal political processes, manyano membership does not activate workers toward change and, in fact, militates against this. While many of the manyano members were active in the union, like Eunice Dhladhla, they saw these aspects of their lives as separate and disconnected, while others referenced the role of the manyano in relation to their public working lives in ways that deactivated them politically. For example, Sophia Ncobo in explaining why she belonged to the manyano but not the union said: "In the manyano we don't talk about these kinds of [political] things. We pray, we don't fight and make trouble. Because God is loving, and for peace."

Similarly, Doris Radebe suggested the ways in which manyano activity and the deference to spiritual salvation—by privately reconciling the conflicts produced by these workers' traumas—limited workers' agitation against the state for a public reconciliation of their positioning as mother-workers: "We solve our problems together, by praying to God. Only God can save your problems, you see. We have got many problems as domestic workers. Our children are very far away. We support them and give them a better future by working so hard, every day. . . . Your troubles become so heavy, then when you pray you can feel God listening."

Doris later added, when I asked about the role of men in relieving the troubles and burdens of child care: "Men, they are useless. *Shuh*, they just make you pregnant, then they run away into their bottle of drink. See, that's why we get strength from being amongst ourselves. . . . We don't even complain about them. We just get the strength from each other." These mother-workers therefore continue to struggle privately. Mabel Mabena said, "We struggle to grow our children. That's all we can struggle for. We cry so God can hear us, and help us give our children a better future."

To dismiss manyano activity as escapism or merely pragmatic in its construction of a sense of community and provision of social support, however, privileges only a certain version of the ways in which motherhood and faith may be important idioms for different constituencies of women. Ultimately, in their manyano activity, South African domestic workers express the pain and pathos of laboring as a class of "mother-workers." In it, they make legible the traumas they face as mothers and workers, and attempt to reconstruct their worth as both.

Conclusion

Formalization of Paid Domestic Work versus Socialization of Reproduction?

In 1994, the *New York Times* reported on its front page that democracy had meant little to nothing for South Africa's domestic workers. "In the months since South Africa's humblest workers went to the polls for the first time," reported the *Times*, "many defying their employers to vote for Nelson Mandela, life has changed little for the people who form the human scaffolding of South Africa's white elite" (October 10, 1994).

As the largest single sector of women's employment in the country, the over one million domestic workers in South Africa were widely regarded as among the most oppressed, exploited, and marginalized sectors of the working class, and there was an urgent expectation for democratization to recognize their plight. In 1994, at the time of the *Times*' concern about South African domestic workers' unchanged positioning, the state's efforts for the sector were lethargic. But, by the time of the study on which this book is based, just a decade later, the post-apartheid South African state had crafted one of the most significant efforts anywhere in the world to formalize, modernize, and professionalize paid domestic work.

This signaled the emancipatory vision of the post-apartheid state, but also pointed to its challenges. While domestic workers have been the beneficiaries of an extensive democratic statecraft attempting to turn "servants" into workers, their positioning as migrant "mother-workers" remains potently unaffected. They have been included within the definition of worker, and their wages and working conditions have improved, yet they remain a cheap reproductive labor force in a continuingly race- and gender-segmented domestic labor market. They have enacted their inclusion at the same time as they narrate their continuing exclusion within the "new" South Africa.

184

They have benefited from the empowering effects of their political incorporation at the same time as it has signaled their subjectification to state power. And, while they have been mobilized as a category by the politics of transition, they have become increasingly depoliticized as a collective. This polysemy of the democratic statecraft for domestic workers is captured in the experience of Hazel Sondlo, with whom this book started, in just one of her experiences of negotiating the limits of her work with her employer—maternity leave.

When Hazel found out she was pregnant, one of her first thoughts, as with most South African domestic workers, was what would happen when her employer found out. "There was a time when if they found out you were pregnant, they just told you to go," she recollected. But, like many of the domestic workers in this study, Hazel knew she would not have to suffer the same fate in a democratic era. Thanks to the post-apartheid state's extensive efforts to recognize "servants" as workers, Hazel could hold her employer accountable in law should she be dismissed unfairly, and she was furthermore entitled to four months' paid maternity leave.

But, Hazel was ambivalent about approaching her employer directly to claim her right to maternity leave. Instead, she chose a less direct strategy. She was mopping the kitchen one day while her employer scrambled about trying to find a lost shoe. Suddenly, Hazel feigned dizziness. Her employer was jolted out of the urgency of her panicked search, and asked, "Hazel, are you okay?"

"Yes, madam," said Hazel. "It's just the baby. I'm pregnant. Three months." Her employer was stunned for a moment. Most likely a bit disconcerted that Hazel did not tell her sooner and probably worried about the implications of Hazel's ability to work as the pregnancy progressed, she said, "You should take it easy." Enjoying the cultivation of a distinct hierarchy of advice and empathy, her employer still managed to prioritize her own interests in ensuring the continuity of Hazel's employment: "But, you know, these days if you go to the clinic regularly and do what the doctors say, you can be just as active, even right until the day of delivery, and even afterwards."

Hazel chose not to say anything. Instead, she stared steadfastly at her employer in a way that communicated without words that she had no intention of working right up to the day of delivery and thereafter. Two months later, while her employer lazed about, Hazel told her that she knew a cousin who could come work for her while she was on maternity leave. Her employer was immediately unnerved. She did not recall approving maternity leave, yet here was Hazel already planning around it?!

Her employer didn't say anything right away, but later that afternoon approached Hazel and seemed agitated. "I can't afford . . ." her voice tapered off, perhaps as she considered the implications of maternity leave for Hazel. "Hazel, I didn't plan for this. I'm not sure this arrangement is going to work out." The anger of being imposed on by Hazel's choice to have a child inflected her tone and body language.

Hazel chose not to say anything. Instead, she started the following week to ask her employer's neighbors about work prospects, knowing that this information would find its way back to her employer. Strategically using the informal networks between employers, she was covertly communicating to her employer that she had one of two choices: allow her maternity leave or risk losing a trusted, reliable employee. After two months of this surreptitious negotiation, Hazel's employer approached her as she was leaving one day and said that she had found a way to support three months' maternity leave, but no more. Hazel knew she was entitled to four. Rather than the silent communication to this point, she now said something. "Ok, madam," she deferred, her body language demure as she walked down the driveway, but concealing a triumphant spirit in which she knew that she had struck a deal that was suitable to her and her employer, however less than ideal for both.

Had Hazel approached her employer without the protections of her newly acquired rights against unfair dismissal, the unexpected penalty to her employer of Hazel's choice to have a child may well have led to the outcome that was so commonplace under apartheid—instant dismissal. The different outcome in this instance was in no small part a consequence of Hazel's emboldened position as a worker with rights. But, there were also limits to Hazel's claiming of those rights. She could very well have asserted her right in law to four months' paid maternity leave and taken her employer to the CCMA had she refused, yet she chose not to. She chose an implicit form of negotiation and chose to take less paid leave than was due to her. Why?

"The relationship with your employer is a very difficult one," said Hazel. "You are young, and you don't understand how relationships work. It's about compromise. It's about feelings. Yes, I am a worker. Yes, I can get four months. But, I'm a part of the family, so I compromised." Like most domestic workers, Hazel did not literally mean she was a part of the family. She understood full well that deep hierarchies and asymmetries of power made her anything but a part of the family. But, in her remarkable explanation, by invoking the trope of "part of the family," she signaled the oxymoron at the core of this analysis of South African domestic workers in a democratic era. The rights that protected Hazel necessitated a management of the highly personalized relationship with her employer through an abstract and depersonalizing political technology. So, on the one hand, she enjoyed the protective aspect of the formalization of her work through her status as worker, but on the other, she distanced herself from a complete erasure of the personalized relations with her employer, even when it meant accepting less than what was her right. This contradictory collision of depersonalizing rights and personalizing intimacy complicated any simple political resolution to the "dilemma" of paid domestic work in post-apartheid South Africa.

On the Subject of Rights, and the "Dilemma" of Domestic Work

Gabrielle Meagher (2002) once asked, "Is it wrong to pay for housework?" "Yes" and "no" answers to that question structure an implicit, albeit tense, debate between scholars of paid domestic work. In one camp, there are those who prefer the socialization or equalization of care (whether that be through public responsibility and provision, or the equalization of responsibility for care between men and women within households). In the other camp, there are those who are not as convinced that such socialization or equalization is either possible or desirable, and hope to see paid domestic work upgraded in status and respect so that it need not be exploitative or dehumanizing. But, despite this otherwise irreconcilable disagreement, scholars on both sides of this invisible political line do share one consensus. They all seem to agree that there should be recognition of paid domestic work as a form of *work* like any other, requiring, at minimum, its formalization. Those explicitly disowning the utopian ideal of abolition, such as Pierette Hondagneu-Sotelo, argue that "formalizing the informal employment arrangements in paid domestic work is a necessary first step toward upgrading the occupation. Such 'formalizing' entails bringing paid domestic work into conformity with state codes and regulations governing employment. This is a modest but essential reform," she argues (2001, 211).

Others, arguing that "we should first challenge the public/private dichotomy and advocate the publicizing of care" (Lan 2006, 248), agree, however, that the formalization of paid domestic work as a form of employment like any other is a minimum "agenda of action" en route to the socialization of care. Paid domestic work is certainly a form of work. But, is it a form of work that can be formalized, by the state, like any other?

In post-apartheid South Africa, it was not only the intimacy of paid domestic work that severely complicated the possibility of that "modest but essential reform" on which the politics of paid domestic work seems to converge. In the impotence of the committed South African state to overturn the personalized relations of servitude lay a story about the limits of rights—that political technology presumed a panacea by much scholarly and political advocacy for domestic workers.

In South Africa, rights as a political technology for the modernization of "servitude" into employment contained contradictory potentials. On the one hand, rights did, as in the case of Hazel and so many others, provide protection that allowed workers to disrupt the sedimented forms of power in the relationships with their employers. But, this rights-based approach also arguably represented a conservative (i.e., status quo–maintaining) politics that constrained the possibilities of a more radical overturning of paid domestic workers as a reproducing class.

John Comaroff demonstrates, with great analytical insight, the ways in which the colonial project in South Africa was accomplished through the "discourse of rights" and argues that—despite its contradictions and paradoxes—is redeployed as the primary technology of the state post-apartheid: "The colonial discourse of rights—its contradictions, paradoxes, and perversities intact—continues to make itself felt as a new dawn rises on the South African postcolony" (1995, 234).

Together with Jean Comaroff (2000), they argue that this utilization of rights as an instrument of colonial and postcolonial rule is not unique to South Africa but part of contemporary "millennial capitalism," which induces a specific political culture. For Comaroff and Comaroff, the nation-state under modernity was produced by a "culture of legality." But, in an era of "millennial capitalism," they argue, states are defined by a "fetishism of the law," and "like all fetishes, the chimerical quality of this one lies in an enchanted displacement, in the notion that legal instruments have the capacity to orchestrate social harmony. . . . Hence, too, its hegemony, despite the fact that it is hardly a guarantor of equity. As an instrument of governance, it allows the state to represent itself as the custodian of civility against disorder" (2000, 329).

Patricia Williams, however, in *The Alchemy of Race and Rights,* does not see legislative rights as a technology of control for states but as a libertarian tool for the disenfranchised. "For the historically disempowered," she argues, "the conferring of rights is symbolic of all the denied aspects of their humanity: rights imply a respect that places one in the referential range of self and others, that elevates one's status from human body to social being" (1991, 153).

How do we reconcile these opposed conceptions of rights and the law, and its place in transformative democratic practice? Comaroff and Comaroff suggest that "critical disbelief, in pursuit of a reinvigorated praxis, is the beginning of a solution" (2000, 335). In this book, critical disbelief produces a very different reading of the disconnects between the aspirations of rights, and their accomplishments.

It has, for instance, been argued that paid domestic work in post-apartheid South Africa is most defined by an "access gap"—or the disconnect between legislating rights on paper and accessing them in practice—that issues from "employer unwillingness" (Fish 2006a, 196).[1] This book, however, began from a more skeptical approach to the subject of rights and produces a profoundly different explanation of the "access gap" as well as a different conceptualization of the powers of both the state and its newly constituted subjects. Domestic workers in post-apartheid South Africa do not fail to claim their rights because they are "vulnerable" and therefore lacking in capacity. In part, they do not claim their rights precisely because of processes that constitute them as rights-bearing subjects. On the one hand, domestic workers were interpolated as "vulnerable," presuming compromised capacity, at the same time as that construction bestowed on them rights, which, in order to be claimed, necessitated uncompromised capacity. The terms of being incorporated into the definition of political agent therefore limited domestic workers' capacities to inhabit the possibilities it suggests. At the same time, very aware of this impossible logic of rights extended on the basis of injury (Pratt 2004; see also McClure 1995) and confronted with the irreconcilable confrontation between disembodied rights and embodied intimacy, domestic workers consciously disowned the more disabling and subjectifying aspects of the democratic statecraft.

The disconnect between rights in theory and rights in practice is not to be located, then, in the failure of domestic workers' political incorporation but can be seen as a reflection of the same. While these workers' compromised positioning suggested the ambivalent possibilities of realizing rights, this was not as a reflection of the power of employers versus workers' lack thereof. In fact, it suggested the practices of power of both the state and workers. It also suggested the limits of the state intervention for the location of care within the body politic.

When Jacklyn Cock studied "maids" and "madams" in apartheid South Africa, she did so because "the situation of black and white women in

South Africa presents a challenge to any oversimplified feminist notion of 'sisterhood.' That challenge is sharpest in the institution of domestic service where the wages paid and the hours of work exacted by white 'madams' from their black 'maids' suggest a measure of oppression of women by women" (1980a, 1).

Angela Davis (1981), however, from a radical black feminist position, argued that this "oppression of women by women" issued from the failure of public responsibility for care. Women were locked into private relationships of paid domestic work that exacerbated inequalities because liberal capitalist states diffused the public and private conflicts over care work to the privatized relationships between women. In addition to claims, then, that the racialization of paid domestic work represented a challenge to the feminist project of "sisterhood," Davis (1981) suggested that the failure of the socialization of responsibility for care was, in many ways, the most pervasive and successful anti-feminist project. Davis therefore concluded: "The abolition of housework as the private responsibility of individual women is clearly a strategic goal of women's liberation . . . movements for institutions such as subsidized public child care, contain an explosive revolutionary potential" (1981, 243–44).

The formalization of paid domestic work through rights, by this accounting, cannot aspire to much more than the maintenance of the patriarchy of liberal capitalism, in which responsibility for, and provision of, care is deferred to families and—because of the private patriarchies within households—to women. In South Africa, the "modest but essential reform" of rights for domestic workers as workers was coterminous with a logic that refused the socialization of care. The dual-care regime produced by the labor reforms reinforced the inequalities of care between domestic workers and the employers for whom they worked. The individualized protection of labor rights therefore provided a necessary bulwark of protection for many workers, but it also simultaneously reinforced the political economy of care rather than disrupted it. Formalizing rights for domestics as workers cemented their position in the political economy of reproductive labor and constrained the possibilities for a more radical redistribution of care.

On the Powers of the State, and Workers

In much the same way as the experiences of South African domestic workers interrogated the radical limits of rights, it also exposed the multiply implicated forms of power that inhere in the democratic state. While some analyses berate the post-apartheid state for not doing enough to ensure compliance, this book recognizes the remarkable range of reforms for the sector instituted by the democratic dispensation. That domestic workers' lives have not changed much under democracy is therefore clearly no longer a reflection of the failure of the state to recognize their plight or to enforce their rights. While there are many continuities with the apartheid era, there have been significant shifts in workers' access to labor rights, a formalized labor relations system, and agencies of the state. As shown, the state has embarked on an extensive effort in relation to the sector, and workers have not been passive victims of the wills of employers, but have strategically negotiated their entry into political personhood by instrumentally claiming their rights and engaging protective state agencies.

These inclusive efforts, however, simultaneously embodied logics that subjected workers to a parallel form of state power. While a simplistic explanation of the continued positioning of domestic workers post-apartheid may defer to a blaming of the state for failed implementation, this study shows that workers' continued and altered positionings are reflective of the state's different powers. The state, being multivalent and multiply imbricated in different registers of power, is not unilinearly subjectifying. Its constituted subjects, in this case, refigured and recoded the logics of state discourses and defended their own meaningful social practices while they instrumentally utilized the state's apparatuses where beneficial for them.

As an agent of regulation for both protection and control, the state therefore displays dual and simultaneous powers to both emancipate and subjectivate. It is these dual powers that domestic workers' ambivalent embrace and rejection of state efforts reflects. In observing this duality and contradiction, there is a recognition of domestic workers' capacity to creatively negotiate structures, to identify modes of subjectifying power, and to respond to them as practitioners of power themselves.

Nthabiseng Motsemme wonderfully exposes the politics of representation of black women in post-apartheid South Africa. "Women's narrations of their lives highlight the need for a layered approach to make graphic the complexity of their lives," she argues (2002, 669). This, she urges, must involve a real recognition of this complexity, rather than the appropriation of these experiences and their co-option into a narrative of victimization, especially when it is appropriated to "make racism more compelling" (669).

The representation of third-world women through the trope of victimization, as Chandra Mohanty argues, plays an important role in creating "assumptions about Western women as secular, liberated and having control over their own lives," while presenting non-Western women as oppressed and powerless (1991, 74). With South African domestic workers, often constructed as victims, this politics of representation becomes more acute. Efforts to challenge the marginalization of domestic workers can potentially marginalize them even further. While these are a group of workers whose life stories are indeed trails of tears, to subsume them within a victimization narrative is to deny their creativity.

While domestic workers do indeed remain vulnerable, trapped in an institution with marked power imbalances that remain defiant to the principles that define South Africa's nascent democracy, they are not inert recipients of the wills of employers or the state. They are active, and where there is continuity or change, it is as much a reflection of their practices, the most interesting of which issued unexpectedly from the intimacy of their work.

On Flexible Intimacies

In Ann Stoler's *Carnal Knowledge and Imperial Power* (2002), the intimate is exposed as a strategic site of colonial governance. Drawing on instances of colonial relations of domestic service, there is a theoretical reflection on "matters of intimacy as matters of state" (Stoler 2001). By examining the attempted modifications of the intimacies that inhere in paid domestic work as a project of democratic statecraft in the postcolony, there is a recognition of the similar interdependencies of intimacy and governance in the making of not only political and domestic orders but also political subjectivities. For, in the end, South African domestic workers did not neatly inhabit the subject statuses presumed by the democratic statecraft of reconstructed work-based intimacies. They strategically negotiated the efforts of the postcolonial state to draw the intimacies of their work into the vocabulary of employment like any other.

In *The Purchase of Intimacy*, Viviana Zelizer (2000) interrupts the logics that are uncomfortable with the intersections of love and money, contract and affect, commerce and intimacy. The "hostile worlds" thesis, she argues, holds that intimacy and money exist in such separate spheres that any contact between them inevitably leads to contamination and degeneration. The "nothing but" thesis, its polar opposite, sees intimate relations involving money as nothing but rationally conducted exchange, indistinguishable from any other similar monetary transaction.[2] Zelizer offers a language and template for making sense of some of the handling of paid domestic work as a form of work that blurs the distinction between the worlds of commerce and sentiment. When mothers purchase the love of other women to care for their children, when families commodify what is usually understood as a labor of love—cleaning and cooking—and when waged work is understood as love, intimacy and money are forced into an uneasy and complex coexistence.

When scholars and activists resolve this enforced but uncomfortable cohabitation of presumably hostile worlds by deferring to the necessary primacy of rules of market, commercial exchange, and waged contracts, they are, in some ways, using the "nothing but" arguments Zelizer identifies. That is, uncomfortable with the coexistence of care and commerce, the intimate relations presumed by commodifying care work can be explicable only if coopted into the logic of rational market exchange, into the language of employment like any other.

South African domestic workers suggested the limits of this "nothing but" thesis by expressing how intimate relations can remain only uncomfortably organized through the language of commercial exchange like any other. At the same time, they exposed a greater hostility between the spheres of contract and affect than Zelizer's disputation of the "hostile worlds" thesis suggests. The regulation of the domestic workplace through the logics of employment (as a specific form of contractual monetary exchange) was somewhat inconsistent for these workers because it sought to reconcile the simultaneity of intimacy and commerce by the reduction of one to the logic of the other.

Yet, the various forms of intimacies that structured their work and family lives were also diverse and attenuated. While some theorists remain intrigued by the transformations of intimacy in late modernity—its increasing liquidity (Bauman 2003) and/or plasticity (Giddens 1993)—South African domestic workers suggested the always existing flexibility of the intimacies they inhabited. In their work, they strategically and instrumentally manipulated intimacy with their employers. But, they also articulated the sometimes genuine forms of love and affection they cultivated for the children they cared for, the families they worked for, and indeed, the work they performed. In their private lives, they recoded the abstract wage as a form of affective intimacy. And, their intimate love for their children structured forms of faith-centered sociality. Together, they weaved a rich tapestry of intimacies that colored the contours of their lives as workers and mothers. The juxtaposition of the intimacy regime presumed by the modernizing efforts of the state, on the one hand, and the flexibility of the intimacies that structured these mother-workers' lives, on the other, produced contradictory consequences. In defying state logics that failed to recognize the practices of power that derived from the intimacy of their work, domestic workers challenged the ongoing practice of power in South Africa's democratic statecraft. And, in so doing, they force us to reconsider whether efforts to emancipate them should begin by protecting them as waged workers or disrupting the logic of the market implied therein.

Appendix

Some Notes on Method

Reducing the crucial discussion on methodology to an appendix risks creating the impression that it is treated as an afterthought. This is not the case. The complexities of the processes used to garner the material for this study warrant a special, even if artificially separate, discussion. As a sociologist schooled in standard qualitative methods, the proverbial "field" I entered unsettled my own sense of methodological certainty. Despite careful a priori consideration of a systematic set of methods and techniques for gathering the information that would answer the questions identified, what eventually came to constitute the "methodology" was unavoidably more unsystematic, improvised, and eclectic.

As mentioned in the text, the research for this study was conducted over a period of eighteen months between February 2004 and August 2005 in South Africa's largest city, Johannesburg. Various historical studies have demonstrated the regional specificities of the development of domestic service in South Africa, suggesting the value of a locale-specific study. Jacklyn Cock's *Maids and Madams* (1980), focused as it was on the institution in the Eastern Cape, proved the utility of a detailed context-specific exploration of the sector.

Since the earliest history of the city and domestic work, Johannesburg provided a dominant regional space for the development of paid domestic work (Van Onselen 1982), especially in relation to the emerging order of racial capitalism. As Achille Mbembe and Sarah Nuttall argue, "it is in Johannesburg that the relations of capital, technology, labor, and the unequal distribution of wealth engendered the greatest conflict," and where—as focal themes in this study—"the critical nexus between the body politic, the creation and distribution of wealth, and systematized human degradation" is most apparent (2004, 353). As South Africa's largest metropolitan area, its most vibrant economic locus, and most racially, ethnically, and culturally diverse, Johannesburg provided the richest context for the exploration of this contested institution. Furthermore, as the center of the province with the highest rates of in-migration, this distinctively migrant labor force makes itself available for study most readily in the urban constellation of Johannesburg.

At the same time, the racial profile of employers, employees, and the distribution of live-in, live-out, full-time, and part-time work as recorded in a number of surveys in Gauteng province, of which Johannesburg is the largest metropolis, is consistent with the national profile of the sector. So, while still placing limits on generalization to a national level, the profile of domestic work in Johannesburg does not pose obvious constraints to understanding it as relatively typical to the institution across the urban areas of the country (except in the Western Cape, where the racial profile of employees and employers looks rather different than in the rest of the country).

But, the manifestations of domestic work in South Africa across its various urban topographies are only inconsistently understood and therefore may well look different (in the porous border towns of Bloemfontein or Polokwane, for instance, or in the small towns of the country's coastal and desert plains). At the same time, the features of the sector in its rural instantiations (of domestic servants on farms, or in small towns in the country's rural heartland) remain completely unexplored.

Nonetheless, in Johannesburg, the density of the relations between domestic workers and the democratic state produced particularly rich ground for ethnographic investigation of the core problematic of the study. Since the aim was to understand the effects and meanings of political incorporation for domestic workers, and therefore to detail the relationships between the state and workers, domestic workers were the primary participants. While both colloquial and official definitions recognize gardeners and drivers (mainly male) as "domestic workers," this study was limited to the workers who worked *within* private homes, doing the cooking, cleaning, and caring within the household. The majority (approximately 90%, Markdata 2000) of domestic workers in the country fall into the latter limitation, and are invariably black women. Since the aim of the study was to explore the relationships between the state and domestic workers, employers were not included as part of the research design.

Because there was an implicit effort to understand change, life histories were used as a primary method, collected in all instances by myself, in some cases with the aide of a translator, and over multiple sessions. These were supplemented by in-depth interviews, all conducted with domestic workers who were working in Johannesburg at the time. These workers were sampled purposively based on a matrix that would ensure, within limits, adequate sampling of various categories of workers. These axes included: the structure of employment (live-in, live-out), terms of employment (full-time, part-time), race of worker (African and Colored), race of employer (African, Colored, Indian, White), and class of employer (working class, middle class, and upper class). But this schematic classification renders more orderly a process that became decidedly more messy.

At first, I approached workers by myself and "blindly"; that is, outside of networks or referrals. Workers offered a mixture of unanticipated reactions, ranging from outright disdain, to disinterestedness and cautious cooperation. The multiplicity of responses were produced in part by my own marked positioning in terms of social location and power. As a young, middle-class, university-based, English-speaking, "Indian" South African, my identity generated layers of tensions that made the fieldwork extremely complicated. Workers that I initially approached immediately read me as part of the employing class, and responded to me as such. They either dismissed me altogether, or enthusiastically embraced me assuming I was seeking to hire them or was able to offer assistance for their individual employment-related issues. Some were disdainful of my presence and unwilling to participate once learning that no compensation, referrals for jobs, or specific advocacy for their labor relations issues were on offer.

At the same time, I was asked on more than one occasion by older domestic workers whether I was married, my answer in the negative immediately generating for workers a sense of offense. A "young" woman asking much older women about the most intimate aspects of their lives was a disruption of acceptable generational hierarchies. It was very clear, as well, on numerous occasions that my identity as an "Indian" South African placed severe limits on the extent of workers' comfort with me. In one instance, as I approached a group of assembled workers in a public park in Killarney, they loudly complained in isiZulu and Sesotho as I explained my interest in talking to them. I could not understand the content of their disaffections, until a helpful worker who recognized my plight pulled me aside to explain that "since 'Indians' are the 'worst employers,'" they were angry at my insolence for approaching them to discuss their lives as domestic workers. At the same time, my basic abilities in indigenous languages failed to generate relations of trust, and while Afrikaans and English made a number of interviews still possible, the quality of these interviews were inconsistent, and workers were distrustful.

As a result of these challenges, I shifted strategies. First, I sought to approach workers through networks of trust, rather than "blindly." Utilizing the church and the union as entry points for these networks proved remarkably more enabling. While constantly conscious of not oversampling union or church members, these access points proved invaluable. This strategy could not resolve the complications produced by my own social positioning, but entry through relations of familiarity and trust allowed a greater level of conscious awareness of the "difference" that structured the encounters between me as researcher and workers as "subjects" of inquiry.

I also enlisted the assistance of a graduate student at the University of the Witwatersrand who had worked as a domestic worker herself to fund her studies. Her position as an African woman, amazing social skills, and competency with indigenous languages opened new possibilities for a different quality of research, even though it produced mediated encounters between myself and the workers in ways that both enabled and complicated a more fully ethnographic encounter. On recognizing the radical difference in the qualities of interviews conducted in second languages of English and Afrikaans, compared with those conducted in the first languages of participants, all remaining interviews were conducted in the participant's language of choice, with translation assistance when necessary, and all were then translated later by another research assistant, other fellow workers, and helpful union officials.

On establishing close relationships with nearly five dozen workers, I not only recorded their life histories but "followed" them for more than a year as they went to union, *manyano*, and *stokvel* (revolving credit association) meetings, church services, and grocery and clothes shopping; as they played *fah-fee* or simply chatted on park benches and street corners; as they went from one job to another, took care of their children or households, and—on two occasions—partied in celebration. I spent time with them in their homes, and sometimes chatted with their friends, relatives, and neighbors. In addition, in-depth interviews were conducted with an additional two dozen workers and at two focus groups.

All workers, except three, were interviewed in public spaces such as street corners or public parks (usually as they played *fah-fee*), union offices, church, or at their homes, always in a location of their choice. The life histories were collected over periods of between two and four sessions, each between thirty minutes and two hours in duration. In-depth interviews ranged from fifteen to ninety minutes each. All tape-recorded interviews were transcribed. I quote at length throughout the book from these transcripts, and two points are noteworthy: (1) All names, except for officials and those quoted from public sources, have been changed to pseudonyms to ensure workers' anonymity, and (2) Some of the narratives have been slightly edited, but this is only to ensure their readability.

This was supplemented by intensive research into state processes. A total of twelve interviews were conducted with officials of the state and related agencies, including officials directly involved with drafting the various pieces of legislation that crafted inclusion for domestic workers. This included officials from the Ministry of Labor, UIF, CCMA, as well as from the Services Sector Education and Training Authority (Seta) service providers. And, in an unplanned technique, this involved ethnographic engagement with the state. I attended as many state-run information workshops, "inspection blitzes," government celebrations, and the like as I could find time for, and found myself an observer of constituent relations between the state and its subjects. At times I made my way to state-sponsored events on my own; at times I followed the workers; and in a few cases, I followed state officials I had come into contact with. Among state officials, my position at a university provoked a certain performativity, on the one hand, and a presumed sense of shared sentiment, on the other. Officials on more than one occasion addressed me as sympathetic to their expressed frustrations working with, as they termed it, "difficult" domestic workers.

This ethnographic work was supplemented with extensive documentary research into the legislative apparatuses of the state, historically and in the contemporary period, including archival research at the National Archives, Robben Island Museum and Archives, and the Historical Papers Collection at the University of the Witwatersrand, housing the records of the Black Sash, South African Council of Churches, and various relevant materials for the South African Domestic Workers Union (SADWU). Copious volumes of material documenting and detailing the state deliberations and policy discussions for domestic workers were made available by the Department of Labor's head office in Pretoria, and reams of newspaper clippings and organizational information was made available for endless perusing by the South African Domestic Service and Allied Workers Union (SADSAWU) in Johannesburg. This was supplemented by a review of all newspaper articles dealing with domestic work, utilizing *SA Media* from 1976 to the present.

Remaining "immersed" in the context for the duration of the writing-up of the project also ensured that the process of "fieldwork" was not temporally dislocated from the more sustained period of analyzing and understanding the material I had collected. Of course, it is not possible to neatly separate out the more than twenty-five years of lived experience of domestic service as a South African. An ongoing relationship with the Johannesburg branch of the domestic workers' union also does not fit into any clearly delimited understanding of "fieldwork" but invariably enriched and deepened my understanding of the community of workers I had come to know quite well, but who still approached me with a delicate mixture of caution and expectation. While never intended or understood as an ethnography in the anthropological sense, if this work is to be analyzed in those terms, it was clear that my own positioning never allowed me to be an "insider" among domestic workers. In some ways, this imposes a necessary irreducibility between workers' and my own political sensibilities, and that has certainly kept alive the political dialogue and debate between us.

Notes

Introduction

1. The names of all workers are pseudonyms in order to protect their anonymity and confidentiality.

2. The Bantu Authorities Act of 1951 established these ten ethnically divided "homelands," often also referred to as Bantustans.

3. As a cornerstone of apartheid's efforts to strictly regulate and control the movement of black Africans in South Africa, laws were enacted that required black Africans to carry a "pass" legalizing their presence in the urban areas of South Africa.

4. This book utilizes the racial classifications that define historical and contemporary categorizations of race in South Africa, in which all nonwhite populations are classified "black" and then subdivided into "Coloured," "Indian," and "African." The continued use of these categorizations is not to reify or lend legitimacy to them, but reflects the lived realities of these social constructions and their reinstantiations in post-apartheid South Africa.

5. In the geography of expansive white suburban properties, live-in domestic workers were invariably accommodated in the one-roomed structure in the backyard, separated from the main house, and often referred to as the servant's quarters. Workers often used "the backyard" as a simile for live-in domestic service.

6. The official estimate for the paid domestic work sector, reported by the *Labor Force Survey* in September 2007 (Statistics South Africa) was 1,057,000. According to the same survey, domestic workers as a single category of employment represented 8 percent of the total South African workforce.

7. To distinguish "domestic work," which can be performed unpaid within the home, from the institution under investigation here, I use the term "paid domestic work." I use the term *domestic workers* for ease of discussion, however, to refer only to paid domestic workers.

8. The new Labor Relations Act (1996), and the Basic Conditions of Employment Act (1997).

9. Sectoral Determination Seven, Domestic Worker Sector (2002). Department of Labour, Republic of South Africa.

10. The Domestic Workers' Plan—a public-private partnership between a South African financial services company, Old Mutual, and the government's Presidential Working Group on Women—was launched on September 25, 2007.

11. For more on the methods employed, see the appendix.

12. Because I was interested in the macropolitics of the relationship between the democratic state and domestic workers, rather than the micropolitics of the relationship between employers and their employees, I did not conduct any in-depth interviews with employers. Instead, I remained attentive to the ways in which domestic workers themselves chose to represent their relationships with their employers.

13. Rollins (1985) exposed the extent to which the relationships "between women" within paid domestic work reinforced racial hierarchies between the African American women she studied and their employers, suggesting the role of psychological as much as material oppression in the dynamics of power between employers and employees. Glenn (1986) continued this explication of the fracturing of gender by race in her analysis of three generations of Japanese American women in paid domestic work. And Romero (1992) explored the inequality-reifying relations of domestic service between Chicana women and their employers. At the same time, various other studies of paid domestic work sought to highlight the classed splintering of gender, in the United States (Wrigley 1995), Latin America (Chaney and Castro 1989; Gill 1994), and Africa (Hansen 1989).

14. Mary Romero (1992) presciently analyzed the "dilemma" of household work, in which all women had to find a way to manage the responsibility for the home at the same time as the possibility of paid employment. I use the term "dilemma" to capture the similarly intractable problem that emerges when women confront the possibility of paid domestic work as a way of resolving their gendered responsibility for domestic labor.

15. Gabrielle Meagher's (2002) question, "Is It Wrong to Pay for Housework?" both captures this dilemma and reviews the competing perspectives. See also Joan Tronto's (2002) analysis of "the 'nanny question' in feminism."

16. The scholarship abounds with this claim. Even when recognizing socialization of reproductive work as the long-term solution, there is a deference to the modernization of paid domestic work as a minimum solution to the dilemma of domestic work. For instance, when Gabrielle Meagher (2002) asks, "Is It Wrong to Pay for Housework?" she answers that it need not be because "formalized and modernized paid housework is the best alternative available" (60). This is a common theme for many who dismiss the abolition of paid domestic work as utopian, from the earliest debates on the subject to Pei Chia Lan's (2006) argument that part of the solution "is to formalize and professionalize domestic and care work" (248). See also, for instance, Pierette Hondagneu-Sotelo's (2001) discussion of this debate and Mary Romero's (1992).

17. From the title of the book by Rhacel Parreñas (2001a).

18. As Mahmood Mamdani's *Citizen and Subject* (1996) details, the forms of political governance that separated urban and rural contexts ensured a bifurcated state mobilizing citizenship as the basis for an urban regime of law and rights, in contrast to the rural regime of extraeconomic coercion and a "tribalized native authority" (18–21). For black domestic workers, this created a distinct relationship between citizenship rights and labor market positioning, in which tenuous citizenship prescribed a despotic labor regime.

19. Women who do part-time, generally day work—washing laundry, ironing, or cleaning—are often referred to as "chars" in South Africa.

20. There is also in contemporary Johannesburg a small but significant number of foreign migrant domestic workers from the Southern African hinterland, especially Zimbabwe. Since the lack of historical research cannot confirm whether this is a "new" trend, it is not discussed in this study but is the subject of another research project I am currently involved in.

21. Recent discussions suggest that an important aspect of the contemporary profile of the occupation in South Africa is the changing racial composition of employers. It is important to point out that while the transition from mainly white to mainly black employers has been documented in other settler colonies following democratization (see Hansen 1989; Pape 1993), in South Africa, the qualitatively different character of settler colonialism has not resulted in the transformation of the racial composition of employers to the same extent. First, "blacks" have employed domestic workers since the early days of apartheid, so this does not constitute a "new phenomenon" but rather a relative increase in an existing pattern. It therefore does not suggest a transformation from domestic work being organized around race, to suggesting new configurations of class. Second, what is far more compelling about paid domestic work is not the relatively insignificant shift in the racial profile of employers, but the enduringly persistent continuities in the racial profile of employees.

22. An important additional form of "work" beyond cooking, cleaning, and child care performed by domestic workers in South Africa is home security. In a country ravaged by violent crime, domestic workers perform the additional function of serving as security guards for the homes and possessions of their employers (see Hansen [1990, 364] for discussion of a similar experience in Zambia). "Madams and Mamas," a neighborhood watch group that utilizes domestic workers as daytime security guards is one example of this. Altbeker (2005), after having spent a year on the streets with the South African Police Service, also documents the extent to which the police rely on domestic workers as auxiliaries for reporting criminal activity and for maintaining the necessary daytime presence in homes that deters criminals.

23. The sexual abuse of domestic workers is common in South Africa (Motsei 1990) and referred to in studies of domestic workers in many other contexts (see, e.g., Gill 1994, 16).

24. See also Jonathan Grossman's (1996) analysis of "continuity and change" for South African domestic workers, and Allison Jill King's (2007) study of the micropolitics of employer-employee constructions of *Deference and Disdain*.

25. See Qayum and Ray (2003) for an insightful discussion of the coexistence of a political culture emphasizing discourses of democracy and the "culture of servitude" represented by paid domestic work in the Indian postcolony, as an example of the fruitfulness of this approach.

26. See also Andall (1998) for the ways in which "government regulation" of Cape Verdean women in Italy in the 1970s served to cement migrant domestic workers' exploitation rather than challenge it.

27. Chang (2000), in an overview analysis, provides a "gendered analysis of how government policies regulate the lives of women in the increasingly global market" (ix) and shows how states create, rather than eschew, the low-waged service work of migrant domestics.

28. Hondagneu-Sotelo's (2001) claim that the failure of such regulation by the U.S. government represents an opportunity, rather than a hindrance, is an interesting deviation from this argument.

29. Mendez (1988) exposed the limits of the "modernization" of domestic service through the market as a mechanism for transforming the exploitations produced by the intimate dependencies of paid domestic work. Salzinger (1991) explored a similar "modernizing" effort by domestic worker cooperatives. But a similar examination of modernization by the state has not been attempted.

1. The Apartheid State and Modern Servitude

1. South African Native Affairs Commission, 1903–1905. Vol. 1, *Report of the Commission* (Cape Town, 1905), p. 83.

2. Roseline Naapo, "The Lonely Worker," *SADWU Newsletter*, 1986.

3. For a description of the racial classifications used, see introduction, note 4.

4. South African Native Affairs Commission, 1903–1905. Vol. 1, *Report of the Commission* (Cape Town, 1905), p. 83.

5. AB1236 Community of the Resurrection Mission District Work Returns Scrapbook. Historical Papers Collection. University of the Witwatersrand.

6. South African Native Affairs Commission, 1903–1905. Vol. 1, *Report of the Commission* (Cape Town, 1905), p. 83.

7. See Gaitskell's (1984) discussion of a similar role of missions in domesticating African "girls."

8. The term "piccanin" means "small boy child," but it was used widely in South Africa in reference to, and to infantilize, African men, mainly servants.

9. The "reference book" was the pass book that was required by law, confirming the urban status of a black African. Employers taking possession of the pass book effectively bound a worker to that employer, as it was the most important document confirming legal presence in the city, and no other employment could be sought without it.

2. Beyond the Backyard

1. All employers' names have been changed to protect workers' anonymity.

2. Various surveys show rates between 63 percent (CASE 2001) and 67.8 percent (Markdata 2000) across the provinces.

3. For example, a report by the Community Agency for Social Inquiry (CASE 1999) argues: "The demise of apartheid brought about many social and economic changes, including the lifting of restrictions on where people may live. This, in turn, has had an impact on domestic workers who may now be in a position to commute rather than live in their employer's backyard."

4. *Mapantsula* (1988), directed by Oliver Schmitz (Johannesburg: One Look Productions).

5. See Preston-Whyte (1982, 167) for an example of the already-established nature of this pattern by the late 1970s in Durban, and her argument that at least some of this was also due to the spatial reconfiguration of the city into ever more prevalent blocks of flats that did not provide sufficient space to house all domestic workers on a live-in basis.

6. All names of state and union officials have not been changed, as consent was given to use their real names.

7. This is similar to Dill's (1988) documentation of the failure of live-out work for African American domestic workers in the United States to transform the personalized nature of the employment relationship.

8. Arlie Hochschild (1989) coined the phrase "second shift" to describe the situation where women engaged in paid employment during the day returned home to an unequal distribution of household labor, and therefore having to work a second shift at home.

9. The 1991 *October Household Survey* reported that while 55 percent of employing households employed their workers on a part-time basis, the figure for full-time work was 36 percent. This is roughly commensurate with the *Labor Force Survey* (2003), which showed that 48.6 percent of domestic workers worked full-time, while 55.9 percent worked part-time

10. Central Statistical Services, *Statistics of Houses, Domestic Servants, and Flats, 1972–1980.* Government Library, University of the Witwatersrand, Johannesburg.

11. Central Statistical Services, *Survey of Household Expenditure*, 1975–1985. Government Library, University of the Witwatersrand, Johannesburg.

12. 79.8 percent in one study (Markdata 2000), and 82 percent in another (CASE 2001).

13. For example, the Northern Cape and Limpopo provinces—amongst the least urbanized—have live-out rates of 84.4 percent and 82.6 percent (Markdata 2000).

14. Workers with more employers were more likely to be part-time, while those working for a single employer were more likely to be full-time (i.e., working live-out for a single employer throughout the week).

3. Protecting "Vulnerable" Workers?

1. Focus Group with Domestic Workers, Kwazakhele, Eastern Cape, 1993 (MCA 10–929), Mayibuye Archives, Robben Island Museum.

2. New Labor Relations Act (1996) and the Basic Conditions of Employment Act (1997).

3. Sectoral determinations promulgated as part of the Basic Conditions of Employment Act (1997) specify sector-specific conditions of employment, including, among other things, minimum wages.

4. The mandatory increases, at 8 percent per annum, were well beyond inflation at the time.

5. The inclusion of domestic workers in the UIF followed a campaign initiated by the Commission for Gender Equality, abbreviatedly referred to as the GMAC-UIF (Gender Monitoring and Advocacy Coalition for the inclusion of domestic workers in the Unemployment Insurance Fund (UIF). But, the inclusion of domestic workers in the UIF also represented a strategic effort as part of the processes of democratic consolidation and state-making.

6. This project formed part of the Domestics Chamber of the Services Seta (Sector Education and Training Authority) (see note 19).

7. All currency exchanges from South African rands (R) to U.S. dollars ($) are calculated at 6 to 1 (the average exchange rate between 2004 and 2005, at the time of the research and initial writing).

8. Downloaded from http://www.serviceseta.org.za/docsmedia/Document/02_10_2003/domestic_marketing_company_brief.doc (August 14, 2005).

9. While all other provisions of Sectoral Determination Seven came into effect from 1 September 2002, the minimum wage requirement of the determination came into effect from 1 November 2002.

10. Between R1 and R500 [$0–$83] per month.

11. From 67 percent to 47 percent.

12. Between R501 and R1000 [$83–$166] per month.

13. From 27 percent to 42 percent.

14. Less than R500 ($83) a month.

15. Furthermore, given trends in other sectors of the economy, what is significant about these figures is that it represents, as Hertz (2004) summarizes, an 18.7 percent increase in mean monthly earnings for domestic workers, higher than for any other workers in similar occupations, whose earnings increases did not keep pace with consumer inflation.

16. Indeed, so overwhelming was the response that to accommodate the influx, the call center tripled the number of staff, installed an additional fax facility to prevent overload, and upgraded the Internet facility (*Sunday Times*, July 2, 2003).

17. See chapter 7 for an extended discussion of employers' enforcement of the invisibility of workers and the implications for the denial of workers' personhood.

18. In reference to the popular cartoon strip in South Africa, *Madam and Eve*, which satirizes the relationships between "maids" and "madams."

19. As part of the government's efforts on skill development, various Sector Education and Training Authorities (Seta) were established. The Services Seta was mandated to further skills development in the services sector.

20. Thirty-nine percent of domestic workers earned between R501 and R1000 [$83—$166] a month, while a further 23.5 percent earned under R500 per month [$83]. This means that, despite the improvements in wages, a vast majority of domestic workers (62.5%) in South Africa still earned below R1000 [$166] a month (*Labor Force Survey* 2007).

21. This is a reference to the ruling party African National Congress's 2004 election campaign "A better life for all."

22. "Council" houses provided by the apartheid state in black locations were notoriously small, cramped, lacking in amenities, and therefore colloquially nicknamed "matchboxes."

23. Rollins (1985) used the term "maternalism" to describe employers' acts of apparent benevolence as subtle forms of power and control.

24. The protection of "vulnerable workers" is considered one of the central tenets of the Ministry's policies and efforts in general, and includes other workers as well, such as farm workers and wholesale and retail workers.

25. As Amanda Gouws (2005) argues, the discourse of vulnerability is closely tied to the pathologization of "victims" in need of state "intervention," 78–82.

26. The vast majority of commuters in Johannesburg are transported each day by ubiquitous mini-bus taxis—small vans that carry about a dozen passengers. Taxi ranks are the transfer points at which taxis and commuters congregate in large numbers.

27. It is interesting to note how in the workers' tribute, "Lioness of the Household," the roar of the worker is expressed: "O yes I dare your roaring is heard everywhere everywhere / Whether it is in the upper rooms of the luxurious homes you run / You roar forward you roar / Till you can see your own reflections / On the floors on the walls on the doors." The "roar" is expressed within the confines of the domestic workplace (in the rooms of the luxurious homes they run) and within her work (shining floors and walls until her visibility is confirmed in the reflection of her image in them). It is meaningful that workers locate their capacity and agency to roar back in their work, and in the private workplace.

4. Intimate Work

1. See Romero (1992, 107–9) for a nice discussion of the kinds of emotional labor extracted from Chicana workers in the United States.

2. The heading for this section draws on the subtitle of Ann Stoler's (2002) book, *Carnal Knowledge and Imperial Power: Race and the Intimate in Colonial Rule*, and the title of Achille Mbembe's (2001) book, *On the Postcolony*.

5. Paid to Care

1. It is difficult to argue that "national care chains" in South Africa benefit only middle-class households because white and Indian working-class households also rely—although at a much cheaper price—on domestic workers. For ease of discussion, *middle class* is used here in a relative rather than absolute sense.

2. *Privatized*, here, means that the responsibility for care lies with either the family or the market, in contradistinction to *socialized* where there is "public" responsibility for care.

3. White Paper for Social Welfare, Republic of South Africa, August 1997. http://www .welfare.gov.za/documents/1997/wp.htm (accessed September 16, 2005).

4. Central Statistical Services, Government Library, University of the Witwatersrand, Johannesburg.

5. Ibid.

6. Johan Martins, "Total Expenditure of Households in Gauteng according to Outlet." Research report no. 329, compiled for the Bureau of Market Research, University of South Africa, Pretoria, August 2004. http://www.unisa.ac.za/contents/faculties/ems/docs/Press329 .pdf (accessed May 19, 2008).

7. Ibid.

8. This is a practice generally common among African women in South Africa. Domestic workers use it as an inventive solution to child care while working.

9. Some of the workers renting domestic workers' rooms in the suburbs were able to share their rooms with their spouses, but their landlords would not allow their children to stay on the property as well.

10. Only one worker lived with a young child, but she was, in another indication of the "national care chain," raising him for her younger sister who was working as a sex worker in Hillbrow.

11. Only domestic workers with children were asked, but not all domestic workers with children were asked whether they received the Child Support Grant.

12. Lund Committee on Child and Family Support (1996), *Report of the Lund Committee on Child and Family Support*. Pretoria: Department of Welfare, 78.

13. Ibid., 26.

14. See Hassim (2005) for documentary evidence of the stigmatization and constructions of the "deserving" versus "undeserving" poor that results from the CSG's limitation to only the poorest of households.

6. Demobilizing Domestic Workers

1. Bridget Kenny (2004) uses this term to describe the demobilization of retail workers on the East Rand in the 1990s, but it is useful to describe a similar (though less dramatic) trajectory among organized domestic workers.

2. South African Institute of Race Relations (SAIRR) Part II AD 843/RJJ4.8, Historical Papers Collection, University of the Witwatersrand, Johannesburg.

3. South African Domestic Workers Association (SADWA), the Western Cape–based Domestic Workers Association (DWA), the Natal-based National Domestic Workers Association (NDWA), the Port Elizabeth Domestic Workers Union (PEDWU), and the East London Domestic Workers Union (ELDWU).

4. South African Domestic Workers Booklet, *Fighting for Our Rights* (n.d.), published by Community Resource Information Center.

5. Ibid., 6.

6. This reflects the minimum wage levels at the time of the research, in 2004.

7. From the "Resolution on Child Care," quoted in *Forward Worker* 1(2).

7. "Like the Heart in the Body"

1. While *manyano* is the isiXhosa term for the Methodist prayer union groups, it is used frequently to describe the phenomenon as a whole.

2. According to Gaitskell, the Methodist manyano uniform carried a particular spiritual significance: "black skirts signifying sin, red blouses the saving blood of Christ and

white hats the women's resultant purity" (1990, 261). The Anglican prayer union, the Women's Help Society, uniform in the 1920s consisted of black skirts and headscarves, and white jackets (Gaitskell 1990).

3. See Holness's testimony as well that "the majority of the Manyano women I know are domestic workers" (1997, 21).

4. While often referred to as their "day" off, domestic workers got only the afternoon [i.e., after 2 pm] off.

5. See also Preston-Whyte (1982) for a description of the importance of the manyanos to domestic workers and an attempt to explain it as providing a locus of Black social and recreational life given the constraints against the same under apartheid.

6. In the racialized structures of women's associations within, for instance, the Methodist church, manyanos were effectively for African women, with separate associations for "Coloured" and White women. Various efforts since the 1970s attempted a unification of these racially separate women's organizations, but none have succeeded. Instead, each of the racially separate women's groups have redefined their roles internally, and a fourth, nonracial group has emerged as an alternative (Theilen 2005, 85).

7. See Walker (1995) for a critical discussion of the ways in which women's struggles in South Africa, more generally, have been recognized to issue from their positioning as mothers.

8. In 1995, a submission was prepared for the South African Constitutional Assembly (the body tasked with drafting the new Constitution) by an African National Congress (ANC) branch after oral testimony and group discussion among predominantly domestic workers.

9. Renaming was a pervasive practice of racist dehumanization during apartheid, not limited to domestic work.

10. It is likely that some of these *kopano* [manyano equivalent in Lesotho] women were domestic workers as well.

11. Helen Bradford argues that "women's prayer unions provided a key arena in which black women, excluded from politics and formal organizations to a far greater extent than men, could develop the self-confidence to challenge social relations oppressing them both as blacks and as women" (1987, 308).

12. "Mother-work" was first coined by Molly Ladd-Taylor (1994, 2), but deepened by Cameron MacDonald (1998, 26). I use the term *mother-workers* to refer not only to the work of mothering but also to the class of working women constituted by engagement in this form of work.

Conclusion

1. Fish suggests that "employer unwillingness" takes three forms: (1) "the power asymmetries in the workplace" that "render policy inconsequential" (195); (2) the "colonial mentality" (196) of employers that refuses formalization of the employment relationship; and (3) the failure of effective government oversight, partly as a result of the role of government officials as employers themselves.

2. This is one of three permutations of the "nothing but" thesis proposed by Zelizer (2000). I reference only the first because it is most relevant to the discussion here.

References

Abu-Lughod, L. 1990. "The Romance of Resistance: Tracing Transformations of Power through Bedouin Women." *American Ethnologist* 17:41–55.

Adler, G., and E. C. Webster. 2000. *Trade Unions and Democratization in South Africa, 1985–1997.* Basingstoke: MacMillan.

Altbeker, A. 2005. *Dirty Work of Democracy: A Year on the Streets with the SAPS.* Cape Town: Jonathan Ball.

Andall, J. 1998. "Catholic and State Constructions of Domestic Workers: The Case of Cape Verdean Women in Rome in the 1970s." In *The New Migration in Europe: Social Constructions and Social Realities,* edited by K. Koser and H. Lutz, 124–42. New York: St-Martin's Press.

——. 2000. *Gender, Migration, and Domestic Service: The Politics of Black Women in Italy.* Burlington: Ashgate.

Anderson, B. 2000. *Doing the Dirty Work? The Global Politics of Domestic Labour.* London: Zed Books.

Attwell, P., ed. 1997. *Take Our Hands: The Methodist Women's Auxiliary of Southern Africa, 1916–1996.* Cape Town: Salty Print.

Bakan, A. B., and D. Stasiulis, eds. 1994. "Foreign Domestic Worker Policy in Canada and the Social Boundaries of Modern Citizenship." *Science and Society* 58:7–33.

——. 1995. *Negotiating Citizenship: Migrant Women in Canada and the Global System.* Toronto: University of Toronto Press.

——. 1997. *Not One of the Family: Foreign Domestic Workers in Canada.* Toronto: University of Toronto Press.

Barnes, A. S. 1993. "White Mistresses and African-American Domestic Workers: Ideals for Change." *Anthropological Quarterly* 66(1): 22–36.

Bauman, Z. 2003. *Liquid Love: On the Frailty of Human Bonds.* Oxford: Polity.

Beinart, W. 1987. "Women in Rural Politics: Herschel District in the 1920s and 1930s." In *Class, Community, and Conflict: South African Perspectives,* edited by B. Bozzoli, 324–57. Johannesburg: Ravan.

References

Benson, S. P. 1983. " 'The Customers Ain't God:' The Work Culture of Department Store Saleswomen, 1890–1940." In *Working Class America*, edited by M. Frisch and D. Walkowitz, 185–211. Urbana: University of Illinois Press.

Berger, I. 1992. *Threads of Solidarity: Women in South African Industry, 1900–1980.* Bloomington: Indiana University Press.

Bittman, M., G. Matheson, and G. Meagher. 1999. "The Changing Boundary Between Home and Market: Australian Trends in Outsourcing Domestic Labour." *Work, Employment and Society* 13(2): 249–73.

Blackett, A. 1998. "Making Domestic Work Visible: The Case for Specific Regulation." In *Labour Law and Labour Relations Programme Working Paper 2*. Geneva: International Labor Organization.

Blum, A. S. 2004. "Cleaning the Revolutionary Household: Domestic Servants and Public Welfare Policy in Mexico City, 1900–1935." *Journal of Women's History* 15(4): 67–90.

Boddington, E. 1983. *"Domestic Service: Changing Relations of Class Domination, 1841–1948: A Focus on Cape Town."* Master's thesis, University of Cape Town.

Bozzoli, B. 1983. "Marxism, Feminism, and Southern African Studies." *Journal of Southern African Studies* 9(2): 139–71.

Bozzoli, B., with Nkotsoe, M. 1991. *Women of Phokeng: Consciousness, Life Strategy, and Migrancy in South Africa 1900–1983.* Johannesburg: Ravan.

Bradford, H. 1987. " 'We Are Now the Men:' Women's Beer Protests in the Natal Countryside, 1929." In *Class, Community, and Conflict: South African Perspectives*, edited by B. Bozzoli, 292–323. Johannesburg: Ravan.

Brandel-Syrier, M. 1962. *Black Woman in Search of God.* London: Lutterworth Press.

Brown, W. 1992. "Finding the Man in the State." *Feminist Studies* 18(1): 7–34.

——. 2002. "Suffering the Paradoxes of Rights." In *Left Legalism/Left Critique*, edited by W. Brown and J. Halley, 420–34. Durham: Duke University Press.

Bubeck, D. E. 1995. *Care, Gender, and Justice.* Oxford: Clarendon.

Budlender, D. 2004. *Investigating the Implications of Ten Years of Democracy for Women: The Role of the Department of Labour.* Cape Town: Institute for Democracy in South Africa.

Bujra, J. M. 2000. *Serving Class: Masculinity and the Feminisation of Domestic Service in Tanzania.* Edinburgh: Edinburgh University Press.

Burawoy, M. 1979. *Manufacturing Consent: Changes in the Labor Process under Monopoly Capitalism.* Chicago: University of Chicago Press.

Burchell, G., C. Gordon, and P. Miller, eds. 1991. *The Foucault Effect: Studies in Governmentality.* Chicago: University of Chicago Press.

CASE. 1999. Domestic Workers and the Basic Conditions of Employment Act. Johannesburg: Community Agency for Social Enquiry.

CASE. 2001. *Training Needs of Domestic Workers.* Commissioned by Department of Labour and GDZ, Community Agency for Social Enquiry.

Chaney, E. M. 1985. "Agripina." In *Sellers and Servants: Working Women in Lima, Peru*, edited by X. Bunster and E. M. Chaney, 11–80. New York: Praeger.

Chaney, E. M., and M. G. Castro, eds. 1989. *Muchachas No More: Household Workers in Latin America and the Caribbean.* Philadelphia: Temple University Press.

210

Chang, G. 2000. *Disposable Domestics: Immigrant Women Workers in the Global Economy.* Cambridge: South End Press.

Childress, A. 1986. *Like One of the Family: Conversations from a Domestic's Life.* Boston: Beacon Press.

Chin, C. B. 1998. *In Service and Servitude: Foreign Female Domestic Workers and the Malaysian "Modernity Project."* New York: Columbia University Press.

Clark-Lewis, E. 1987. " 'This Work Had an End': African Domestic Workers in Washington, D.C., 1910–1940." In *To Toil the Livelong Day: America's Women at Work, 1780–1980,* edited by C. Groneman and M. B. Norton, 196–212. Ithaca: Cornell University Press.

Cobley, A. G. 1997. *The Rules of the Game: Struggles in Black Recreation and Social Welfare Policy in South Africa.* Westport, CT: Greenwood Press.

Cock, J. 1980a. *Maids and Madams: A Study in the Politics of Exploitation.* Johannesburg: Ravan Press.

———. 1980b. "Deference and Dependence: A Note on the Self Imagery of Domestic Workers." *South African Labour Bulletin* 6:9–21.

———. 1981. "Disposable Nannies: Domestic Servants in the Political Economy of South Africa." *Review of African Political Economy* 21:63–83.

———. 1988. "Trapped Workers: The Case of Domestic Workers in South Africa." In *Patriarchy and Class: African Women in the Home and Workforce,* edited by S. B. Stichter and J. L. Parpart, 205–19. London: Westview Press.

Colen, S. 1990. "Housekeeping for the Green Card: West Indian Household Workers, the State, and Stratified Reproduction in New York." In *At Work in Homes: Household Workers in World Perspective,* edited by R. Sanjek and S. Colen, 89–118. Washington: American Ethnological Society.

Coley, S. M. 1981. "And Still I Rise: An Exploratory Study of Contemporary Private Black Household Workers." PhD diss., Bryn Mawr College.

Comaroff, J. 1995. "The Discourse of Rights in Colonial South Africa: Subjectivity, Sovereignty, Modernity." In *Identities, Politics, Rights,* edited by A. Sarat and T. R. Kearns, 193–236. Michigan: University of Michigan Press.

Comaroff, J., and J. Comaroff. 2000. "Millennial Capitalism: First Thoughts on a Second Coming." *Public Culture* 12(2): 291–343.

Constable, N. 1997. *Maid to Order in Hong Kong: Stories of Filipina Domestic Workers.* Ithaca: Cornell University Press.

Corrigan, P. D., and D. Sayer. 1985. *The Great Arch: English State Formation as Cultural Revolution.* Oxford: Blackwell.

Cruikshank, B. 1999. *The Will to Empower: Democratic Citizens and Other Subjects.* Ithaca: Cornell University Press.

Dalla Costa, M., and S. James. 1972. *The Power of Women and the Subversion of the Community.* Montpelier, VT: Falling Wall.

Davis, A. 1981. *Women, Race, and Class.* New York: Random House.

De Fiore, J. 2002. "Las Madres en el Barrio: Godmothers, Othermothers, and Women's Power in a Community of Caregiving." In *Child Care and Inequality: Rethinking Carework for Children and Youth,* edited by F. M. Cancian, D. Kurz, A. S. London, R. Reviere, M. C. Tuominen, 27–50. London: Routledge.

References

Department of Labor. 2000. *Skills Development Survey.* Unpublished report. Republic of South Africa.

———. 2002. *Investigation into Minimum Wages and Conditions of Employment of Domestic Workers.* Republic of South Africa. Available at http://www.gpsa.co.za/articles/exec_summ_domestic_workers.htm (accessed January 27, 2005).

De Souza, J. F. A. 1980. "Paid Domestic Service in Brazil." *Latin American Perspectives* 7(1): 35–63.

De Villiers, F. 1989. "From Domestic Worker to Head of the Domestic Workers' Union." In *Lives of Courage: Women for a New South Africa,* edited by D. E. H. Russell, 168–77. New York: Basic Books.

Dill, B. T. 1988. "'Making the Job Good Yourself': Domestic Service and the Construction of Personal Dignity." In *Women and the Politics of Empowerment,* edited by A. Bookman and S. Morgen, 33–42. Philadelphia: Temple University Press.

———. 1994. *Across the Boundaries of Race and Class: An Exploration of Work and Family Among Black Female Domestic Servants.* New York: Garland Publishing.

Dudden, F. 1986. "Experts and Servants: The National Council on Household Employment and the Decline of Domestic Service in the Twentieth Century." *Journal of Social History* 20(2): 269–89.

Ehrenreich, B. 2003. "Maid to Order." In *Global Woman: Nannies, Maids, and Sex Workers in the New Economy,* edited by B. Ehrenreich and A. R. Hochschild, 85–103. London: Granta.

Ehrenreich, B., and Hochschild, A. R. 2003. *Global Woman: Nannies, Maids, and Sex Workers in the New Economy.* London: Granta.

Epprecht, M. 1993. "Domesticity and Piety in Colonial Lesotho: The Private Politics of Basotho Women's Pious Associations." *Journal of Southern African Studies* 19(2): 202–24.

Fish, J. N. 2006a. *Domestic Democracy: At Home in South Africa.* London: Routledge.

———. 2006b. "Engendering Democracy: Domestic Labour and Coalition-Building in South Africa." *Journal of Southern African Studies* 32(1): 107–27.

Fisher, B., and J. Tronto. 1990. "Toward a Feminist Theory of Care." In *Circles of Care: Work and Identity in Women's Lives,* edited by E. Abel and M. Nelson, 35–61. Albany: State University of New York Press.

Flint, S. 1988. "The Protection of Domestic Workers in South Africa: A Comparative Study." *Industrial Law Journal* 9:1–15.

Ford, M. 2004. "Organizing the Unorganizable: Unions, NGOs, and Indonesian Migrant Labour." *International Migration* 42(5): 99–117.

Fraser, N. 1989. *Unruly Practices: Power, Discourse, and Gender in Contemporary Social Theory.* Minneapolis: University of Minnesota Press.

Gaitskell, D. 1979. "'Christian Compounds for Girls': Church Hostels for African Women in Johannesburg, 1907–1970." *Journal of Southern African Studies* 6(1): 44–69.

———. 1982. "'Wailing for Purity': Prayer Unions, African Mothers and Adolescent Daughters, 1912–1940." In *Industrialisation and Social Change in South Africa: African Class Formation, Culture, and Consciousness, 1870–1930,* edited by S. Marks and R. Rathbone. White Plains: Longman.

——. 1983. "Housewives, Maids or Mothers: Some Contradictions of Domesticity for Christian Women in Johannesburg, 1903–39." *Journal of African History* 24: 241–56.

——. 1984. "Upward All and Play the Game: The Girl Wayfarers' Association in the Transvaal 1925–1975." In *Apartheid and Education: The Education of Black South Africans*, edited by P. Kallaway, 222–64. Johannesburg: Ravan.

——. 1990. "Devout Domesticity? A Century of African Women's Christianity in South Africa." In *Women and Gender in Southern Africa to 1945*, edited by C. Walker, 251–72. Cape Town: David Philip.

Gaitskell, D., J. Kimble, M. Maconachie, and E. Unterhalter. 1984. "Class, Race, and Gender: Domestic Workers in South Africa." *Review of African Political Economy* 27–28:86–108.

Gamburd, M. 2000. *The Kitchen Spoon's Handle: Transnationalism and Sri Lanka's Migrant Housemaids*. Ithaca: Cornell University Press.

Giddens, A. 1993. *The Transformation of Intimacy: Sexuality, Love, and Eroticism in Modern Societies*. Stanford: Stanford University Press.

Gill, L. 1994. *Precarious Dependencies: Gender, Class, and Domestic Service in Bolivia*. New York: Columbia University Press.

Glenn, E. N. 1986. *Issei, Nisei, War Bride: Three Generations of Japanese American Women in Domestic Service*. Philadelphia: Temple University Press.

Goffman, E. 1961. *Asylums: Essays on the Social Situation of Mental Patients and other Inmates*. Harmondsworth: Penguin.

Goldblatt, B. 2005. "Citizenship and the Right to Child Care." In *(Un)thinking Citizenship: Feminist Debates in Contemporary South Africa*, edited by A. Gouws, 117–36. Burlington: Ashgate.

Gordon, S. 1985. *Talent for Tomorrow: Life Stories of South African Servants*. Johannesburg: Ravan Press.

Grossman, J. 1996. " 'My Wish Is That My Kids Will Try to Understand One Day': Domestic Workers in South Africa Communicating the Experience of Abuse, Resistance and Hope." Paper presented at 9th International Oral History Conference, Göteborg, Sweden, March.

——. 2004. "The Denigrated Compassion and Vision of the Backyard: South Africa's Domestic Workers in the New Global Village." Unpublished paper, Cape Town.

Gouws, A. 2005. "Shaping Women's Citizenship: Contesting the Boundaries of State and Discourse." In *(Un)thinking Citizenship: Feminist Debates in Contemporary South Africa*, edited by A. Gouws, 71–90. Burlington: Ashgate.

Hansen, K. T. 1989. *Distant Companions: Servants and Employers in Zambia, 1900–1985*. Ithaca: Cornell University Press.

——. 1990. "Domestic Trials: Power and Autonomy in Domestic Service in Zambia." *American Ethnologist* 17(2): 360–75.

Hartmann, H. 1976. "Capitalism, Patriarchy, and Job Segregation by Sex." *Signs* 1:137–69.

Hassim, S. 2004. *Voices, Hierarchies and Spaces: Reconfiguring the Women's Movement in Democratic South Africa*. Durban: Center for Civil Society.

——. 2005. *Gender, Welfare and the Developmental State in South Africa*. Geneva: United Nations Research Institute for Social Development.

——. 2006. *Women's Organizations and Democracy in South Africa: Contesting Authority*. Madison: University of Wisconsin Press.

Hattersley, A. 1969. *An Illustrated Social History of South Africa*. Cape Town: A. A. Balkema.

Hertz, T. 2004. "Have Minimum Wages Benefited South Africa's Domestic Service Workers?" African Development and Poverty Reduction: The Macro-Micro Linkage, Forum Paper. Available at http://www.tips.org.za/events/forum2004/Papers/.

Hirson, B. 1990. *Yours for the Union: Class and Community Struggles in South Africa, 1930–1947*. London: Zed Books.

Hochschild, A. R., with Anne Machung. 1989. *The Second Shift*. New York: Viking.

Hochschild, A. R. 2000. "Global Care Chains and Emotional Surplus Value." In *On the Edge: Living with Global Capitalism*, edited by W. Hutton and A. Giddens, 130–46. London: Jonathan Cape.

——. 2003. "Love and Gold." In *Global Woman: Nannies, Maids, and Sex Workers in the New Economy*, edited by B. Ehrenreich and A. R. Hochschild, 15–30. London: Granta.

Holness, L. 1997. "Women's Piety and Empowerment: An Observer's Understanding of the Methodist Women's Manyano Movement." *Journal of Theology for Southern Africa* 98:21–31.

Hondagneu-Sotelo, P. 1994. "Regulating the Unregulated? Domestic Workers' Social Networks." *Social Problems* 41:50–64.

——. 2001. *Doméstica: Immigrant Workers Cleaning and Caring in the Shadows of Affluence*. Berkeley: University of California Press.

Hondagneu-Sotelo, P., and E. Avila. 1997. " 'I'm Here but I'm There:' The Meaning of Latina Transnational Motherhood." *Gender and Society* 11(5): 548–71.

Hooyman, N., and J. Gonyea. 1995. *Feminist Perspectives on Family Care: Politics for Gender Justice*. Thousand Oaks, CA: Sage.

Katzman, D. M. 1978. *Seven Days a Week: Women and Domestic Service in Industrializing America*. New York: Oxford University Press.

Kenny, B. C. 2004. "Divisions of Labor, Experiences of Class: Changing Collective Identities of East Rand Food Retail Sector Workers through South Africa's Democratic Transition." PhD diss., University of Wisconsin-Madison.

——. 2007. "Claiming Workplace Citizenship: 'Worker' Legacies, Collective Identities and Divided Loyalties of South African Contingent Retail Workers." *Qualitative Sociology* 30(4): 481–500.

King, A. J. 2007. *Deference and Disdain: Domestic Service in Post-Apartheid South Africa*. Aldershot: Ashgate.

Kruger, J. 1998. "From Single Parents to Poor Children: Refocusing South Africa's Transfers to Poor Households with Children." Paper delivered at 2nd International Research Conference on Social Security, International Social Security Association, Jerusalem, January 25–28.

Kruger, J., and S. Motala. 1997. "Welfare." In *First Call: The South African Children's Budget*, edited by S. Robinson and L. Biersteker, 65–114. Cape Town: Idasa.

Kuumba, M. B. 2002. "Dismantling the Master's Narrative: Teaching Gender, Race, and Class in the Civil Rights Movement." In *Teaching the Civil Rights Movement: Freedom's Bittersweet Song*, edited by J. B. Armstrong, S. H. Edwards, H. B. Roberson, R. Y. Williams, 175–89. London: Routledge.

Ladd-Taylor, M. 1994. *Mother-work: Women, Child Welfare, and the State, 1890–1930.* Urbana: University of Illinois Press.

Lan, P-C. 2006. *Global Cinderellas: Migrant Domestics and Newly Rich Employers in Taiwan.* Durham: Duke University Press.

Leatt, A. 2004. *Granting Assistance: An Analysis of the Child Support Grants and its Extension to Seven and Eight Year Olds.* Cape Town: Rondebosch Institute.

Lindio-McGovern, L. 2003. "Labor Export in the Context of Globalization." *International Sociology* 18(3): 513–34.

Lund, F. 1993. "State Social Benefits in South Africa." *International Social Security Review* 46(1): 5–23.

———. 1998. "Social Welfare and Social Security." Draft paper prepared for the Conference on the Politics of Economic Reform. Cape Town.

Lund, F., S. Ardington, and M. Harber. 1996. "Welfare." In *The Women's Budget*, edited by D. Budlender, 97. Cape Town: IDASA.

Lund Committee on Child and Family Support. 1996. *Report of the Lund Committee on Child and Family Support.* Pretoria: Department of Welfare.

Lynch, K., and E. McLaughlin. 1995. "Caring Labour and Love Labour." In *Irish Society: Sociological Perspectives*, edited by P. Clancy et al., 250–92. Dublin: Institute of Public Administration.

Macdonald, C. L. 1998. "Manufacturing Motherhood: The Shadow Work of Nannies and Au Pairs." *Qualitative Sociology* 21(1): 25–53.

Magona, S. 1994. *Living, Loving and Lying Awake at Night.* New York: Interlink Books.

Mamdani, M. 1996. *Citizen and Subject: Contemporary Africa and the Legacy of Late Colonialism.* Kampala: Fountain.

Markdata. 2000. *Domestic Workers and Employers Report.* Commissioned by Department of Labor, Republic of South Africa.

Marks, S., ed. 1987. *Not Either an Experimental Doll: The Separate Worlds of Three South African Women.* Durban: Killie Campbell Afrikaner Library.

Mbembe, A. 2001. *On the Postcolony.* Berkeley: University of California Press.

Mbembe, A., and S. Nuttall. 2004. "Writing the World from an African Metropolis." *Public Culture* 16(3): 347–72.

McClure, K. 1995. "Taking Liberties in Foucault's Triangle: Sovereignty, Discipline, Governmentality and the Subject of Rights." In *Identities, Politics, Rights*, edited by A. Sarat and T. R. Kearns, 149–92. Michigan: University of Michigan Press.

Meagher, G. 2002. "Is It Wrong to Pay for Housework?" *Hypatia* 17:52–66.

Mendez, J. B. 1998. "Of Mops and Maids: Contradictions and Continuities in Bureaucratized Domestic Work." *Social Problems* 45(1): 114–35.

Meyer, M. H. 2000. *Care Work: Gender, Labor, and the Welfare State.* London: Routledge.

Milkman, R., E. Reese, and B. Roth. 1998. "The Macrosociology of Paid Domestic Labor." *Work and Occupations* 25(4): 483–510.

References

Mohanty, C. T. 2003. *Feminism without Borders: Decolonizing Theory, Practicing Solidarity.* Durham: Duke University Press.

Moss, B. 1999. "'And the Bones Come Together:' Women's Religious Expectations in Southern Africa, c. 1900–1945." *Journal of Religious History* 23(1): 108–27.

Motsei, M. 1990. "The Best Kept Secret: Violence Against Domestic Workers." Paper presented at the Center for the Study of Violence and Reconciliation Seminar, University of the Witwatersrand, July 25.

Motsemme, N. 2002. "Gendered Experiences of Blackness in Post-Apartheid South Africa." *Social Identities* 8(4): 647–73.

Murphy, K. 2000. *Domestic Workers in South Africa.* Indiana: Kroc Institute for International Peace Studies.

Murray, S. B. 1998. "Child Care Work: Intimacy in the Shadows of Family-Life." *Qualitative Sociology* 21(2): 149–68.

Ortner, S. B. 2006. *Anthropology and Social Theory: Culture, Power, and the Acting Subject.* Durham: Duke University Press.

Ozyegin, G. 2001. *Untidy Gender: Domestic Service in Turkey.* Philadelphia: Temple University Press.

Padayachie, R., E. Atmore, L. Biersteker, R. King, J. Matube, S. Muthayan, K. Naidoo, D. Plaatjies, and J. Evans. 1994. *Report of the South African Study on Early Childhood Development: Recommendations for Action in Support of Young Children.* Washington, DC: World Bank.

Palmer, P. 1989. *Domesticity and Dirt: Housewives and Domestic Servants in the United States, 1920–1945.* Philadelphia: Temple University Press.

Pape, J. 1993. "Still Serving the Tea: Domestic Workers in Zimbabwe 1980–90." *Journal of Southern African Studies* 19(3): 387–404.

Parreñas, R. S. 2000. "Migrant Filipina Domestic Workers and the International Division of Reproductive Labour." *Gender and Society* 14(4): 560–80.

——. 2001a. *Servants of Globalization: Women, Migration, and Domestic Work.* Stanford: Stanford University Press.

——. 2001b. "Transgressing the Nation-State: The Partial Citizenship and 'Imagined (Global) Community' of Migrant Filipina Domestic Workers." *Signs* 26(4): 1129–54.

——. 2001c. "Mothering From a Distance: Emotions, Gender, and Intergenerational Relations in Filipino Transnational Families." *Feminist Studies* 27(2): 361–90.

Peberdy, S., and Dinat, N. 2005. *Migration and Domestic Workers: Worlds of Work, Health, and Mobility in Johannesburg.* Migration Policy Series No. 40. Cape Town: Southern African Migration Project.

Peires, J. B. 1976. *The Dead Will Arise: Nongqawuse and the Great Xhosa Cattle-Killing Movement of 1856–57.* Bloomington: Indiana University Press.

Posel, D., and D. Casale. 2005. "Women and the Economy: How Far Have We Come?" *Agenda* 64:21–29.

Pratt, G. 2004. *Working Feminism.* Philadelphia: Temple University Press.

Preston-Whyte, E. 1976. "Race Attitudes and Behaviour: The Case of Domestic Employment in White South African Homes." *African Studies* 35:71–89.

——. 1982. "Segregation and Interpersonal Relationships: A Case Study of Domestic Service in Durban." In *Living Under Apartheid: Aspects of Urbanization and*

Social Change in South Africa, edited by D. M. Smith, 164–82. London: Allen and Unwin.

——. 1991. "'Invisible Workers:' Domestic Service and the Informal Economy." In *South Africa's Informal Economy*, edited by E. Preston-Whyte and C. Rogerson, 34–53. Cape Town: Oxford University Press.

Qayum, S., and R. Ray. 2009. *Cultures of Servitude: Modernity, Domesticity, and Class in India*. Stanford: Stanford University Press.

——. 2003. "Grappling with Modernity: India's Respectable Classes and the Culture of Domestic Servitude." *Ethnography* 4(4): 1–36.

Rees, R. 1998. "'We Want a Union:' Finding a Home for Domestic Workers." *South African Labour Bulletin* 22(6): 52–57.

Rollins, J. 1985. *Between Women: Domestics and Their Employers*. Philadelphia: Temple University Press.

Romero, M. 1988. "Day Work in the Suburbs: The Work Experience of Chicana Private Housekeepers." In *The Worth of Women's Work: A Qualitative Synthesis*, edited by A. Statham, E. M. Miller, H. O. Mauksch, 77–91. Albany: SUNY Press, 77–91.

——. 1992. *Maid in the U.S.A.* New York: Routledge.

Ruiz, V. L. 1987. "By the Day or Week: Mexicana Domestic Workers in El Paso." In *To Toil the Livelong Day: America's Women at Work, 1780–1980*, edited by C. Groneman and M. B. Norton, 268–84. Ithaca: Cornell University Press.

Ryklief, S., and B. Bethanie. 2002. "A License to Exploit? An Analysis of the Proposed Minimum Wages and Conditions of Employment for Domestic Workers." *Bargaining Indicators*. Volume 7. Cape Town: Labor Research Service.

Salzinger, L. 1991. "A Maid by Any Other Name: The Transformation of 'Dirty Work' by Central American Immigrants." In *Ethnography Unbound*, edited by M. Burawoy, 139–60. Berkeley: University of California Press.

Sanjek, R., and S. Colen. 1990. "Introduction." In *At Work in Homes: Household Workers in World Perspective*, edited by R. Sanjek and S. Colen, 1–13. Washington, DC: American Ethnological Society.

Schechter, T. 1998. *Race, Class, Women and the State: The Case of Domestic Labour*. Montreal: Black Rose Books.

Schwarzenberg, S. 1987. "Rawls and Ownership: The Forgotten Category of Reproductive Labor." In *Science, Morality and Feminist Theory*, Supplementary Volume of the *Canadian Journal of Philosophy*. Calgary: University of Calgary Press.

Scott, J. 1985. *Weapons of the Weak: Everyday Forms of Peasant Resistance*. New Haven: Yale University Press.

Secombe, W. 1974. "The Housewife and Her Labor Under Capitalism." *New Left Review* 83:3–24.

Seidman, G. W. 1994. *Manufacturing Militance: Workers' Movements in Brazil and South Africa, 1970–1985*. Berkeley: University of California Press.

——. 1999. "Gendered Citizenship: South Africa's Democratic Transition and the Construction of a Gendered State." *Gender and Society* 13:287–307.

——. 2007. *Beyond the Boycott: Labor Rights, Human Rights, and Transnational Activism*. Albany: American Sociological Association/Russell Sage.

References

Shindler, J. 1980. "The Effects of Influx Control and Labour-saving Appliances on Domestic Service." *South African Labour Bulletin* 6:21–36.

Silvey, R. 2004. "Transnational Domestication: Indonesian Domestic Workers in Saudi Arabia." *Political Geography* 23:245–64.

Smith, P. R. 2000. "Organizing the Unorganizable: Private Paid Household Workers and Approaches to Employee Representation." *North Carolina Law Review* 79:45–110.

Stoler, A. L. 2001. "Matters of Intimacy as Matters of State: A Response." *Journal of American History* 88(3): 893–97.

——. 2002. *Carnal Knowledge and Imperial Power: Race and the Intimate in Colonial Life*. Berkeley: University of California Press.

Sundkler, B., and C. Steed. 2000. *A History of the Church in Africa*. Cambridge: Cambridge University Press.

Swaisland, C. 1993. *Servants and Gentlewomen to the Golden Land: The Emigration of Single Women from Britain to Southern Africa, 1820–1939*. Oxford: Berg.

Theilen, U. 2005. *Gender, Race, Power, and Religion: Women in the Methodist Church in Southern Africa in Post-Apartheid Society*. Frankfurt: Peter Lang.

Tronto, J. 1998. "An Ethic of Care." *Generations* 22(3): 15–20.

——. 2002. "The 'Nanny Question' in Feminism." *Hypatia* 17(2): 34–51.

Van der Berg, S. 1997. "South African Social Security Under Apartheid and Beyond." *Development Southern Africa* 14(4): 481–503.

Van der Waag, I. 2007. "Wyndhams, Parktown, 1901–1923: Domesticity and Servitude in an Early-Twentieth-Century South African Household." *Journal of Family History* 32(3): 259–95.

Van Onselen, C. 1982. "The Witches of Suburbia: Domestic Service on the Witwatersrand, 1890–1914." In *New Babylon, New Nineveh: Studies in the Social and Economic History of the Witwatersrand 1886–1914*, vol. 2, 1–73. Johannesburg: Ravan.

Von Holdt, K. 2003. *Transition From Below: Forging Trade Unionism and Workplace Change in South Africa*. Pietermaritzburg: University of Natal Press.

Walker, C. 1990. "Gender and the Development of the Migrant Labour System, 1850–1930: An Overview." In *Women and Gender in Southern Africa to 1945*, edited by C. Walker, 168–96. Cape Town: David Philip.

Weber, M. 1946. *From Max Weber: Essays in Sociology*, edited and translated by H. H. Gerth and C. W. Mills. New York: Oxford University Press.

Wells, J. 1991. "The Rise and Fall of Motherism as a Force in Black Women's Resistance Movements." PhD diss., Columbia University.

Whisson, M. G., and W. Weil. 1971. *Domestic Servants: A Microcosm of 'the Race Problem.'* Johannesburg: South African Institute of Race Relations.

Williams, P. J. 1991. *The Alchemy of Race and Rights: Diary of a Law Professor*. Cambridge: Harvard University Press.

Willis, P. 1977. *Learning to Labour*. Farnborough: Saxon House.

Willsworth, M. 1979. *Transcending the Culture of Poverty in a Black South African Township*. Master's thesis, Rhodes University.

Wolpe, H. 1972. "Capitalism and Cheap Labour-Power in South Africa: From Segregation to Apartheid." *Economy and Society* 1(4): 425–56.

Wrigley, J. 1995. *Other People's Children*. New York: Basic Books.

Yeoh, B., and S. Huang. 1998. "Negotiating Public Space: Strategies and Styles of Migrant Female Domestic Workers in Singapore." *Urban Studies* 35(3): 583–602.

Zelizer, V. 2000. "The Purchase of Intimacy." *Law and Social Inquiry* 25(3): 817–48.

Index

Index

Index

gender
  composition of domestic work, 33
  and race, 202n13
  rights, 10
  rural areas, 29–30
  struggles, 68–69
Gender Monitoring and Advocacy
    Coalition for the Inclusion of Domestic
    Workers into the Unemployment
    Insurance Fund (GMAC-UIF),
    155–56
generational continuities, 120–21
gift-giving, 14, 105
Girl Wayfarers Movement, 36
global care chains. *See* care chains
globalization, 6–7, 11, 92
Gordon, Suzanne, 50–51, 63, 151
Government Notice No. 742 (1889), 26
Gqosho, S., 168
Growth, Employment and Redistribution
    [strategy] (GEAR), 122

Helping Hand Club, 36
Hertzog, J.B.M., 36
hierarchies of power, 99
HIV/AIDS, 76, 129, 136, 142
homelands. *See* Bantustans
hostels, 34, 35–36
"hostile worlds" thesis, 192
houseboys, 28, 33, 45, 60, 148–49. *See also*
    domestic workers: African men as
household expenditure, 126
housing, 81–82

ICU. *See* Industrial and Commercial
    Workers' Union
immigrant labor, 14, 24–25, 27, 31–32, 57,
    111, 113
immigration policies, 25–26
India, 10, 14
Industrial and Commercial Workers' Union
    (ICU), 149
industrial relations, 154
influx control, 38, 39, 41, 48. *See also*
    passes
inspection blitzes, 91, 94
instant dismissal, 72–73, 77. *See also*
    unfair dismissal
intensification of work, 57
International Labor Organization (ILO), 11

intimacy
  commerce, 193
  depersonalization, 114
  dialectic of, 98
  domestic work, 19
  flexible, 192–94
  race, 117–18
  rights, 187–90
  transformations of, 193
  and worker's power, 13–15
intimate work, 96–107
  ambiguities of, 98, 99, 116–17
  culture of, 110–13
  family secrets, 97–98
  negotiating working conditions, 101–3
  servitude, 100
  and the state, 96
  as a strategic resource, 98–99
  workers' power, 13–15, 18
  workplaces, 95–96
  See also emotion work
isolation of domestic work, 73–74, 177
Italy, 59
izigebengu, 148

Joint Council of Europeans and Natives,
    36–37
Joint Standing Committee on the Improve-
    ment of the Quality of Life and Status
    of Women, 69

Keep the Home Fires Burning Campaign
    (2004), 132–33
Khoikhoi, 27
kopano movement, 170, 179. *See also*
    manyanos

labor bureaus, 31, 38, 39, 40, 41
labor legislation
  history of, 30–38
  legislative protection, 11, 70
  regulation of domestic work, 40–42, 144
  and trade unions, 153
  See also individual Acts of Parliament
labor market policy, 16
labor relations
  formalization of, 72–73
  pre- and post-apartheid, 94–95
  See also trade unions
Labor Relations Act (1996), 74, 201n8

Index